World, Class, Women

World, Class, Women
Global Literature, Education, and Feminism

Robin Truth Goodman

ROUTLEDGEFALMER
NEW YORK AND LONDON

Published in 2004 by
RoutledgeFalmer
29 West 35th Street
New York, NY 10001
www.routledge-ny.com

Published in Great Britain by
Routledge
11 New Fetter Lane
London EC4P 4EE
www.routledgefalmer.com

RoutledgeFalmer is an imprint of the Taylor and Francis Group.

10 9 8 7 6 5 4 3 2 1

Library of Congress Cataloging-in-Publication Data is available on file.

ISBN 0-415-94490-2 (hbk.)
ISBN 0-415-94491-0 (pbk.)

Contents

Acknowledgments

I am grateful to Kenneth J. Saltman for his patience, encouragement, and indispensable editing. Also, to Sheila Macrine, Barry Faulk, and Mark Cooper for their suggestions and references, and to Nancy Huse for turning me on to *Benigna*. I thank Leigh Edwards and all the members of the Florida State University English Department faculty who offered invaluable time and critiques of a piece of this text at the Pink Lady Faculty Research series. I also thank the Women's Studies Department at the University of South Florida, the annual conference on Literature and Film at Florida State University, the Crossroads of Cultural Studies conference, and the Popular Culture Association's annual conference for allowing me the opportunity of presenting parts of this work, and for comments. I thank the Office of Research at Florida State University for their financial support in completing this work. I am grateful to Jack Clifford and Debra Brock for technical support. And, of course, to my parents, with all of my love.

Introduction

This indigenous woman, whose name is Maria, is working at a modern industrial loom amid a long line of similar women. She is making sweaters at a new maquiladora named Trans Textil Internacional in the old colonial city of San Cristóbal de las Casas, in Chiapas. The sweaters Maria knits are entirely for North American consumers, there being no local market. In fact, all the materials such as cotton come from the United States and Europe; the role of Maria and the other workers in the factory is simply to knit, cut, stitch and assemble. Companies like Liz Claiborne, the Limited, Guess and Victoria's Secret will buy Maria's sweaters for between $8.50 and $12 apiece and sell them at $80–100.

Maria makes 6 pesos, or less than 60 US cents, for each of the six sweaters she can finish in a day. She receives no benefits. She has two children back home in her village and used to commute every day, but the transportation cost most of her pay, so she now lives with two other workers in a cuartito, *or small room, near the factory[. . .]*

This is Ground Zero of globalization.
—Tom Hayden, "Seeking a New Globalism in Chiapas," *The Nation*

[J. K. Rowling] had bought a new property, which [. . .] was a highly desirable London residence in Kensington, estimated to have cost $6.75 million. The Georgian-style house is in a terrace of twenty-five new millionaire homes and boasts an underground swimming pool, under-floor heating and 24-hour security. Madonna rented one for a while which gave the terrace celebrity status[. . .] Like many people who appreciate the value of money because they have worried about it on a daily basis in the past, Joanne is not prone to extravagance and this house is a little more of a splash-out than a new ring or a dress [. . .] She looks rich [. . .] Her skin is polished and immaculate, her clothes have designer labels and her jewellery is real diamonds[. . .] It is an ivy-covered Georgian mansion that might have been built to protect privacy. A stone wall surrounds it, eight feet high and 250 feet long, complemented by a security panel and an intercom on a pair of splendid black gates with a coronet on top[. . .] You can imagine little Jessica arriving home from her primary school and having to punch in the top-secret code in order to get into her home.
—Sean Smith, *J. K. Rowling: A Biography*

World

This book looks at the breakdown between the public and the private spheres of modern neoliberal power, particularly in how it relates to feminism. *World, Class, Women* investigates the intersections between the private power championed by some contemporary postmodern feminist theory (through discussions of, for example, identity, psychology, subjectivity, entrepreneurship, emotions, and caring) and the organization of private power—particularly corporate and military power—which has led to a current crisis in politics. The current phase of capitalism witnesses a depletion of supports for the public. Poorer countries make their economic infrastructures attractive to foreign investors by lowering wage levels, deregulating the environment, bashing labor organization, cutting taxes, cutting spending, and the like in order to increase potential private profitability. Richer countries have also cut taxes and social services as private companies have taken over many of the functions formerly performed by public institutions.

The privatization of public functions has been as much the product of an ideological and symbolic assault on public spaces and public initiatives as of a material deregulation of corporate growth. *World, Class, Women* considers the way some versions of feminism, following on the lessons taught by the corporate media, have produced meanings about privacy as the basis for new formulations of the public sphere, including public culture, public political participation, and public schooling. As the meanings of public education are woven within public debates about the free market, global competition, and the workforce, such feminist perspectives have reimagined empowerment as a transcendence of the public sphere through private accumulation, private initiative, private identities, and private consumption. Often, the drive to privatize is moralized and promoted through the symbolics of mothering, domesticity, and nurturance adopted from commercialism as much as from certain feminist inscriptions of politics. This symbolics of motherhood works to put the responsibility for social problems onto women: Rich mothers get blamed for working and abandoning their children while poor mothers get blamed for not working and collecting welfare so that they do not have to abandon their children. Such ideological formulations of motherhood and the private as imagined above through J. K. Rowling have been adopted rather than critiqued by such contemporary feminist scholarship, even as they symbolically affirm the material impoverishment of women globally which has been the consequence of the privatization of the public sphere. In other words, just as J. K. Rowling's designer labels are produced through Maria's poverty, a feminist celebration of "success" as moving off the welfare roles and "making it" by winning the golden calf of entrepreneurship and hyperconsumerism provides the ideological and material rationale for Maria's contract status, her lack of benefits, the privatization of her work, and the chilling political system that blames and punishes her for her poverty. Contingently, dependency is turned into a personal weakness as the structural economic relations of production are, within such treatments, replaced by private psychological narratives. *World, Class, Women* seeks to understand how such constructions of women's private worlds are functioning pedagogically, what kinds of politics can be constructed through their symbolic placement, how they make sense of power relations, whose interests they currently serve, and what alternative models can be promoted.

The feminist investment in the personal and in theories of women's private lives happened simultaneously with the new postmodern focus in cultural theory with its interests in the margins, in fragments, in subjecthood and identity, and in local sites of power. It also happened simultaneously with a change in capitalist relations, which Samir Amin identified as when, starting in 1975, the mechanisms creating postwar growth and prosperity—social-democratic welfare projects, Third World industrialization under the rubric of "development,"[1] and the Soviet project—gave way to global financial and management agreements with five major monopolistic goals—monopolies in technology, financial markets, access to natural resources, media and communications, and weapons of mass destruction. Under this new type of organization of capitalist relations, Amir states, "the conflict between globalized economic space and the fragmentation of spaces for political and social management is unbearable" (1997: 39).

As neoliberalism has meant a diminishment of public supports for ordinary people, it has, at the same time, intensified public supports for specified industries, a movement of funds that is legal in the United States through funneling funds through the military for subcontracting and has, as well, promoted international trade agreements to protect certain private interests through patent rules. The corporate control of the way international trade law is being written is evident also in some of the legal structures, as, for example, under the Free Trade Area of the Americas or FTAA agreement (under whose authority Maria's job was created), "corporations can sue governments directly for lost profit resulting from the passage of laws designed to protect public health and safety, working conditions or environmental standards" (Barlow: 7). This is the same legal principle behind the new reality that, for instance, private educational companies in the United States will be able to sue public schools in the Third World because of "unfair competitive advantage," reconceiving the very idea of the public according to a competitive private-business model.

The separation in theory, that Amin remarks, between thinking about how global economics works on a grand scale and thinking the culture of the fragment and the personal has meant that global economic management is usually seen as divorced from everyday life and that agency itself can often be considered only within a sphere of action divergent from global maneuvers, decision-makers, and oligopolistic corporate operators, leaving aside the shaping of visions for a viable public. The feminist turn away from master narratives partook of a more general turning away from the grand narratives of history in which Marxism played a large part. Discrediting master narratives by discarding Marxism, however, most of these feminist theories bursting on the scene of contemporary cultural analysis also discarded looking at the other historical factors leading to the grand narratives of monopolistic power: the global diminishment of public supports in which both welfare and development were embedded and what such changes meant for gender oppression: political disenfranchisement, the interpretation of needs as dependencies, the maligning of nondisciplinary state functions, and the growing feminization of the workforce as labor worldwide is increasingly impoverished under regimes of capital flight and public disinvestments.

The need to come up with other terms to guide the future of feminism is crucial to confronting what this book considers as a crisis in contemporary politics and a crisis in democracy. For this, *World, Class, Women* turns back to first-wave feminism to recover the idea of the "civic" through which feminist education was originally developed. It also looks to literatures from the Third World for thinking through the place for the public in politics and for discerning what are the shortcomings of imagining politics without it. Many others have noted the prevalence of a politicized private sphere in Third World literatures. For example, Fredric Jameson controversially wrote that "*the story of the private individual destiny is always an allegory of the embattled situation of the public third-world culture and society*" because "all third-world texts are necessarily[. . .] *national allegories*" (69). As well, Partha Chatterjee asserted that postcolonial literature investigates the feminine and the private because

> [anticolonial nationalism] divides the world of social institutions and practices into two domains—the material and the spiritual. The material is the domain of the "outside," of the economy and statecraft, of science and technology, a domain where the West had proved its superiority and the East had succumbed[. . .] The spiritual, on the other hand, is an "inner" domain bearing the "essential" marks of cultural identity. (6)

However, *World, Class, Women* differs from these analyses by (1) connecting this privatization of the nation-state to politics beyond the national; (2) thinking the relationship of women's private lives with the public functions of the contemporary redistributive state, not only the aesthetics of nationalism, which are often the products of private sentiment; and (3) contesting the relegation of women, women's lives, and women's narratives to the sphere of domesticity. Instead of focusing on women and women's issues as the symbolic extension of the liberal ideal of privacy in the Third World, *World, Class, Women* invites a politics of the public sphere around women and women's issues.

I have found the idea of the public to be still vibrant in some Third World literatures because, with less media saturation, there has been less identification with the private power of capital and a larger sense of separation from its interests. Additionally, there has been a more in-depth critique that privatization is benefiting imperialism to the detriment of the interests of the state and the public, and more political movements against it, as shown by the recent demonstrations against water privatization in Bolivia, Colombia, El Salvador, and other places. In Africa, as Samir Amin has pointed out, the weakening of public institutions for the purpose of the outward-looking integration into world markets has meant "[a] surplus could be extracted from the labor of the peasants and from the wealth offered by nature without the investments of modernization (no machines or fertilizer), without genuinely paying for labor (reproducing itself in the framework of traditional self-sufficiency), and without even guaranteeing the maintenance of the natural conditions of reproduction of wealth (pillage of the agrarian soils and the forests)" (2002: 44). From the perspectives of these common Third World situations, it is possible still to identify survival itself with the future of the public sphere and, as women are the hardest hit by such structural adjustment policies, to identify the future of the public sphere itself as dependent upon the future direction of feminism.

Class

There are six major reasons why *World, Class, Women* focuses on schools and pedagogy: 1) education—as the current political debates surrounding schools suggest—is a place where the struggle between public and private power is currently being waged, and where, contingently, it is possible to plot out what is at stake in maintaining a public sphere and what a public sphere might look like today; 2) the domestic dialogue in the United States on privatizing public education furnishes much of the ideological cushioning behind privatization movements that have been used to implement a broader imperial structure of financial, economic, and political reform through the privatization of state functions in the Third World; 3) as education has been thought about as part of the socialization of children, it reveals that the divide between public and private power is marked by the symbolic power of femininity and, as well, participates in creating a much broader ideological conception of feminized labor; 4) feminism began as a radical discourse about education, particularly because discussing education required thinking about civic access on which rests the very notion of political freedom for women; 5) critical pedagogical theory has offered much insight about the way meanings are produced to favor private over public interests, particularly dissecting the political economy of the media and the way private interests are taking over the public role of citizen-learning. As Henry Giroux elaborates,

> For many young people and adults today, the private sphere has become the only space in which to imagine any sense of hope, pleasure, or possibility. Market forces focus on the related issues of consumption and safety. Reduced to the act of consuming, citizenship is "mostly about forgetting, not learning." And as social visions of equity cede from public memory, unfettered brutal self-interests combine with retrograde social policies to make security a top domestic priority[. . .] Increasingly, notions of the public cease to resonate as a site of utopian possibility, as a fundamental space for how we reactivate our political sensibilities and conceive of ourselves as critical citizens, engaged public intellectuals, and social agents. (2001: xii)

Additionally, critical pedagogical theory has induced thinking about other sites of learning outside of the schools, allowing cultural and literary texts to be considered as framing issues and the ways they can be understood, producing the line between what can and cannot be said, constructing meanings, and formulating identities. Giroux, again:

> Broadly defined, culture in this perspective breaks down the divide between elite and popular culture and extends the reach of what counts as a serious object of learning from the library and the museum to mass media and popular culture. Similarly, the politics of culture not only reconstitutes and maps how meaning is produced, it also investigates the connections between discourses and structures of material power, the production of knowledge and the effects it has when translated into daily life. (2000: 27)

And 6) feminist pedagogical theory offers some of the most egregious examples of the way popular understandings and metaphors of femininity and domesticity as well as depictions of femininity within some versions of postmodern feminism are currently wielded to support the expansion of corporate power and the privatization of public power.

There are many examples of this throughout this book, typified by such statements as this one by Lynda Stone as she talks about the waning of civics classes in public schools and their replacement by moral "character" education: "Overall, there is less emphasis on educating for citizenship, largely because, paradoxically, public affiliation is a private matter of identity" (75). Stone then goes on to explore how commercialized, trademarked dolls substitute for teaching about citizenship because they return to the notion of the identity via the body that feminism has contributed to new configurations of democratic participation. In other words, reducing politics to a private matter has meant the transformation of the citizen into the consumer. Another case in point is Maxine Greene's essay "Lived Space, Shared Spaces, Public Spaces," in which she identifies the "public" as a "coming together, bringing a space into being" where "we see aspects of each other, possible paths of becoming, and that there is always, always more" because "[w]ithout opportunities to reflect on the phenomena of our beginnings—the sounds, the colors, the fluid outlines of things, the textures—we would lose touch with our becoming, our formation, with who we have chosen ourselves to be" (2000: 298). By personalizing public space, by focusing only on personal experience as defined through the senses, this perspective necessarily negates any political evaluation of what kinds of institutions we need, how money ought to be distributed, and what kinds of obstacles to "becoming" are produced in the social relations operative in the current regime of capital. With Wendy Brown, I am "suggesting that political conversation oriented toward diversity and the common, toward world rather than self, and involving conversion of one's knowledge of the world from a situated (subject) position into a public idiom, offers us the greatest possibility of countering postmodern social fragmentations and political disintegrations" (51).

Jo-Anne Dillabough and Madeleine Arnot trace the legacy of the private/public distinction in how it has influenced feminist theories of education. Reacting to male dominance in the public sphere, much of the feminist theory they review, they conclude, has focused on the private sphere, often essentializing women as mothers and failing to question embedded clichés of motherhood and household relations. What they call "radical" feminism took up sexuality and sexual control as well as the gender coding within such relationships. Another trend in feminist educational theory is what Dillabough and Arnot call "liberal," where catchphrases about equal opportunity have meant that feminist equality would be achieved in the equalizing of work relations, so that schooling "was to be used as the 'training ground for the [female] entrepreneur'" (27). In the more humanist branches, an analysis of the state was brought into play, but only in terms of who should control reproductive rights. In other words, the private sphere became the mainstay and dominant paradigm of feminist analysis as feminists were interested in "exposing women's uneasy relationship to public decision-making, to patriarchal machineries and modes of regulation in education and to male public discourses in schools" (26).

Now, however, the tools have not yet been substantially prepared to wrought a feminist analysis of the so-long-neglected public sphere, and not a public sphere whose sole aim would be in training middle-level management for service-sector jobs or contract labor (e.g., "the entrepreneur") or in protecting the private life of reproduction or in defining public political participation solely through the vote but rather a democratic public sphere determining the institutional infrastructure where citizens' conditions of life would be negotiated. Whether or not feminism could have predicted it, the concept of the private sphere as free of public authority or as the refuge of a battered identity has now been appropriated to sustain neoliberal ideologies that demonize the public sphere as having too much authority and too many restrictive powers. Such an ideological apparatus helps to propel deregulation and privatization as the public common sense and the only future hope, providing the basis for the increased exploitation and impoverishment of women globally and postponing liberation indefinitely.

Because critical pedagogy is centrally concerned with using education to further democratic projects and economic redistribution, it is essential, given the gender of poverty, that it develop materialist theories of gender not exclusively based in psychoanalysis or liberal ideas of assimilation, tolerance, inclusion, and consumption. *World, Class, Women* looks at postcolonial literature and feminist writings about schools in order to theorize how the shrinking of the public sphere, the diminishing powers of the nation-state, the waning of democracy and the public sphere, the rise of the global corporation, and the reign of corporate ideologies influence access to learning, what counts as knowledge, the socialization and reproduction of labor, and, subsequently, both the meaning of subjectivity and the possibilities of a radical feminism.

Furthermore, thinking about schools helps to bifurcate that indelibly unbreakable connection between the nation and the state. *World, Class, Women* is not so much concerned with the theory debates on postnationality, and certainly does not consider the era of nationhood as over. Nor does it want to engage with the role of nationalism as a culture in antiimperialist and postcolonialist movements. Rather, by thinking about education, this book looks at the culture of the state at a time when the nation-state itself is being stripped of its care-giving functions now increasingly relegated to individual consumers and to markets. How is the state now allied with the public and how does it unravel the public; how does international market deregulation reshape the state's operations, its allegiances, and its redistributive functions; how does the struggle between public and private interests shape the future of the state; what are presently thought as state roles, guarantees, limits, and obstacles; how do public institutions work differently now under neoliberalism; and in what sense can the state serve the advent of a global democratic public. As Stanley Aronowitz and Peter Bratsis have indicated,

> Marxist state theory and, increasingly, the state as an analytical object have been victims of an improper burial. They have been buried by a conservative shift inside and outside of the academy. They have been buried by an assumed decline of the state in the face of globalizing and localizing forces. They have been buried by a shift of emphasis, within the left, away from the study of "political power" to a more disaggregated vision of power as a dispersed and undifferentiated phenomenon[. . .] We are in the midst of a veritable avalanche of descriptive and theoretical writing on globalization. From William Greider's journalistic accounts of the spread of transnational corporate power to all corners of the globe to the dense theoretical work of Hardt and Negri, and almost everything in between, there is a general agreement that world capitalism has entered a new era, marked by the partial or complete displacement of the old regulatory institutions of the nation-state [. . .] Yet, the nation-states remain a mainstay of global arrangements. (xi-xxi)

In the face of the general takeover of cultural thought by concepts such as decentralization and deterritorialization, which conform to the realities of contemporary production, trade, and migration, the failure in contemporary cultural theory to engage with the state has meant an erasure from theoretical consideration of some of the dominant meaning-making institutions and their global transformations, not only, as Aronowitz and Bratsis go on to point out, in terms of education, but also health care, welfare, the military, the International Monetary Fund and the World Bank— which are "composed of the finance ministers of the leading capitalist powers, who in turn retain close ties with the chief transnational corporations" (xxi)—and the defense of territory "administered by the state as the context for capital accumulation, international power relations, and political struggle" (xxv). Adds Andreas Kalyvas, "This absence of theoretical work on the state conforms rather well with the absence of more conjunctural and contextual political writings, firmly rooted in the immediate political problems of actual politics, exploring potential strategies of resistance, tactics of mobilization, and struggles of radical transformation of the capitalist-instituted reality, including its central site of domination, the state" (123–124).

Additionally, theories of schooling necessarily construct social theories of consciousness, and social theories of consciousness are much needed to contend the pervasive power of neoliberal ideologies stimulating us rapidly and constantly, as well as the determinism embedded in many postmodern maps of the subject, a determinism that is making it ever more difficult to think about agency. The absence of theories of consciousness is remarkable in much current cultural analysis, as, for example, Foucault's subjected subject does not respond to power through thinking against it but rather embodies its language, only able to think or exist as an identity—even as an identity in resistance—constituted through power's watchful expectations. Another example is in Michael Hardt and Antonio Negri's much-debated volume *Empire*. Here, the authors recognize the need to imagine a supranational sovereign democratic public to replace the sovereignty of the modern nation-state. They call this democratic public sphere "the multitude." Modeled on a Deleuzian "body without organs," "the multitude" is spontaneous, diverse, decentered, and imminent, emerging automatically in opposition to the growth of Empire and its accumulation of wealth while reflecting its forms (like Peruvian economist Hernando de Soto's informal markets analyzed in chapter 4):

> Empire creates a greater potential for revolution than did the modern regimes of power because it presents us, alongside the machine of command, with an alternative: the set of all the exploited and the subjugated, a multitude that is directly opposed to Empire, with no mediation between them[. . .] When we look closer at how this constitutive process of subjectivity operates, we can see that the new spaces are described by unusual topologies, by subterranean and uncontainable rhizomes—by geographical mythologies that mark the new paths of destiny. (393–397)

As Hardt and Negri deny any conception of exteriority or difference in Empire (capital, they say, can no longer expand, but only network, marking the finality of the imperial eras), the analysis of ideology is made impossible along with the self-conception of a laboring class coming to learn of its own position within the relations of production and coming to see itself projected outside of its objective relations as the new revolutionary subject. "The multitude" is, rather, just a response that Empire forms in its own image, undifferentiatable formally from the practices of neoliberalism. "The multitude" is "the synergies of life, or really the productive manifestations of *naked life*" (366), an engagement of pure productive energy without division and so without consciousness of itself and seemingly, like the market, without ideology or borders.

Rejecting outright the old Marxian idea of the vanguard (another exteriority), Hardt and Negri cannot substitute some other intellectual formation to replace or transform the role of the multitude's intellectuals or universities or to explain the process through which the revolutionary force comes to understand either the form of its oppression or its transformative mission. When asked at a 2003 conference of the Marxist Reading Group in Gainesville, Florida, Hardt explained that the revolution would not start in the university but did not indicate how the multitude, devoid of educational institutions, would become aware of the need for change or what kind of change. Even while shaping their manifesto through the work of Spinoza, Deleuze, and Foucault (among others in the philosophical tradition), Hardt and Negri brush off intellectual life altogether in the life of the multitude. This contrasts sharply with, say, Uruguayan novelist and political theorist Eduardo Galeano's primer *Upside-Down* (1998), which showcases the school as the locus for communicating the way global power operates as the first step towards spinning ideas to counter it. It also contradicts Nigerian novelist Ngugi wa Thiong'o who, while challenging the revolutionary role of the vanguard, and agreeing that colonial schools and universities alienate people and mystify knowledge and need to be contested, nevertheless indicates that they should be replaced by an education which gives "people the confidence in their ability and capacities to overcome obstacles or to become masters of the laws governing external nature as human beings" (56). In other words, Ngugi prioritizes seizing back the public nature of public schools and other institutions by restoring public intellectualism rather than abandoning the political reason of the public altogether or refusing to imagine a social change which would bring forward new directions of thought and intellectual input. Thinking through the school helps to return postmodern cultural theory to a politics of consciousness without resorting to the pure interiority and sensualism of the consumerist subject.

Women

Feminism has traditionally been wary of universalisms, for the most part trying to avoid the universalist conscription of history which Hegel locates in the state by reverting instead to discussions of atomism and particularity. Much postmodern feminism therefore sought to define women as a culture-on-the-margins by endowing theoretical value on the private lives of women. In its Western version, second-wave feminism designed its goals around personal fulfillment and critiqued personal relationships formed under patriarchy. It turned to psychology and psychoanalysis as a way of thinking alternatives to patriarchy through tracing relations of power and resistances to power in personal histories, individual socialization, and subjective formation. Its main arch, in other words, was thinking power as private. Following the sexist division of labor in industrialism, male power was supposed to be public, so private power was supposed to allow the liberation of the feminine. This meant that analysis of feminist agency, in particular, was to avoid thinking the public and rather focus on the places where private power has historically been symbolically and philosophically framed: domesticity and the family, on the one hand, and, on the other, psychic interiority—the spirit, the emotions, the subject, identity, self-love. Within such versions of feminism, not only was the personal deemed political but also *the personal became all that remained of the political.*

One of the ways such feminist perspectives get constructed is by affirming what counts as "women's worlds," producing and affirming an image of private life that has since become an ideological support for envisioning corporate rights and shaping corporate policy. These types of postmodern feminisms succeeded in repeating a patriarchal gesture of associating femininity with the privacy of the liberal subject and, at the same time, in incapacitating a critical language for engaging with problems of public power, with wider historical and institutional political-economic contexts that play upon the thinking of privacy, and therefore with redistributive policy.

Furthermore, the feminist espousal of private power fed a much more insidious, mass-media-induced distrust of the public sphere, a distrust that benefited the accumulation of private corporate power. As Nancy Fraser has remarked, the private of the family was linked with the private of property and the economy divided from the public of administrative state organs or public opinion institutions (124). The idea of domesticity fabricated in the feminist assurance in decentered discourse or in the emancipatory potential of peripheral experience allowed feminism to neglect consideration of how the global corporate power structure was appropriating this same ideology of domesticity to cheapen labor, for example, or cut supports or avoid taxes in the name of the privacy of private enterprise. It did not allow reflections on how favoring independence as the value guiding social change would lead to the demonization of state-supported programs sullied with the label of "dependency." It did not account for how venerating interiority would reduce agency to a standard-of-living measure rather than of social transformation. It did not contemplate how the popularity of reflections on subjectivity was part of a broader global trend to blame social problems on individual failings, taking attention away from political causes like disinvestments in public institutions. It did not ponder how the turn to the body as the ultimate natural refuge of identity, subjectivity, and privacy was paralleling a much broader tendency of corporatizing the body down to its very genetic structure, as Donna Haraway has pointed out, turning "living organisms" into "a patentable 'composition of matter'" (90) while obfuscating "the capacity for multisided, democratic criticism and vision that [would] fundamentally shape the way science is done" (94).

The aggrandizing of the private comes to a head in such theories as Lauren Berlant's as she observes that the public has been sentimentalized as it symbolically merges into talk about private feelings, particularly private feelings about nationalism. As she writes in an article with Michael Warner,

"National heterosexuality is the mechanism by which a core national culture can be imagined as a sanitized space of sentimental feeling and immaculate behavior, a space of pure citizenship. A familial model of society displaces the recognition of structural racism and other systemic inequalities" (549). The problem with this theory is that it assumes that the public sphere has already disappeared instead of analyzing what is making it disappear now, what remains of it, what is important about it, what we can do to revitalize it, and what its future looks like. Even more evasively, Cynthia Enloe's article "Masculinity as Foreign Policy Issue," which circulated widely on the internet after the September 11 attacks (to much feminist approbation), analyzes why the United States shies away from issues which its values dictate that it support—e.g., banishing land mines, backing the international criminal court, disarming, acknowledging the rights of children—because military officials are afraid of appearing "unmanly" before their compatriots and allies: "This is not about hormones," she insists. "It is about the male politician's angst about not appearing 'manly.' This, in turn, is about American political culture." Such a perspective serves only to reduce the political economy of representation to a private issue of feelings, avoiding the questions of institutions, distributions, media consolidations, and the reduction of state functions to military discipline under the arm of global capital.

Part of the feminist appropriation of the private had to do with the way existing models of the public sphere, most notably Habermas's, divided the public sphere of material reproduction from the private sphere of symbolic reproduction, separating the social from the more naturalized domestic as Nancy Fraser has pointed out, and therefore providing the conceptual basis for the privatization of women's work. The feminist skepticism over Habermas fell into line with a distrust of his model of the public sphere of democratic public deliberation based in universal values developed through investigations in canonical humanism and communicational transparency. Existing theories of the private seemed to eclipse the saliency of thinking the public sphere in this way.

The repercussions of this apprehension, within feminist cultural theory, around the public sphere can be seen in the recent fall from glory of Guatemalan freedom fighter and indigenous advocator Rigoberta Menchu. In 1985, Rigoberta Menchu, aided by Venezuelan activist Elizabeth Burgos-Dubray, published a *testimonio* relating her experiences coming to political consciousness organizing for indigenous rights in Guatemala. She chronicled how she and the indigenous people of Guatemala formed public resistance against incursions of the Guatemalan military backed by the United States as well as by the large landed gentry profiting from the *latifundista* or plantationlike migrant-labor system for which the poor *campesinos* in need of work were forced to travel seasonally to the rich coastal regions where they labored for the exploitative export economy. Upon publication, Rigoberta Menchu became a hero, even winning the Nobel Peace Prize in 1992.

In 1999, anthropologist David Stoll published an ethnographic study of the Guatemalan highlands where he refuted Menchu's story by claiming it a lie. According to Stoll, Menchu's story was designed to sell the ideological platform of the international left—particularly that of Fidel Castro, who was supported by Burgos-Dubray, and the Guatemalan guerrilla group EGP (*Ejercito Guerrillero de los Pobres,* or Guerrilla Army of the Poor)—to international solidarity in Europe and the States, becoming "a way to mobilize foreign support for a wounded, retreating insurgency" (xiii), as the guerrillas had been committing political assassinations and depriving peasants of vital lands.

Much of Stoll's criticism revolves around a particular distortion in Menchu's tale. Possibly influenced by Paulo Freire and *teleogia de la liberación,* Menchu maintains that most of her education grew out of interactions, rituals, and practices in her highland, Mayan community because her father saw national schooling as a way of ending indigenous customs. In his research in Guatemala, Stoll discovered that Menchu actually attended a private Catholic convent school, and so she could never have been present as a personal witness to the events that she describes, the atrocities committed by the Guatemalan military, the torture and killing of peasants like her brother, the armed incursions and kidnappings, the fumigations, the terror. In other words, by situating Menchu within a discourse of private power, Stoll is able to undo her scathing critique of Guatemalan public institutions and their support of large-scale agribusiness private interests as well as her stoic portrait of what it means to build an oppositional, politicized public sphere. Since the private story was refuted, the pedagogical potential of the public proposition was also diluted and even, finally, expunged altogether.

The radical possibilities of a democratic public sphere are tied to the fate of women. Franz Fanon, perhaps, saw this best when he was outlining the historical procession of revolutionary consciousness. In "Concerning Violence," Fanon maligns the educational system as an arm of the oppressors and taught that among the colonized, pure force in the form of the policeman and the soldier was what taught submission. Nevertheless, the native comes to full consciousness of his oppression and discovers the truth of the national cause. In this essay, native consciousness appears imminent, embodied, and then suddenly discovered through a dialectic with history, but Fanon does not seek to explain its mechanisms nor its construction. Fanon envisions the revolutionary subject as male while, as Anne McClintock has observed, presuming "that subjectivity itself is neutral with respect to gender" (363). Anticolonial consciousness begins as false-consciousness, where the black man envies the white man, desires to take his place, "to sit at the settler's table, to sleep in the settler's bed, with his wife if possible" (1968: 39). Yet, Fanon provides more of a road map for developing revolutionary consciousness in "Algeria Unveiled." Here, the consciousness necessary to throw off oppression came when the militant woman brought what she had learned through revolutionary struggle back to her family. "Behind the girl, the whole family— even the Algerian father, the authority for all things, the founder of every value—following in her footsteps, becomes committed to the new Algeria" (1965: 60). Just as she dons the veil for secrecy during missions, or takes it off to hide her identity in the European quarter, the Algerian woman, for Fanon, allowed privacy to be mobilized for public purposes, and for the public to be the dominant form shaping private consciousness. For this, "deciding to incorporate women as essential elements, to have the Revolution depend on their presence and their action in this or that sector, was obviously a wholly revolutionary step" (1965: 49).

Forecast

The first chapter resurrects a theory of the civic from first-wave feminism in order to show how contemporary radical theories of education can provide working points for imagining women's liberation. The idea of the civic, which was central to early feminist notions of equality, can be thought more closely as informing the way that critical education theory has fashioned a politics of the public sphere than as evolving into the introspection of feminist pedagogy's interest in feelings, caring, and subjective conflict. The next two chapters give examples of how corporate media and culture have been undermining the possibility of imagining a public sphere. The second chapter, for example, reads the magic of Harry Potter as teaching that kids can and should embody the magic of capital, marking their freedom through school privatization, trade deregulation, consumption, competition, corporatization, white supremacy, welfare scapegoating, and escape from public oversight. Chapter 3 explores what Mobil Corporation had at stake in supporting and promoting Keri Hulme's 1984 Maori novel *The Bone People*. This novel has been hailed by scholars in postcolonialism and multiculturalism alike as a celebration of family, spiritual healing, feminist independence, and Maori recognition. This chapter shows how the widely read novel celebrates international finance and presents nature as ripe for corporate exploitation while attacking public institutions and labor.

The next two chapters discuss how theory and literature can piece together visions of the public to construct a language of critique against privatization. Chapter 4 is principally concerned with the way market reforms have been envisioned through the commodification of knowledge, which ideologically supports school privatization. Picking up on the way the oil industry in particular has infiltrated certain arms of nation-states even to the point of violence as analyzed in chapter 3, I criticize Peruvian economist Hernando De Soto's utopic call for deregulation and privatization by reading it against Nigerian novelist Buchi Emecheta's novel about women's postcolonial labor markets, *The Joys of Motherhood*. The fifth chapter applies some of the theoretical points made in the first chapter to the contemporary context by showing how a public sphere can be thought in opposition to ideologies of privacy and domesticity, which locate women's empowerment in relations of the home. Such ideologies have worked to support a reconceptualization of labor as feminized, that is, as temporary, contractual, and outside of traditional productive sites, responsible for its own overhead, and isolated. Continuing to criticize feminist pedagogy's exaltation over caring because of its implications for women's labor and for feminizing labor in general, chapter 5 looks at South African novelist Bessie Head's ethnographic study *Serowe: Village of the Rain-Wind*, in order to show how she thinks through the politics of a public sphere through a story about building a school.

World, Class, Women is interested in nudging feminism and feminist theory in a different direction and repoliticizing it in face of the crisis of capitalism we currently confront. In this, it points out how some of the values and terms of certain second-wave postmodern feminisms are being appropriated and resignified in ways that are detrimental to women worldwide. *World, Class, Women* understands that feminist politics are necessary to tackling the dangers of corporate governance, consolidation, and militarism, but also sees the direction that much feminism is now taking risks falling into ideological complicity with unemancipatory and undemocratic trends. It therefore challenges feminism to rethink the public.

CHAPTER 1

Critical Pedagogy and the Feminist Legacy

Here we are only concerned with the obvious fact, when it comes to considering this important question—how we are to help you prevent war—that education makes a difference.
—Virginia Woolf, *Three Guineas*

In 1938, as Europe was about to lead the world into a brutal conflagration, Virginia Woolf recognized the urgency for a fundamental educational change. This educational change would necessarily include economic transformation. As well, Woolf understood that without this change, there would be an inevitable spiraling toward escalating militarism and widespread destruction. Today, as the United States has sparked off a major global conflict that will probably ignite others, Virginia Woolf's lessons remain unlearned.

In an essay entitled "Crossing the Boundaries of Educational Discourse: Modernism, Postmodernism, and Feminism" published in 1992, Henry Giroux acknowledges critical pedagogy's indebtedness to feminism. Feminism has, Giroux remarks, "asserted the primacy of social criticism" (63), suggested "a complex relationship between material social practices and the construction of subjectivity through the use of language" (65), "provided a theoretical context and politics for enriching postmodernism's analyses of reason and totality" (66), and welcomed "the postmodern emphasis on the proliferation of local narratives, the opening up of the world to cultural and ethnic differences, and the positing of difference as a challenge to hegemonic power relations parading as universals" (68). Indeed, not only has the particular postmodern feminism to which Giroux refers contributed to thinking the radical in politics and education, but feminist thought was originally formulated as a radical theory of education.

The reason to consider the history of feminist thought as it has influenced and could influence critical pedagogy is not only to expand the canon of theory or traditions within critical pedagogy. Neither is the purpose here simply to include "silenced others" in an endless parsing of differences, or, as Kathleen Weiler has proposed, "challenging the structure of traditional canon [. . . and] suggesting alternative classroom practices" (2001: 68). Additionally, as Virginia Woolf well knew, the history of feminist thought offers an imperative to reconceptualize the relationship between the private and the public spheres built up with industrialism, and this reconceptualization is vital to the future of education. Mary Wollstonecraft herself taught that politics, civic virtue, and justice resided in such a reconceptualization, for, she argued, only when women escaped from domestic confinement and dependence would they exercise the free will on which equality, antiauthoritarianism, and civic knowledge could be built. Mary Wollstonecraft did not seek to unmoor a doctrine of separate spheres in which mothering would be to women what soldiering was to men. Yet, in making this equation, Wollstonecraft saw that in order to broaden political participation and economic access, redefining women's labors as civic labors was central, and so women's positions were not to be marginalized, dominated, and locked away from public reason. My project here is to reassess the history of feminist thought and, in so doing, to retrieve the elements, ideas, and symbolic connections that are useful to a theory of liberation, a feminist politics, a culture of democracy, and a rethinking of the meanings of education.

Following on Wollstonecraft's polemic, the legacy of feminist thought teaches that the nonregulated private sphere undermines the civic potential of education because it reaffirms a gender system based on inefficiency, excessive and wasteful indulgences, despotism, violence, and savagery. In a sense, Wollstonecraft is picking up where Foucault left off (so to speak), identifying the private bedroom as the extension of power rather than a refuge or resistance from it, only Wollstonecraft then metaphorizes the bedroom, in the mode of the classical tradition of political theorists like Aristotle, to show that the relationships of the private bedroom model the broader relationships of authority and tyranny in politics. Feminism then argues that civic virtue needs to be embedded in the private sphere in order for the public to stop conforming to the dictatorships of private power, so that feminist discourse would infuse private identity with the order of the public and the concept of democratic participation for the purposes of politics and freedom. Remarks, for example, Charlotte Perkins Gilman in her 1898 classic *Women and Economics,* "[W]hen we see how much of our improvement is due to gains made in hygienic knowledge, in public provision for education and sanitary regulation, none of which has been accomplished by mothers, we are forced to see that whatever advance the race has made is not exclusively attributable to motherhood" (1998: 93). Requiring an attention to public institutions, deliberations, and social nets in the feminist reconceptualization of the private sphere, educating women to know equality and to resist deception would depend on building public supports that would vitally reform social relations even in the home and the possibilities of progress. Feminism was, from its beginnings, a call not only to educate more, but also, by educating more, to educate differently.

This demand for civic ideas to be the basis of private exchange inverts the current liberal, corporate ideologies that Zygmunt Bauman has criticized as the "therapy for present ills" where "we live also through a period of the privatization of utopia and of the models of the good" (1999: 7), where, in other words, public potentials are thought of in private terms. "The art of reforging private troubles into public issues," he warns "is in danger of falling into disuse and being forgotten; private troubles tend to be redefined in a way that renders exceedingly difficult their 'agglomeration,' and thus their condensation into a political force" (1999: 7). This state of affairs results, says Bauman, from the "passing of control over crucial economic factors from representative institutions of government to the free play of market forces" (1999:19), in other words, from the privatization of public power, which gives rise to feelings of insecurity.

An example of how the logic of the private is so prevalently operating can be found in a recent demonstration I went to at the university where I work, Florida State University. The demonstration was organized by students who were living in tents on the campus green in order to protest the agency the university was employing to monitor the sweatshops where the university's sports clothing was manufactured (the students favored the WRC, or Workers' Rights Consortium). The university was using police action to remove the students from the green, including shutting off the water and locking the buildings after hours, claiming that the "tent city" was unsafe and unsanitary even though the university has a custom of allowing students to camp out on the green the night before football games. During the protest, where students were going to march to the administrative office to dialogue with the police, I overheard two students talking. One of the students said to the other that the "tent city" students should be allowed to stay on the green because they paid tuition and so in a sense they "owned" the green. In other words, these students could not think of political action as outside of private rights, and they could not imagine the public—as in the public university—belonging to them through any other means besides private ownership. They could not think, for instance, of their protest as a protection of their constitutional rights to assembly or as part of a tradition of civil disobedience, or that the public university itself should promise a space for the expression and discussion of opinions and redress in democratic deliberation. In other words, the system of private ownership, which they were protesting in sweatshops, was providing the only available logic in which they could frame the logic of their politics, their participation, and their protest.

For Bauman, the growth in therapeutic culture is directly related to the widespread inability to think the public. This inability incites the growth in such cultures of insecurity where "power is increasingly removed from politics—a circumstance which accounts simultaneously for growing political apathy, the progressive disinterestedness of the electorate in everything 'political' except the juicy scandals perpetrated by top people in the limelight, and the waning of expectations that salvation may come from government buildings, whoever their current or future occupants may be" (1999: 19). The intensification of corporate governance over public issues is played out in a therapeutic culture, which passes the responsibility for public problems onto private individuals and which also blames social insecurities on private crimes (e.g., family dysfunctionality causing psychological maladaptions), meaning that public communities are envisioned as full of "fear, suspicion, and hate" (14) because of individual failings and so needing micromanagement by private concerns, "interventions," and market remedies.

The problem is, of course, that corporate power does not fix such social insecurities but rather creates them, driving wages down, demanding the lowering of government spending and the tax base, endangering the environment, busting unions, and the like, all giving legitimation to the growth of the disciplinary security state which, in its turn, incites even greater insecurity. In the face of this breakdown in the cultures of democracy, Giroux has expounded on the need for public schools to defend public cultures, as public services are increasingly defunded and noncommercial spaces are disappearing. For Giroux, as corporate culture has come to dominate political institutions including schools, it is vital, for the survival of democracy, to develop a sense of public agency as autonomous from the imperatives of the market: "[t]he continued devaluation of education as a public good points to the need for educators to work together to reclaim schools as democratic public goods" (2000: 26). Drawing on Antonio Gramsci, Giroux has developed a sense of the public necessary for democratic action and agency, where "common sense and consent were being constructed within public spheres marked by the emergence of new technologies and specific, yet shifting, educational practices" (2000: 110) but also where "alternative cultural spheres might be transformed into sites of struggle and resistance" (2000: 111). Like Wollstonecraft, Woolf, and Gilman, Giroux wants education to stand for the different kinds of thought and action that different configurations of private and public power would promise.

Wollstonecraft warned that there would be neither freedom nor peace as long as women were barred from free and rational thought by domestic domination, because submission to a singular command in marriage, as in the military, obstructs ambition, creating instead extravagance, vice, and uselessness: "I shall scarcely excite surprise," she notes, "by adding my firm persuasion that every profession, in which great subordination of rank constitutes its power, is highly injurious to morality. A standing army, for instance, is incompatible with freedom; because subordination and rigour are the very sinews of military discipline; and despotism is necessary to give vigour to enterprises that one will directs" (17). Likewise, Giroux understands the domination of the private—this time, of private and corporate ownership—impeding the ability of students to think the end of oppression and to reclaim a political role. The tyranny of the king, which Wollstonecraft found so abhorrent and inimical to free thought, and the tyranny of fascism, which Woolf feared, has returned here as the tyranny of the global corporation.[1]

Woolf, Wollstonecraft, and Gilman specifically relegated the idea of the private to the home. As Woolf explains, "Your class [men] possesses in its own right and not through marriage practically all the capital, all the land, all the valuables, and all the patronage in England. Our class possesses in its own right and not through marriage practically none of the capital, none of the land, none of the valuables, and none of the patronage in England" (18). A comparison between Giroux's critical pedagogy and this early feminist thinking of educational change demonstrates how that idea of the private has circulated into other power dynamics besides the home, and how Woolf's idea about masculine power as consolidated capital accumulation now is oriented through a culture of corporatism. The private, in Giroux's analysis of power, stands both for the opposite to the public—a space devoid of dialogue, deliberation, participation, and institutional access as the backbone of democratic culture—and for a depoliticized version of the personal, where private action and sentiment are circumscribed as outside of broader economic, cultural, and historical struggles. In defense of the private as the basis of property and thus of a liberalized notion of identity, corporate culture has defended its own transcendence of the law of the nation-state, its hostility to taxation and regulation, and its right to finance political campaigns in order to influence candidates' policy initiatives. Though the early feminist movement had not yet conceived a politics of the public sphere, one can still look to this critique for alternatives to the concentration of private power. By considering the way feminist thought has historically contended the power of the private, I here build on Giroux's insightful analysis of the way power operates by defining and dividing the public from the private. I argue that the private in Giroux's sense still carries in it some of the attributes of femininity with which early feminist writing attributed it, as well as the same dangers to democracy.

Intertwined with the privatization of public power, the feminization of corporate labor has, in fact, contributed to its depoliticization. Where flexibility and mobility are more and more considered as the virtues of capital, some of the historical features of domestic production have been absorbed into current corporate practices. As well, corporations have manipulated attributes and moral attitudes of gender to produce value in the workforce. Observes Angela Davis,

> Although the "housewife" was rooted in the social conditions of the bourgeoisie and the middle classes, nineteenth-century ideology established the housewife and the mother as universal models of womanhood. Since popular propaganda represented the vocation of *all* women as a function of their roles in the home, women compelled to work for wages came to be treated as alien visitors within the masculine world of the public economy. Having stepped outside their "natural" sphere, women were not to be treated as full-fledged wage workers. The price they paid involved long hours, substandard working conditions and grossly inadequate wages. Their exploitation was even more intense than the exploitation suffered by their male counterparts. Needless to say, sexism emerged as a source of outrageous super-profits for the capitalists. (229)

Melissa W. Wright has shown how "housewife" discourses of feminine helplessness, victimization, and temporalness on the one hand, and promiscuity and moral depravity on the other, have justified the *maquiladoras'* cheapening of labor on the Mexican border. As male workers are seen as more "loyal," they are trained in higher skilled jobs with greater technological involvement. "She, however," remarks Wright about the female Mexican worker, "is stuck in the endless loop of her decline[. . .] First, [the Mexican woman] establishes the standard for recognizing the production of value in people and in things: Value appreciates in what is not her. Second, she incorporates flexibility into the labor supply through her turnover" (127). The willful changing of jobs on the part of the women workers was not encouraged by low wages, lack of child care, lack of training, or bad working conditions, the managers insisted, but rather by the girls' own cultural waywardness, their lack of "loyalty."

Wright is here discussing how over two hundred women workers in the industrial city of Juarez were murdered and their bodies discarded in the desert over a period of five years in the late 1990s. The corporate managers responded by blaming their deaths on the cultural dissolution that they maintained the women represented, where, they claimed, the demise of values led women to seek "experiences." Even when a woman was killed by the company's own bus driver, the corporate managers could displace responsibility for the murders onto the women themselves by suggesting that going out at night meant lack of loyalty to the culture, the patriarchy, and the family in the same way that lack of loyalty to the corporation meant high job turnover among women workers. As such, the Mexican woman laborer "can be nothing other than a temporary worker, one whose intrinsic value does not mature, grow, and increase over time. And therefore, as a group, Mexican women represent the permanent labor force of the temporarily employed" (143). With the growing needs of capital to cut costs in order to counter falling rates of profit, the contingency of women to the private sphere and to the domestic has justified a deepening of their exploitation through corporate expansion. The private lives of women—alongside stereotypical associations of the "feminine" and the reduction of women to their sex—are used along the Mexican border to defend the privatization of production, the deregulation of public oversight, the privatization of public services like transportation, the reason for labor's de-unionization, and capital's lack of commitment, or "loyalty," to the community from which it profits or to its safety.

The feminist critique of critical pedagogy has not recognized critical pedagogy's potential to oppose gender oppression because of its comprehensive analysis of and resistance to the power of the private. In fact, coming out of Deweyan progressivism and feminist consciousness-raising of the 1960s and 1970s while linking educational theorizing to the new social movements, a field called "feminist pedagogy" has been staging a critique against critical pedagogy precisely for what its adherents interpret as critical pedagogy's antifeminism. Elizabeth Ellsworth, for example, has argued, "To the extent that our efforts to put discourses of critical pedagogy into practice led us to reproduce relations of domination in our classroom, these discourses were "working through" us in repressive ways, and had themselves become vehicles of repression" (1994: 301), and Patti Lather has reproached critical pedagogy for "its reinscription of prescriptive universalizing," concluding that "critical pedagogy in the contemporary moment is still very much a boy thing" (2001: 184). "Feminist pedagogy" has accused critical pedagogy of not paying due attention to such core educational concerns as nurturance, feeling, authority, relationships, voice, difference, self-esteem, marginalization, cognition, experience, and resistance. Yet, this assumption of "privatized" attributes—caring and psychology (emotion, relationality, interiority)—to the feminine is re-creating the historic and discursive context for deepening gender oppression. As Jane Gallop has observed, "Maternal pedagogy might appear utopian but it is also subject to traditionally gendered prescription" (35). Feminist pedagogical critique creates social visions that, in celebrating the current position of women and the meanings of femininity, reinforce oppressive economic relations.

In his early work *The Consumer Society,* Jean Baudrillard discusses how the market destroys social relations and then offers them back up in images of solicitude. For Baudrillard, advertising provides an "ideology of a society which is continually taking care of you" (167) through a manipulation of emotions and motivations that he calls "terroristic." As capitalism destroys families by destroying the political institutions that support them, for example, the consumer society presents instead proliferating scenarios of motherly enticement and tenderness which cover up for the impoverishment of social life and replaces real attachments. For Baudrillard, this replacement is pedagogical: "If you don't know what it is to be happy," Baudrillard cites in a TWA advertisement, "we'll teach you. We know better than you" (169). The production of advertising as mothering effectively reveals the compatibility between, on the one hand, the destruction of support networks, fields of functional relationships, and public security systems, and, on the other, their anxious and accelerated replacement by signs and ceremonial narratives of sincerity, warmth, authenticity, humanity, and sentiment. The simulation of motherhood at the same time suppresses knowledge of its own magical production as it turns us all into orphans by reducing the compassionate role of the state. When unconcerned with its own political complicities, pedagogical theory worried centrally about reproducing the experience of human connection plays into a broader assault on these same values as they get subsumed in their own simulation.

Even as "feminist pedagogues" do not realize the need to contend the power of the private, the domination of the private is repeated in the historical cheapening of women's labor. As Pierre Bourdieu has explained why schools reproduce old relations of gender,

> Men continue to dominate the public space and the field of power (especially economic power—over production) whereas women remain (predominantly) assigned to the private space (domestic space, the site of reproduction)[. . .] or to the quasi-extensions of the domestic space, the welfare services (especially medical services) and education[. . .] [T]his is because [the sexual division relating to disciplines, careers and jobs] act[s] through *three practical principles* which women, and also their social circles, apply in their choices. The first is that the functions appropriate to women are an extension of their domestic functions—education, care and service. The second is that a woman cannot have authority over men[. . .] The third principle gives men the monopoly of the handling of technical objects and machines. (93–94)

"Feminist pedagogy" simply reaffirms the gender relations that have created the symbolic justification for the corporate-sponsored worldwide impoverishment, demeaning, and devaluing of women through discourses of domesticity. In this sense, "feminist pedagogy" stands against the tradition of feminist thought which Giroux has inherited as he rethinks the public/private divide so essential to thinking liberation and social change.

Law and Order

In a post–September 11 world, privacy has become a coveted and much contested terrain that needs—now as never before—to be protected *at all costs* in the name of civil liberties and democracy. The Patriot Act provisions for extending criminal enforcement will allow greater police authority in wiretapping and Internet snooping without warrants as well as greater immunity for police search-and-seizures performed under orders, more leeway for arresting suspected terrorists and holding them without charges, and more encouragement for neighbors to spy on neighbors (Welch). Additionally, a bill being considered in the state of Oregon legislature proposes to prosecute street-blocking demonstrators under an antiterrorism bill, thereby redefining civil protest and freedom of assembly as national security threats and automatically subjecting protest marchers to at least twenty-five years of prison (Douglas).

The historical symbolic linking of women with privacy has meant that the attack waged on privacy has also been waged against women, their rights, and the public institutions that protect them. The Bush administration is defining the global abortion rights of women as, like terrorism, a rationale for U.S. imperialist strong-arming and even, sometimes, economic restructuring and structural adjustments, making the world freer for the private interests of corporatism. For example, in a 2002 meeting in New York, the UN Special Session on Children was trying to negotiate a commitment to provide services to young people infected with HIV. However, "[d]uring discussion of a section referring to children in postconflict situations, Washington harped on the word 'services' because it might imply emergency contraception or abortion" (Block, 21). Analyzing the history of reproductive care in Puerto Rico, historian Laura Briggs has written about how U.S. imperialism has historically been propelled by an ideology of "rescue" of women's bodies, where women's reproduction, cultural morality, and discourses of overpopulation have been used to justify interventions like sterilization clinics:

> The Puerto Rican policy innovation, of persuading U.S. firms to employ a (largely female) work force outside the mainland and away from U.S. consumers and the mainland's apparently reliable political and physical infrastructure, was deemed a success—and contributed to the current situation, whereby virtually all manufacturing for U.S. markets is done in the Third

World. Yet, for all that this is the hard language of policy and economy, it is important to note the extent to which it was accomplished under the rubric of solving the problem of overpopulation. Explicitly, the poverty of the Third World was seen not so much as a legacy of colonialism[. . .] but rather as a problem of overpopulation, which would be solved through a combination of industrialization, techno-scientific solutions (from the birth control pill to the Green Revolution in agriculture), and modernization of the state. (18–19)

The U.S. change toward a policy of intervention that is not about restricting population but rather about aggressively enforcing its growth represents a significant symbolic alteration in imperialist maneuvering. In light of Michel Foucault's insights about modernity's invention of "population"—and therefore life itself—as a target of governance, the new U.S. orientation to impose "pro-life" initiatives means that protected privacy has shifted from a citizen's right to a corporate system. " 'It's like Bush is sacrificing the women of the world to pay his political dues,'" concludes Terri Bartlett of Communications for Population Action International (PAI) (cited in Block, 21). Chipping away at the rights to privacy promised in the *Roe v. Wade* decision, the Bush administration's new rhetoric on reproduction has been used to undermine and defund public services in the Third World, clearing the way, most often through military means, for imperialism: global corporate entry and privatization under the guise of a Christian mission.

This material assault on privacy protections is intertwined with a symbolic assault on the part of the corporate media, where the public is taught to think about privacy rights as threatening to the Bill of Rights, national security, public security, women's safety, moral social structures, the future, and the health and well-being of private enterprise. On the 11 January 2003 episode of NBC's TV drama *Law and Order,* for example, the NYPD finds a skeleton, buried in New York City's Hell's Kitchen, whose DNA is identical to that found in a human hand left in the debris of the World Trade Center collapse. In order to establish that the woman, a receptionist for a Wall Street investment firm, had been killed the night before the attack and that the hand had been dumped on the site before the erection of police barriers, the cops found themselves hacking into the e-mails of the person they suspected of murdering her: her wealthy lover. In the debate about whether or not this evidence should be admissible in court, the city lawyer claimed that the constitutional right to the protection of privacy was fictional, not written in the Constitution, and not intended by the Founding Fathers. The political scholar who had professed this position had used it to justify his opposition to the *Roe v. Wade* Supreme Court decision which, he reasoned, had been based on the false premise of a constitutional right to privacy. There is no constitutional right to privacy, this authority figure explained, pointing to a framed photograph of the Constitution on his office wall—it's just not written there. After the judge decided to admit the e-mails as evidence, the city lawyer confessed that he had not believed a word he had said in the argument, and his female associate empathized by sadly declaring that September 11 made a lot of things different.

The assault on civil liberties here makes women and their reproductive rights into a tragic target of the "War on Terror" while, at the same time, positioning women themselves as terrorists, for their sexuality naturally subjects them to justifiable public scrutiny. It is, after all, a woman's sexual "crime" that justifies both the police action and the state's assault on privacy. The lawyer in *Law and Order* alleges that *Roe v. Wade* is no longer and never was applicable because of the false premise behind the original argument: the constitutional right to privacy. This position does not take into account the history of *Roe v. Wade*'s litigation where privacy has indeed been conceded as a right by law as well as by use and has, along the way, picked up some wider protections through its association with civil rights struggles. However, alongside this one, many political statements that support civil liberties protections or warn that they are threatened are often, in the mainstream U.S. media, labeled as contrary to national interests. For example, the 16 January 2003 installment of Fox News' conservative TV-magazine *The O'Reilly Factor* started with a feature on fourteen empty chemical-weapon rocket delivery cylinders that the UN inspectors had uncovered in Iraq. The reporting and discussion speculated on what else Saddam Hussein was hiding, what the specialists interviewed imagined that such weapons had been/could be/would be used for, and the extent to which this finding would influence the scheduling of the imminent war. The next story indicated that the American Civil Liberties Union (ACLU) had announced that we were living now in a "society of surveillance" as a result of the Bush administration's policies against terror on the domestic front. O'Reilly then asked what unpatriotic intention *the liberals* had in spreading a culture of fear.

This notion that women's escape from private life and legitimate reproduction now represents a threat to corporations akin to terrorism undergirds the *Law and Order* episode about the September 11 murder. The dead receptionist's family fought against the cops because they thought it nobler for her to have died as a result of the terrorist attack—loyal to the country, the company, and the family ideal—than to have her private life exposed as contrary to the moral and domestic norm, cheating on her fiancé (who ended up murdering her because, he cried, he loved her). Responsibility and blame for the murder slide between the terrorists and the woman herself because of her moral depravity that threatens liberal notions of privacy in both their domestic and economic forms. Though she had been orphaned at a young age, her family—not knowing that she was a low-earning receptionist—had expected that she had "made it" on Wall Street, the only "success story" of her siblings. However, the murder victim was as untrue to the corporate dream of class transcendence through work as she was to women's promise of class transcendence through marriage and maternity. Because she tried to "pass" as a "bread earner," her gender conformity was compromised by her prostituted need to earn a living: her rich lover bought her rich clothes and took her to rich restaurants. She therefore exposed the lie that the patriarchal family relation was separated from the public sphere of production, revealing that much had changed since September 11, as privacy was indeed fictional, and this justified the uncovering of her private life through the court's confiscation of her private e-mails: not under corporate/domestic domination, she was a "public woman"—a terrorist. The conclusion here is that corporate privacy is what needs protection as it is threatened and undermined on all sides by citizens gone out of control: women, because of their "loose" sexual behaviors, are a threat to national security. With the collapse of the First Amendment, women's right to privacy is here redefined as contingent to two interlocking conceptions of gender domination: 1) the domestication of their desire in a conventional loyalty to conventional family, patriarchy, and country; and 2) the domestication of women's corporate service through the extension of these gendered roles into the structures of private enterprise.

The U.S. mainstream media is clearly registering a widespread uncertainty over the meanings, usages, privileges, and legal status associated with how the historical legacy of liberal thought since Locke and Hobbes is currently dressing the issue of "privacy," its definitions, its affiliations, its power, and its position in relation to the contemporary politics of terror. Additionally, this popular and intellectual concern over how privacy works and should work—especially at a time of war—touches on the same media's framing of the relation of gender and gender rights to those questions about privacy and, in particular, how the historical legacy of defining women's rights to privacy as domestication is playing out in the current discourses of domestic security. The problem, then, in trying to produce a politics of social change at the current moment, or a movement opposing the current administration's attack on rights and liberties, is that the language of opposition is still couched in a liberal notion of "privacy," which has been appropriated to support the privacy of business over the privacy of citizens.

This notion arises out of liberalism's original positing of identity in terms of property as the source of rights, where in Locke's *Second Treatise on Government,* for example, the laborer's identity initially resides in his ability to alienate and exchange his labor—the property in his body—for wages. "From all which it is evident," writes Locke, "that though the things of Nature are given in common, yet Man (by being Master of himself and *Proprietor of his own Person,* and the Actions or *Labour* of it) had still in himself *the great Foundation of Property*" (298, Paragraph 44). For Locke, labor, by adding value to what is found in nature and in common, creates value in people and in things; value is granted only to what is taken out of the common through labor, as labor constitutes the private as separate from the common.

Chantal Mouffe has elaborated on what this separation between privacy and the public means for politics and democracy.

> Today, the liberal illusion that harmony could be born from the free play of private interests, and that modern society no longer needs civic virtue, has finally shown itself to be dangerous; it puts in question the very existence of the democratic process [. . . I]t has generally been admitted that the "liberty of the moderns" consists in the peaceful enjoyment of private independence and that this implies the renunciation of the "liberty of the ancients," the active participation in collective power, because this leads to a subordination of the individual to the community. (25–37)

Mouffe warns, already in 1993, that under the current regime of "liberal democratic capitalism," the privatization of politics leads to the essentialization of political positions, with the accompanying "risk that the excluded may join fundamentalist movements or become attracted to antiliberal, populist forms of democracy" (6). In developing her theory of "radical democracy" that recognizes "the political" as agonistic, Mouffe's concern here is about posing an alternative to the polarization between those thinking politics as a consensual "public good" that subjugates individualism and those thinking politics solely as a web of intersecting private interests.

To institute the viable political and economic challenge that feminism today requires, "privacy" needs not to contradict or to limit the common but rather to integrate it. Furthermore, "privacy" needs to disassociate itself from the philosophy of property as power and to be used against it. Rather than appearing as a corporate right to transform the public into commercial spaces for private profit, or as a moral right to restrict perceptions of women's labor to private service, "privacy" needs to threaten the independence of corporations and of the corporate state—alongside their propensity to dominate for private interests—with subordination to the concerns, will, and direction of the collective. As well, "privacy" needs to be protected as a constitutive and foundational public right. Demonstrates Giroux, "[A]utonomy is inextricably linked to forms of civic education that provide the conditions for bringing to light how explicit and implicit power can be used to open up or close down those public spaces that are essential for individuals to meet, address public interests, engage pressing social issues, and participate collectively in shaping public policy" (2001: 134). In 1938, as she analyzed why women's colleges were buying into the values, codes, and ideologies of industrial competition, practical research, and private ownership in order to vie for subsidies, donations, and the promise of future jobs, Virginia Woolf understood too the danger to privacy of shutting down public politics: the ideologies using women, femininity, and domestication to fortify protected privacy were fueling a depoliticized culture of commercial growth through war as well as an identification with commercial interests over the politics of equality and peace:

> We are asking why did such an education make the person so educated consciously and unconsciously in favour of the war? Because consciously, it is obvious, she was forced to use whatever influence she possessed to bolster up the system which provided her with maids; with carriages; with fine clothes; with fine parties—it was by these means that she achieved marriage[. . .] Consciously she must accept their [men's] views, and fall in with their decrees because it was only so that she could wheedle them into giving her the means to marry or marriage itself. In short, all her conscious effort must be in favour of what Lady Lovelace called "our splendid Empire" . . . "the price of which," she added, "is mainly paid by women." And who can doubt her, or that the price was heavy? (38–39)

Caring

The economic division between "caregivers" and "bread earners," as Nancy Fraser has pointed out, has led to inequalities in distributions of wealth, from the welfare system to the workplace. In welfare, for example, women are eligible for locally managed family-based programs, which turn them into state dependents while men receive federally administered social-insurance relief, which is less prone to surveillance and controls, more supplemental, and less demeaning. The gendered division of social identities has additionally created specifically gendered contexts for social action, where, for example, (male) workers and (female) consumers mediate between the private life of the economy and the private life of the family as well as between the public life of the citizen and the public life of the state and the opinion institutions. Fraser explores how the inherently gendered caregiving function regulates the meanings of citizenship (the public sphere of deliberation is male), consumerism (the private family mediates buying patterns so that advertising has historically targeted women), the paid workforce (gendered male), and soldiering or defense (women need protections), revealing that

> male dominance is intrinsic rather than accidental to classical capitalism, for the institutional structure of this social formation is actualized by means of gendered roles. It follows that the forms of male dominance at issue here are not properly understood as lingering forms of premodern status inequality. They are, rather, intrinsically modern[. . .], since they are premised on the separation of waged labor and the state from childrearing and the household[. . .]. The preceding analysis shows that, contrary to the usual androcentric understanding, the relevant concepts of worker, consumer, and wage are not, in fact, strictly economic concepts. Rather they have an implicit gender subtext[. . .] It shows that gender identity structures paid work, state administration, and political participation[. . . A]n emancipatory transformation of male-dominated, capitalist societies, early and late, requires a transformation of these gendered roles and of the institutions they mediate. (128)

Contingently, as a result of the contemporary economy's need for flexibility, mobility, and temporalness, "caregiving" has become a trope of the economy at large as the meanings associated with the private life of the home infiltrate both the private life of the economy and the relationships between citizens and states in public institutions such as schools. Not only have women been confined symbolically to the private and therefore to the nonpolitical through their metaphoric link to the domestic, allowing for their deeper exploitation. Also, because they are understood as the only ones responsible, women can then be blamed for the shortcomings of public supports, as when the bourgeoning literature on psychological dysfunctionality attributes the breakdown of the family (and thus of society) to the waywardness of women, their pathology, or their loss of disciplinary control (as in the *Law and Order* episode as well as in the *maquiladora* spectacle analyzed above) rather than to the myriad ways, including welfare reform, that public aid has been cut from under their feet.

In a book advocating that school life needs to be modeled on home life, feminist pedagogue Nel Noddings writes,

> The expectation that women will do direct care when it is necessary remains strong. Where it has given way, the newer expectation is not that men will accept equal responsibility (although, of course, they sometimes do) but that the public will or should somehow provide care so that occupational work will not be interrupted. Many of us agree that such support should be provided. Yet, in countries where public care giving is much more generously supported than it is in the United States, complaints still arise about the lack of human caring—warmth, personal concern—in the care taking. Thus the problem cannot be entirely defined in terms of public responsibility. People long to be cared for by those who have a personal interest in them. (2002: 28–29)

Having split the function of caregiving between women and public supports, Noddings favors that it be women's responsibility because, she says, the public cannot be trusted. She then sets up a dialectical opposition between "caring-for" and "caring-about," where "caring-about" stands for a Kantian or Rawlsian set of rules or principles for just conduct based in [read: male and/or public] reason and "caring-for" means action based in what Hume called "some internal sense or feeling" (24). What Noddings thinks is essential for educational reform is a greater attention paid to homes, not only as a universal provision subsidized by the state and supervised by schools, but also as a set of private, practical lessons in household chores and moral care-values factored into all course curricula and focusing on the neglected "caring-for."

The importance of fostering an "ethics of care" leads Noddings to the insightful conclusions that people can only learn home values when they have a home and that education begins in the home. Noddings is aware that in many homes "much ordinary harm or injury is inflicted in the name of care itself" (2002: 39), though she thinks this can be fixed by proper training; instead of critiquing the ways that patriarchy has fostered violence in the home, she simply remarks that the cause of such pathology is gender socialization and then presents the "radical suggestion" that "schools should educate not only for public life but also for home and private life" (2002: 283). Patriarchal violence, she argues, would be undermined by developing courses that treat "sex education, pregnancy, birth, motherhood and fatherhood, child development, home design and aesthetics, the care of nonhuman living things, nutrition, meal planning and cooking, care of those with special needs (including the elderly), home repair and safety, budgeting and consumer knowledge, moral education, exercise and recreation" (2002: 297). In other words, the problem of patriarchal violence can be solved by teaching people the consumerist values that are inherent to home life practices that have historically been accompanied by such violence: how cooking classes or classes in interior decorating will teach students values to counter domestic violence remains unexplained.

Noddings connects this belief—that the home and its domestic chores are the dominant hope for producing moral relationships, peaceful and caring citizens—to a broader politics where, despite the recurring violence of the private and the current corporate exploitation of such domestic labor, the public would be reorganized according to its better principles. Although slightly worried that forcing people into homes when they live on the street might be coercive and therefore uncaring, Noddings still recommends community housing arrangements that inspire its members to grow by offering incentives: "inspir[ing] hopes and dreams, and mak[ing] it reasonable to suppose that at least some of these may be reached" (2002: 251):

> One can envision a building appointed for single men or women: small private bedrooms, a common dining hall, bathrooms conveniently located for each block of bedrooms, a library and information center staffed by volunteers or by residents who have already acquired the requisite knowledge. No one would be forced to move out, but strong incentives would be provided for "moving on." Everyone would do some kind of work to maintain the community. Some might work outside and pay a small rent until they could move into a situation more nearly self-supporting. (2002: 252).

At first Noddings suggests that the inhabitants themselves would pay for such a policy as they are encouraged to take jobs. Later, she concedes that families could apply for emergency loans from the government as long as the loans stipulated time restrictions, with repayment starting after the advised period of five years. Such a proposition in practice would put the most draconian welfare opponents to shame because they themselves had not even considered solving the so-called welfare problem by forcing poor and working-class people to borrow against their own futures.

Most egregiously, by reducing any role or responsibility for the public, such a policy indicates not only that work and work alone can produce human value, but also that economic mobility results assuredly from good moral values. Unabashedly embracing the corporate-manufactured promise of the American Dream, such a proposal does not answer to the downward pressure on wages, ignoring the classic Marxist critique—that capital needs and so generates a surplus labor force—the Keynsian business cycle with its downward curves calling for government stimulus and safety nets, and the current corporate agenda to decrease labor costs so labor can compete with capital flight and technological replacements. The idea of "care" here simply repeats old stereotypes where women's labor is considered moral and so outside of a public world saturated in systems of money, capital, and power. The ideological lessons of caregiving and personalization of curricula have not led to increased economic solvency or moral improvement as Noddings claims, but rather the opposite: the transfer of public responsibility to private responsibility, as in increased high-stakes testing, which makes students accountable for whether or not schools receive adequate public funding, for example, alongside cuts in urban budgets for public housing, the transformation of welfare to workfare, and widespread cuts to education, all of which make the domestic, single-earner ideal which Noddings describes nothing but a bourgeois fantasy for most people. Furthermore, Noddings's position voids any possibility of critiquing and contending the economics of women's exploitation, the domestic violence engendered through operations of money and power, the ideological manipulation of tropes about family dissolution to support economic privatization and corporate deregulation as privacy rights, or the other oppressions embedded in the constructed differentiation between public and private lives.

In *Women and Economics*, Charlotte Perkins Gilman[2] advocates a similar package to reform education in the model of the home. However, like Wollstonecraft, who understood that "[p]arental affection, indeed, in many minds, is but a pretext to tyrannize when it can be done with impunity" (150–151), Gilman challenged the idealization of the private-domestic in favor of a domestic unit comprised of democratic production and a civic forum. Instead of privatizing the public by diminishing any public role in favor of a philosophy of private initiative as Noddings does in the name of feminism, Gilman seeks to reshape the private in the model of the public, envisioning a movement out of the violence of the private into a viable possibility of a public sphere.

Even so, Gilman's work does fit well within certain nineteenth-century tropes that do not lend themselves to twenty-first-century appropriation, especially when it comes to thinking freedom. Combining evolutionary theory with a utopian interpretation of industrial relations, Gilman naturalizes the division of labor even while she relegates sex-functions and pleasure in general to a regressive evolutionary form. For Gilman, with evolution comes deeper differentiation between the genders and therefore a growing intensity of sex-attraction between them. Simultaneous with increased specialization in work, females, says Gilman, were enslaved to the sex-function, and this, in turn, limited the extent of the environment in which they could voluntarily execute their role in race preservation: sex stymies the self-expression by means of which human progress can unfold. Such a vindictive against sex alongside such an elevation of the division of labor steered Gilman into subordinating the private sphere to the more adaptive social organization found in wage labor and the factory. "As our industrial organization has grown to the world-encircling intricacies of today," she elaborates,

> as we have come to hold our place on earth by reason of our vast and elaborate economic relation with its throbbing and sensitive machinery of communication and universal interservice, the unerring response of the soul to social needs has given us a new kind of loyalty—loyalty to our work. (1998: 137)

Though Gilman's vision might be read as a proto-corporate turn for culture, it also provides a way of thinking about culture as arranged along different lines than those of private profit, private initiative, and equally private consumption.

Gilman's proposal is that day-to-day private labor would be subject to the same division of labor developed in industrialism. Those with talents in cooking would cook for a network of households while others would take care of infants, educate children, clean, or perform maintenance chores. Each occupation would require special training rooted in scientific principles. As each independent function was integrated with the others in order to form a complete working unit, the households would eventually merge together in a common living room and dining area. This vision of the household as inherently social rather than private meant that the household necessarily held together only through civic integrity or the sense of a global service to improve the conditions of life. "It is not the home as a place of family life and love that injures the child," Gilman explains,

> but as the centre of a tangled heap of industries, low in their ungraded condition, and lower still because they are wholly personal. Work the object of which is merely to serve one's self is the lowest. Work the object of which is merely to serve one's family is the next lowest. Work the object of which is to serve more and more people, in widening range, till it approximates the divine spirit that cares for all the world, is social service in the fullest sense, and the highest form of service that we can reach. (1998: 138)

Invoking socialism behind the inspiration of the divine, Gilman used the changing concept of scientific work to explode the myth of the private individual that lurked behind it. The new relations of production would create new cooperative identities, values, and consciousness as a product of deliberative interaction and social rationalism rather than of inexpedient training in privatized household chores, rote and instrumental tasks. What is central here to the construction of this association is the possibility of "the human"—a species concept premised on biological and equal capacities for reason—as the glue in the system and the founding possibility of a feminist politics.

Gilman's plan explicitly opposed the violence and tyranny arising within the patriarchal structure of the home because of its privacy. "[T]he only practical difficulty was father," Gilman wrote to introduce a fictional family. "He was the Master and Owner and Governor. He "commanded and forbade and released prisoners and remitted the customs taxes" like the sultans in the stories, only mostly he imprisoned and put the taxes on" (1994: 34). Published serially (1915) in the magazine *The Forerunner*, which Gilman edited, her children's novella *Benigna Machiavelli* told the story of Benigna, a precocious girl of twelve, who was convinced, even knowing of the Scottish heritage evident in her last name MacAvelly, that she was a descendent of the great Italian prince and had inherited his knowledge of rule. This name-game sets the stage for Benigna's denunciation of patriarchy as she sends her father fleeing back to Scotland by having printed in a Scottish newspaper a solicitation that inferred he may have been left a large property.

Benigna's trick evolves from witnessing her parents' marriage: her mother gets blamed and abused for everything that goes wrong in the household, from falling children to faulty accounting. "[H]e was saying fierce, loud things to Mother, and Mother was crying. 'Answer me that, woman!' Father shouted, waking Benigna. 'Answer me that! Are you dumb—or foolish—or both!' She was crying so she couldn't answer, and he grabbed her by the arm, and she cried out, and I was so scared and fell out of bed" (1994: 15). Benigna specifically attributes the problem to the isolation of the private from the public sphere, where Father was not as prone to drink whisky.

Modeling herself on the exploits of heroes in fairy tales (particularly, the *good* villain), she assigns herself a series of pedagogical tasks that guide her in learning necessary aptitudes and strategies for a project she later defines as management. For example, one of her teachers has a watch that gets broken, and she starts a Secret Society to collect the money to replace it. The Society later performs a play and charges admission, and Benigna tactically organizes getting her parents to leave the house and getting the housekeeper to overlook the children's activities along with how money would be allocated. Benigna's mischief always: 1) teaches her a vital lesson; 2) provides her with a conceptual tool for group enhancement; 3) creates group enhancement through interactive work; and 4) is elaborately rationalized, manipulated, managed, and governed through Benigna's meditations and for the purpose of her learning. Learning, like caring, is indelibly linked to Benigna's process in building a collective opposition to both the intellectual and physical entrenchment of the private.

In the end, Benigna sets up her mother's home as a self-sufficient boardinghouse cum restaurant with provisions for hygiene and healing and evenings of musical entertainment, operating according to a division of labor that privileges and equally values individual talents to the extent that they contribute to the upkeep and future comfort and knowledge of the establishment as a whole. When one of the residents gets sick, the doctor, the nutritionist-cook, and the entertainers all combine efforts to heal. Based on the principle that "[e]very woman should earn her own money when it is possible" (135), Benigna set up protection and education for her sister Peggy as well as provisions for sustenance and shelter for everybody. Peggy's difficulties in learning are never attributed to her personal failings, but rather to the lack of social provisions for an education that would improve the conditions of her life—she immediately rises to the occasion when given an active, working role within the social enclave.

Such a utopic and harmonious home-scene, however, relies on a troubling collapse of a potential public into a race-concept based in evolutionary eugenics. The meaning of the "human" as the force of association and sympathy in the public would need to find other avenues besides building a racial stock or totalizing reason. Certainly, Noddings fares even worse for a just politics of race, for her philosophy of personal initiative has, as the cultural historian Robin Kelley argues, shored up an ideological conviction that racial minorities fail because of personal weakness rather than because of systemic discrimination and oppression:

> For the past sixteen years, at least, we have witnessed a greater concentration of wealth while the living conditions of working people deteriorate—textbook laissez-faire capitalism, to be sure[. . .] As a result of changes in the tax laws, average workers are paying more to the government while CEOs and their companies are paying less. Sweatshops and the slave labor conditions that accompany them are on the rise again[. . . 'D]ownsizing' and capital flight have left millions unemployed[. . .] If racism is essentially a thing of the past, as conservatives and many neoliberals now argue, then the failure of the black poor to lift themselves out of poverty has to be found in their behavior or their culture. In short, the problems facing the vast majority of black folk in today's ghettos [such pundits insist] lie not with government policy or corporate capitalism, but with the people themselves[. . .] (7–8)

Like Gilman—though without rooting socialist politics within evolutionary science and utopian industrialism, Kelley appeals to a language of "humanity" and "community" (4)—rather than an individualizing language of care or a language of mothering completely consumed in stereotypes of pathology and conservative calls to discipline—by working through the context of the city rather than the private home. He thus counters narratives of dysfunctionality which privatize poverty as well as the means to struggle against it and which blame violence on those against whom it is waged.

Pscyhology

Within the Western philosophical tradition, claims Alison Jaggar, the emotions and sensibility have been demoted, if not erased, as sites of knowledge. As scientific objectivity required verification and repetition, body and experience were marginalized as too particularistic, subjective, and variable. Emotions were also suspect because they were associated with the irrational. Feminist epistemology attempts to reclaim the role of emotions in producing judgments, engagements, and actions, and to retrace the history of emotions behind the scientific enterprise. Emotions can, the logic goes, disrupt, resist, or even uproot the patriarchal order based on the domination of reason. Even though emotions are socially constructed and so have led to historical atrocities like imperialism, misogyny, and homophobia, Jaggar allows for a different type of emotion—what she calls "outlaw emotions" that "provide the first indications that something is wrong

with the way alleged facts have been constructed, with accepted understandings of the way things are" (161)—to form the basis of feminism.
These emotions arise out of pain, trauma, compassion, or outrage, experienced as the "gut level" awareness that the world could be different. Jaggar
admits to being vague when she tries to distinguish between the "good"
emotions that lead to universal joy and the "bad" emotions that lead to
injustices, or between "deceptive" emotions that make a slave love his master and authentic outlaw emotions, though she does not seem to fathom
that these judgments themselves are couched in historically specific emotional data (for instance, that many involved in imperialist missions *felt*
that they were saving souls). She does, however, venture that moral emotions are "the highest form of love" because they "draw on heart as well as
hand and brain" (162).

By centering the emotions as a particularly feminized or feminist way of
knowing, such perspectives evoke mothering as the protocol of liberation.
Even more than in pedagogies of care, the psychologization of knowledge
in the name of feminism works to privatize education by voiding the social
and the political as well as isolating the classroom and its social interactions from a broader, global framework of economic and ideological
power in which both schooling and the private are lodged. When feminism
stakes its claims as reaffirming and celebrating the positions women have
been assigned by patriarchal capitalism and the meanings attributed to
those positions, it is simply accommodating itself to conventions of exploitation. The feminist discourse on emotions and knowledge through
emotions performs three basic functions: (1) it restricts consideration of
the public either for analyzing the context of oppression or for imagining
opposition; (2) it produces a commonsense understanding that the
mother-child bond represents and guarantees the liberal ideals of autonomy and freedom for the child. This commonsense understanding, as Valerie Walkerdine and Helen Lucey have shown, supports the regulation of
mothers, and particularly of working-class mothers who, in this paradigm,
are automatically and programmatically pathologized (1989: 29);[3] (3) it
assumes that feminism is, by definition, only fathomable as a result of mid-
dle-class nuclearization. The problem with eliding women and the possibility of their politics with home and family is the same as confining the
oppression of women to home and family relationships: it codes politics
and freedom as the province of class and racial privilege, as bell hooks has
elaborated:

> Feminism in the United States has never emerged from the women who are
> most victimized by sexist oppression; women who are daily beaten down,
> mentally, physically, and spiritually—women who are powerless to change
> their condition in life[. . .] Friedan's famous phrase, "the problem which has

no name," often quoted to describe the condition of women in this society, actually referred to the plight of a select group of college-educated, middle and upper class, married white women[...] She did not speak to the needs of women without men, without children, without homes. She ignored the existence of all non-white women and poor white women. She did not tell readers whether it was more fulfilling to be a maid, a babysitter, a factory worker, a clerk, or a prostitute, than to be a leisure class housewife. (1984: 1–2).

In feminist pedagogical theory, the emotions serve to locate feminist liberation interrelatedly in family relationships, the Unconscious, and the irrational. These conceptual devices are, in these analyses, masking their own origins in politics and history and ignoring their racial and class biases as well as hiding their points of intersection with more repressive movements of contemporary capitalist ideology as it tears away at public power.

In Jaggar's view, the only way to interpret history is through emotive responses. Material struggles, resource needs, and political action are limited to corporealized, internalized states rather than public struggle. Because it is defined through emotions, the "human," for Jaggar, is individualized, naturalized, and physicalized, completely separated from institutional effect or public mediation. Indeed, various strains of feminist pedagogy insist that the exclusion of emotions from institutional knowledge and reason causes the discomfort or alienation that women feel in the classroom. For example, in her autobiographical preamble to her book on multiculturalism where she meditates on the difficulties of growing up as a white girl in America, Christine Sleeter confesses, "I cultivated a strategy to cope with the incompatibility I perceived between being smart and female" (19) (her strategy was to become a cheerleader, but she later realizes this was not a good solution). Following on what she learned from her teacher Alison Jaggar, Jane Tompkins taught a women's studies class on "emotions" where she was "led, by various reporting groups into role-playing, picture drawing, and even on one occasion into participating in a religious ceremony," though what these various activities were supposed to articulate—and how they were supposed to challenge the neoliberal university's exploitation of (largely female) adjunct and contingent labor, which Tompkins describes—remain uncertain, outside of her admission that she found such rituals entertaining and good for building self-esteem.

Anne Seller talks about the thorniness of trying to teach philosophy in a women's studies class, as the philosophy students were interested in engaging complex problems of subjectivity, which alienated the women's studies students who were more enthusiastic about literary theory and psychoanalysis because it provided them with a language to explain "how they felt about their subjectivity" (26). Though praising feminist philosophy as a "place from which we could interrogate institutionalized knowledges and make them answerable not just to women, but to all those excluded constituencies" (26), Sellers remarks that feminist philosophy can sound "unfeminist" "on the grounds that they think too much like men" (29). What she wants instead is a "feminizing philosophy," or "putting women's voices into philosophy" (28) and "finding their own agendas" (29). Sellers is a bit more willing than Jaggar to grant emancipatory potential to philosophic thought. Yet, she still makes a division—a historically gendered division—between thought that is based in reason and so seems part of a masculinist ideology on the one hand, and, on the other, thought that is based in experience, sensation, and emotion and so is considered women's expression and voice, an upsetting of the canonical principles of reason, and so less exclusionary of the marginalized.

Similarly, Maxine Greene has explored feminism in teaching as opposing scientific rationalism with other forms of knowledge: first empiricism (sensuous and common sense experience), then pragmatism (personal calculation of experience), phenomenology (memory of experience), and existentialism (self-consciousness and self-encounter). Though understanding the need for reason as discipline, Greene encourages teachers to use these different forms of knowledge in order to "permit children to pursue their interests, to learn what they desire and not what society imposes on them" (1973: 75), in other words, to recognize the desire in children, a desire that individuates and personalizes them but is generally excluded from considerations of knowledge. As Anthony Elliott has illustrated, such privileging of the self as an emancipatory figure leads toward an "anti-political politics" where "modern women and men[. . .] imagine that problems of identity are, first and foremost, matters for individual attention and personal solution; the culture of identity politics is increasingly made up of isolated and isolating voices, with few cultural resources available for connecting personal troubles to public issues" (17). Additionally, a theory centered in the self promotes the cultural logic that encourages students to make "an enterprise" of themselves. Teaching practices that aim to improve self-esteem usually endorse white and privileged students to feel good and proud without necessarily understanding what creates the privilege to which this "achievement" belongs and without contemplating the way this privilege assures the further privilege of domination.

This gendered division of knowledge between the rational and the emotional does not actually challenge the philosophic canon but rather replicates the very cornerstone classic philosophic debates between the rationalists and the empiricists, the debates culminating in Kant's foundational texts of modern philosophy. The current usage of this old philosophic conflict in such works as Jaggar's, Tompkins', Seller's, Sleeter's and Greene's, is to reduce reason to domination and then to save a place outside of reason for a freedom from domination in pure physical sensation. This idea works, in turn, to help build a vision of freedom as the sensation of a new car or the thrill of a new detergent: it ignores that emotion itself has become the most visible and robust tool of domination in commercial culture. The elevation of emotion to a principled pedagogy disallows the possibility of thinking about how emotion and desire have been manipulated into a culture of advertising and consumption. Giroux has been criticized as a theorist whose excessive rationalism has abandoned "analysis of the emotional investments they [students] experience in relation to particular symbols," neglecting Marx in favor of Habermas but still too enamored by the Frankfurt School (Zembylas and Boler). However, Giroux discusses how not only emotions can be engaged in pedagogy as a way of enabling students to see the relationship between what they learn and how they live, but, at the same time, that students also need to come to an understanding of "the deeper affective investments that make them complicitous with oppressive ideologies" (2001: 106). Following on both Marx and the Frankfurt School, Giroux underscores the need for reason to work against itself rather than to be restricted to the role of domination as well as the need to explore how reason, power, and authority produce emotions to serve specified ends that might not be in the students' interests.

Additionally, as Luce Irigaray has so thoroughly demonstrated, the gendering of this constructed opposition between reason and emotions is less than new. According to Irigarary, the Western philosophical tradition has evoked emotion and sensibility as inversions of reason as part of the way it constructs woman as "man minus the possibility of (re)presenting oneself" (27), and so outside of the representations of concepts through which Kant explores the rational subject. She exposes how Freud's castration complex exemplifies a recurring symbolic pattern in philosophical discourse where femininity holds the place of the nothing-to-be-seen, which reaffirms, through negativity, man's sense of his own survival: "Now the little girl, the woman, has *nothing* you can see. She exposes, exhibits the possibility of *a nothing to see*[. . .] *Nothing to be seen is equivalent to having no thing. No being and no truth*" (47–48). Calling the process variously "sexual indifference" or "hom(m)osexuality" to show the play of sameness, Irigaray traces the tradition through time, revealing the entrenchment of a concept of emotion that mirrors reason but turns it around, the impossibility of difference in the endless repetition and projection of male subjectivity and its reason onto its other. Psychoanalysis, for example, creates femininity as reflecting nothing but the negativity through which male reason represents itself, as when "women have '*less capacity for sublimating their instincts* than men'" (113). Femininity appears as the difference of the

Unconscious, which, for Irigaray, is no difference at all, but just the limit which reason poses for its own self-representation, the emptiness that props up the representation for man of himself as solid, salvageable, conscious, reasonable. "For her, the knowledge would be absolutely 'unconscious,' nonknowledge, but he is able to decipher it to the extent that in some way or other he has tied woman down as the guardian of the negative" (111). On the part of feminist pedagogues who argue for a feminized epistemology, the wish to design a feminism that inhabits the emotions or the Unconscious as a specifically female way of knowing follows a tradition that has historically placed women as the negation of reason, the negation in which reason builds its own image and material dominance.

Irigaray's feminist philosophy has convincingly explained how the separation between emotions and reason has reinforced the oppression of women by subordinating the femininity of emotions to the role of supplementing masculinity as reason, representation, and existence. Nevertheless, disregarding such thinking, much feminist pedagogy has extended this division into various arguments about teaching and psychoanalysis. For example, developing the "object relations" psychology much cited in pedagogical theory, Nancy Chodorow has focused on gender differences in socialization to explain different ethical orientations in boys and girls, where boys think through objectivity and principles and girls make ethical decisions based first on relationships. Chodorow has defended her principle interest in the private sphere and emotional life on the basis that it is the main locus of women's oppression, where the public sphere of the state is less directly meaningful. "I probably would have continued to develop as a Marxist feminist if I had thought that gender inequality inhered primarily in capitalist or capitalist-patriarchal work relations. I would have learned political theory if I had thought that the state was the primary locus of women's oppression or become a cultural critic or philosopher if I thought woman's oppression was located in her otherness" (5). For Chodorow, psychoanalysis is particularly appropriate for analyzing the intensity of experiences because it centers the personal and the familial—"abortion, marriage, divorce, the regulation of sexuality, parenting" (8). It is remarkable how, for instance, "abortion" or "marriage" (never mind "the regulation of sexuality") is locked into private, family relationships rather than public law and, contingently, that decisions about them cannot be considered ethical. Even "parenting" here has been discounted from a public role, an association that would eventually make sense of parents being held accountable, imprisoned, and fined, for their children's infractions or welfare to children who have lost parents (AFDC) being gutted.

The use of femininity in such psychoanalytic perspectives works conceptually to privatize whatever public or political issue is on the table in the name of celebrating and recognizing the emotional. The private is turned into an internal trouble to be accommodated and gratified without reference to the histories of institutional oppression which, in the contemporary formation, include privatization and the types of femininities to which it is linked. Elizabeth Ellsworth, for example, has envisioned the relationship between the Unconscious and Consciousness as personified in the student-teacher relationship, where the student's interior resistances disrupt the rationality of the teacher's lessons. "[Y]ou could say," she proposes, "that teaching is impossible because the unconscious constantly derails the best intentions of pedagogies[. . . The unconscious] brings a passion for ignorance, that is, resistances to knowledge and refusals of one's own implication in it—it brings forgetting[. . .] All learning and knowing takes a detour through the discourse of the Other—through the unconscious and opaque dynamics of social and cultural prohibition" (1997: 55–64). By making dialogue impossible, Ellsworth erases the prospects of democratic deliberation, social contextualization, political resistance, strategic alliance, or a public forum, while downgrading opposition to an individualized, isolated mental operation for the love of ignorance. By focusing on communication, the indeterminacy of language, and the interiority of the psyche, Ellsworth, as Kenneth J. Saltman has pointed out, "does not address how the political economy of schools and of the mass media reproduce intensifying logics of privatization and fundamentalism, which reduce questions of difference, democracy, and the public good to questions of individual consumption[. . . V]iolence originates with the closure of signification" (1998). In other words, Ellsworth never questions or criticizes the collapse of feminism into a private, interior identity based in desire, nor the politics of ignorance where anti-intellectualism can be elevated to a moral principle, schools can be shut down and defunded, and political policy can be formulated without reason, rationale, or evidence. Linking desire to possessive individualism as defining a social order where "the only end of accumulation is to accumulate afresh," Terry Eagleton remarks, "[d]esire comes to seem independent of any particular ends, or at least grotesquely disproportionate to them; and once it thus ceases to be[. . .] intentional, it begins monstrously to obtrude itself as[. . .] an opaque, unfathomable, self-propelling power utterly without purpose or reason, like some grisly caricature of the deity" (159). Ellsworth does not raise the issue of what this privatization has meant historically as it reduces the politics of femininity to the affiliative, the aesthetic, and the affective, nor what kind of larger social context and relations of power such a reduction and interiorization capacitate.

Ignorance *is not* a feel-good libratory gesture nor an escape from the domination of reason, but rather subjects the disempowered and the disenfranchised more resolutely to its authority. Most egregiously, Ellsworth disregards how the attribution of ignorance has been wielded for marginalizing populations, closing schools, shutting down opportunities, gutting social programs, discounting electoral ballots, undermining affirmative action initiatives, blaming teachers for the effects of structural poverty, turning education itself into an assessment testing machine, and the like. As Avital Ronell has noted, "Destructive and clear in its aim, stupidity as an act of naming commits barely traceable acts of ethnocide[. . .] Nowadays, even if it is no longer acceptable to pronounce oneself in overtly racist tones, one can reappropriate stupidity, load it up and point it[. . .] at the minoritized subject. Nothing keeps you down like the mark of stupidity" (27). Currently in the United States (as the following chapter discusses more fully), ignorance has created an aesthetic of power that makes it seem as though a president brought up in extreme wealth and proximity to power-brokers and agenda-setters is really one of the common folk.

Additionally, Ellsworth, like other feminist pedagogues, uses the theories of Jacques Lacan to draw out the subject's misrecognition as the key to freedom. For Lacan, the infant who sees himself reflected in a mirror learns to recognize himself in an image that is whole and so contrary to his experience of his ego as fragmented. The appropriation of this concept by feminist pedagogy is part of a larger appropriation by second-wave liberal feminism theories of the autonomous subject, particularly in thinking through a psychic dimension of women's difference from men as formulating a kind of political intervention. Many second-wave feminist theorists were, in part, reacting against the forms of nineteenth-century feminism, which sought to erase sexual difference in favor of a social theory of political morality based in a universalized idea of the citizen-subject. For example, Julia Kristeva has appropriated the Lacanian Imaginary as a site of feminist resistance because the Imaginary is construed as the Unconscious constructed through maternal relations and disrupting the rule of the Symbolic (language, reason, and the social). Kristeva defines the incompleteness of the Ego as the result of a combination of prerationalist forces—religion, mysticism, the archaic, diabolism, and art—connected with the maternal and the pre-Symbolic Imaginary, where the child experiences, as Lacan theorizes, "a fragmented body-image" (4), exhibited in dreams, fantasies, artwork, and "the schizoid and spasmodic symptoms of hysteria" (Lacan, 5), when all self-knowledge is based in sensory experience, before the unification of the Ego in language. In her recent book *The Sense and the Senseless*, Kristeva blames the rise of market normalization not on corporate power or on the increasing financialization and managerialism of international relations or in cuts to social spending, but rather on a general lack of "an obstacle, prohibition, authority, or law," attributable to the father, which, when overcome, would allow us "to realize ourselves as autonomous and free" (7) as the maternal relation promises. In other words, resistance like power is located in the family through which the social relations of production are exhibited.

Ellsworth translates the Lacanian ego-concept into a pedagogical setting where communication from the teacher turns through a "third term"—the unconscious—that opens up signification and unfixes meaning.[4] Female sexuality as the marker of difference has here been transferred into linguistics and de-eroticized. In the name of feminism, Ellsworth emphasizes that true statements are impossible because they are always misrecognized. Aijaz Ahmad has criticized such contestations because they remove from representation and agency those already denied access to the power of representation like, in this case, people from the Third World:

> This image of language as the enemy of experience, this assertion that representation is always-already a misrepresentation, this shallow pathos about the impossibility of truthful human communication, is of course a familiar Romantic trope which has undergone much aggrandizement—first in those irrationalist philosophies of the late nineteenth century and the early twentieth which preceded the rise of fascism and then again, on a much wider scale, in the reactionary anti-humanisms which have dominated many strands in contemporary avant-gardist thought. In relation to the knowledge of history, then, this image of human communication as a ruse of illusory subjectivity precludes the possibility of truthful statement on the ground that evidence, the criterion of truthful statement in history-writing, is always-already prejudiced by the very nature of language itself. It is significant that these anti-humanisms have come to dominate so much of American scholarship on the eve of the unprecedented imperialist consolidations of the present decade. (194–195)

It is equally significant that such irrationalist and antihumanist philosophies have come to prominence at a time when women—the historical measure of the irrational in much scientific, medical, and psychoanalytic as well as literary discourse, as in André Breton's *Nadja*—have been ever more stringently locked out of representation, increasingly disenfranchised, objectified, impoverished, and systematically exploited on a global level. Putting the feminine into the position of the irrational has worked not so much to bring down reason as to shore up, as Irigaray predicted, the rule of the capitalist reason of accumulation through the processes of dehumanization, negation, linguistic mystification, underrepresentation, and political demobilization, particularly for women.

This is not to say that all postmodern and poststructuralist thought is politically ineffectual because its attention to language and its irrationalities has canceled out all materiality, as Teresa Ebert and Rosemary Hennessy have argued. "[T]he dominant feminist theory in the postmodern moment—ludic feminism," begins Ebert, has largely abandoned the problems of labor and exploitation and ignored their relation to gender, sexuality, difference, desire, and subjectivity[. . .] Following Foucault, Lacan, Derrida, and other poststructuralist theorists, ludic feminism, including much recent socialist feminism, has articulated the social as discourse/textuality and posited desire/pleasure as the dynamic of the social. In so doing, it has displaced economic, labor, and class struggle[. . .] Now, in place of a historical materialist analysis for social change, feminists are provided with models for 'the care of the self,' for 'performing' and 'remetaphorizing' difference, for 'power feminism,' and for 'sexual-agency' feminism, all of which trivialize the situation of women: reducing it to matters of textuality, desire, or volunteerism. (ix–x)

And likewise Rosemary Hennessy has recognized that "[b]y reconfiguring the self as permeable and fragmented subjectivity but then stopping there, some postmodern discourses contribute to the formation of a subject more adequate to a globally-dispersed and state-controlled multinational consumer culture which relies upon increasingly atomized social relations" (6). However, these critics want to retrieve a subject in some respect outside of language—variously materialist, humanist, empirical, nondiscursive, or total—with a utopian access to pure history, a way underneath representation uncomfortably similar to a transcendent knowledge, the providence of a vanguard.

As well, such theory underplays the material role of culture. Manipulated and controlled within larger spheres of economic interest, language—rather than always guaranteeing free expression, desire, or self-definition—produces a politics of distribution through licensing some possibilities, meanings, and judgments over others, opening up some identifications over others, celebrating certain identities while denigrating others, and inserting value. In this sense, language is indiscernible from the empirical. Finding an outside to language is a chore which, following on the history of patriarchy, often locks women outside of power discourses and public agency, reducing them to the same base referential materialism that has been played out in ideals of domestic consumption and the subordination of the laboring body. Feminism should be locating the linguistic context that continually situates femininity as the outside or the inverse of rational subjectivity and so depreciates the worth of the identities which it imbibes and the labor which it frames. Also, it needs to show how language itself is distributed according to the same materialist principles that structure the economy more generally, and so emotions, interiority, desire, and sensation are at least partially formed and mobilized as the private—through the language of mass-mediated representation of the feminine, for example—as part of a general consolidation of power and wealth and their trajectories of accumulation.

Unlike the feminist pedagogues who have claimed ancestry in the history of feminism, in 1792 Mary Wollstonecraft understood that recognizing reason, rather than claiming emotion, was necessary to women's emancipation. For this, she spotlighted education as fundamental to feminist reform, the only way to teach respect for "public good" and "to preserve private virtue" as "the only security of public freedom" (6). "My own sex, I hope," she requests, "will excuse me, if I treat them like rational creatures, instead of flattering their *fascinating* graces, and viewing them as if they were in a state of perpetual childhood, unable to stand alone" (9). As much as it supported practices of domestic life by clearing the way for independent thinking, reason also indicated a release from the tyranny of private life, which restricted women's options to aesthetic display, artificiality, the excitation of desire, contemptible cunning, and the pursuit of flattery.

> [W]hile they [females] have been stripped of the virtues that should clothe humanity, they have been decked with artificial graces that enable them to exercise a short-lived tyranny. Love, in their bosoms, taking place of every nobler passion, their sole ambition is to be fair, to raise emotion instead of inspiring respect; and this ignoble desire, like the servility in absolute monarchies, destroys all strength of character. Liberty is the mother of virtue[. . .] (37)

Suspicious of desire, Wollstonecraft sees it as a kind of manipulation that desperate women enact because of their economic need to inspire love in order to win security in dependency. Women are "designed by sweet attractive grace, and docile blind obedience, to gratify the senses of man" (19). For Wollstonecraft, desire is the inauthentic result of imbalanced hierarchies of power: "should they be beautiful, every thing else is needless" (19). Desire arises out of the trickery and artistry that women perform in their ignorance when marriage is their only option, a condition brought about through the denial of educational access and equality and the false claim that women's natural weakness in reason parallels her natural constitutional weakness and smaller body. Wollstonecraft believes that the deficiency in women's education was a social feature left over from monarchic rule. Concerned centrally with the interconnection between power and desire, Wollstonecraft would understand the centralizing and decontextualizing of desire in feminist pedagogy as unthinkingly obedient to the submissive and exclusionary laws of patriarchy.

Wollstonecraft set her theory on top of the familiar, gendered dichotomy between feeling and thinking, completely damnifying the conventionally feminine attributes of sensibility, desire, and the pleasures of the body in order to prove that women did not inhabit them. As Cora Kaplan summarizes, "Through the assertion that women were not innately or excessively sexual, that on the contrary their 'feelings' were largely filial and maternal, the imputation of a degraded subjectivity could be resisted" (866). The poor education of women has, Wollstonecraft insisted, insured that women were "sacrificed to beauty" (7), and for freedom, women need to be released from this subjugation. This type of rhetorical move resembles the philosophic tradition that Irigaray faults for posing femininity as negation, or as masculinity without representation. However, Wollstonecraft changes this metaphoric relation by separating an authentic femininity from sensibility and linking sensibility, on the one hand, to aristocratic culture—"the education of the rich tend to render them vain and helpless" (9)—and—much more problematically—to the tyrannous seraglio (10), "Mahometanism" (8), or the primitive harem—on the other.

Not only does Wollstonecraft therefore delink femininity to its referencing codes, insinuating that the meanings assumed in femininity are constructed and resignifiable and cannot be accommodated. But associating sensibility with the vainglorious gallantry of the aristocracy also has other important rhetorical effects: 1) it disassociates emotion from femininity, thereby allowing the meaning of femininity to escape from opposition to reason and the public deliberation reason allows; 2) it suggests that independence and identity are not collapsed into the privacy of isolated feelings as the promise of liberation, but are rather called into play in the need for civic action; 3) it sets the reason through which women gain civil independence against the reason of the military, because the reason of the military is based in top-down command authority likened to a parasitical "chain of despots" (17) and therefore expunging independent thought; 4) it also sets reason against a commercialism based in "the desire of dazzling by riches" and "the pleasure of commanding flattering sycophants" (13)—all related to the monarchy and its culture of command.

Certainly, no theory of feminism or equality can rest easy with the conclusion that pleasure, beauty, and desire inhibit true thought, nor that sexual restraint is akin to virtue and reason, nor, most emphatically, that the dangerous passions, sensuality and fleshly pleasures are particularly characteristic of non-European cultures and therefore threatening to civilization. Precluding such thinking is the history of targeting, policing, and abusing sexual minorities as well as the practices of flexing imperialist muscle to impose population controls in poor countries. However, this moralistic and desexualized argument remaining within some strains of contemporary feminism and much feminist pedagogy in particular has been picked up and used, in turn, to scapegoat teachers, women, and sexual minorities for failing schools. The 10 February 2003 Valentine's Day episode of the popular TV drama *Boston Public*, for example, has a white woman teacher who shows particular interest in helping and nurturing one of her students, who, in the serial, most often are represented as the poor, urban, migrant underclasses. When the student confesses in her composition class to having a sexual dream about this teacher, the teacher suddenly realizes that the special nurturance might be causing problems for the student and there is discussion between the teacher and the rest of the faculty about if the special treatment has "crossed the line"; the dangerously unstable line between mothering and seducing has been broached. Though in the end the teacher is acquitted of allegations of oversexualizing her teaching functions when the student is diagnosed as a criminal psychopath, and nurturing is affirmed as an effective teaching method, the teacher is still transferred out of the school and the city because, the principal tells her, of safety precautions. This narrative changes the story behind the current shuffling of both teachers and the student body—predominantly composed of racial minorities—in Boston public middle schools, where—to take the place of the old busing rules, which have been overturned—every year students must take assessment tests and every year they must switch schools and teachers no matter where in the rankings they fall. The *Boston Public* story makes it seem that teachers, particularly female teachers, themselves might very well be responsible for this shuffling, because of the questionable moral structure of teaching in the face of irresistible sexualized adolescents, or even a certain inherent pathology in the maternalized role of teaching, and that the good feminist teacher needs to be in control of a line not to be crossed and so needs to be shifted around often. The Boston public schools have not been seen as declining because students study in the same place with the same teachers over a number of years, but rather because of white flight to the suburbs and private schools following on busing regulations and the subsequent fall in inner-city appropriations. *Boston Public*'s explanation for the shuffling elides the question about the academic results of the shuffling or who is benefiting from creating a culture of schooling that makes it more difficult for mostly working-class and minority students to adapt, to maintain curricular continuity, to feel cared for, or to succeed within urban public education.

Jane Gallop has identified how feminist pedagogy has, indeed, picked up this puritanical side of Wollstonecraft's thought. Gallop explores how the history of feminism benefits from a tension or sometimes an alliance between a "bad girl" feminism—a feminism championing freedoms of the body—and a "good girl" feminism—a feminism based in "female values." Feminist pedagogy, however, expels the side of a feminism advocating pleasure as empowering and adopts exclusively a moralistic feminism that speaks from the place of the nineteenth-century female exemplar, equating desire with "selfless, sexless nurturance" (29). In Wollstonecraft's work, as for the makers of *Boston Public*, the splitting of femininity between a "bad" version and a "good" version is never really complete but rather displaced onto class, making morality into an issue of class struggle through which the emergent middle class would define itself. Not well-positioned historically to conceive a role for sexuality in feminism, Wollstonecraft sees sexuality only as indicating the dangers for feminism of objectifying women in the body, in sex, and in pleasure. She does not then foresee the potential challenge to power instigated when women become subjects of their own desire. Yet Wollstonecraft's reconstruction of femininity is directed toward opening up a sphere of politics rather than defensively projecting its atomization and privatization. As well, Wollstonecraft lays out the groundwork for talking about how the emotions can lend themselves to tyranny, contending that women's identities restricted in their private roles and private expression are a far cry from liberation, that the "social" needs to be a primary category of feminist analysis, and that, contrarily, desire is manipulated in the service of keeping power private.

Critical pedagogy continues to share the critical tradition in which Wollstonecraft originally formulated feminism because it is committed to initiating a discursive practice in which the idea of the public can be imagined, embraced, and concretized. "[I]f she not be prepared by education [. . .]," Wollstonecraft begins, "she will stop the progress of knowledge and virtue; for truth must be common to all, or it will be inefficacious with respect to its influence on general practice[. . . T]he love of mankind, from which an orderly train of virtues spring, can only be produced by considering the moral and civil interest of mankind; but the education and situation of woman, at present, shuts her out from such investigations" (4). This appeal to the public as the ultimate referent for knowledge is repeated, for example, in Pepi Leistyna's ethnography, which chronicles a community planning a multicultural agenda for schools. Instead of dividing the group, Leistyna observes, the issue of gender served to demonstrate the relation of gender and feminist struggle to broader questions of oppression, particularly race and class oppression. While discussing feminist struggles helped to challenge "women, who were predominantly white, to face their own racism," it also created "a public space within which racially subordinated men are compelled to face their beliefs on gender" (120). Leistyna believes, like Chandra Mohanty, that the only way to combat racism, sexism, homophobia, and imperialism is to create "public cultures of dissent[. . .] that are grounded in the *interests* of people and which recognize the *materiality* of conflict, of privilege, and of domination" (1990: 207). bell hooks agrees: "I fear that any feminist transformational process that seeks to change society is easily co-opted if it is not rooted in a political commitment to mass-based feminist movement" (1994: 70–71). In these accounts, as for Wollstonecraft, the issue of gender leads to a sense of a public that is politicized against oppression rather than a closing down of social concerns in favor of a sentimentalization of the private, the emotional, the nurturant, the therapeutic, and the self-expressive.

Much of the recent theoretical speculation on the diminishing role of the nation-state in an age of globalization has made it ever more difficult to invoke the necessity for theorizing the future of public institutions as well as thinking through a resistance to capitalism where defense of the public must furnish a dominant claim. As Andreas Kalyvas has argued, "The vogue of globalization in academic circles has greatly hampered the study of the state ... [T]he rise of postmodern and poststructuralist discourses and concomitant stress on the multiplicity of microtechnologies of power and their diffuse character have substantially undermined the image of the state as a pivotal and sovereign power center and as the main location of political domination" (106). The difficulty of thinking the state has, contingently, made it ever more difficult to think the public. The stakes in overvaluing the sanctity of private life or in undervaluing the thinking of the public in discussions of identity, theory, and politics become clear now in a time of "war on terror" when public spending is being rapidly depleted to fund a deficit in the trillions of dollars supposed to be funneled toward military initiatives. This breakdown in public supports has, in turn, incited insecurity while alleging to route it out, shifting the responsibility for safety onto private citizens (do you know how to contact your family during a terrorist attack? asks the new bureau of Homeland Security. Have you bought enough duct tape to protect yourself in your home?), and planting the seeds for the further buyout of public functions by private companies. Additionally, as the United States unilaterally bypasses the decisions of the UN Security Council, as new telecommunications legislation reforms might allow single companies to control all the media in a given community, as neighbors are encouraged to spy on neighbors as part of new protocols of patriotism, theories that explore power only as decentered and networked across multiple sites seem divested and alienated from critiques of the most dangerous and violent present-day exercises of power. The difficulty in thinking the public further incapacitates certain types of reflection on Third World integration, whose present formulation often takes on the projects of opening markets, commercialization, exploiting natural resources, attracting investments, and providing cheap labor for corporate production, all goals speculating on private value and profitability rather than on public benefits or the strengthening of democratic institutions and yet clearly supported by the state, with its changing legality, its military might, and its allocations. Having looked at the historical role of the public in imagining and shaping the future of democratic feminist politics, the rest of this book goes on to indicate further what is at stake in a public politics that revitalizes the task of thinking counter to the privatization and commercialization of public life.

CHAPTER 2

The Philosopher's Stoned
Harry Potter's Public

"And to the C students, I say, you, too, can be president of the United States."
—President George W. Bush, Yale Commencement, 21 May 2001

The Age of Harry

As he received an honorary degree from his alma mater, the self-proclaimed "Education President" and leader of the "Free World" George W. Bush, addressing the Yale graduating class of the year 2001, announced proudly that education was pointless to success in America. Referring to Vice President Dick Cheney's dropping out of Yale, the president went on: "now we know: If you graduate from Yale [with Cs], you become president. If you drop out, you get to be vice president." He also made "jokes" about his insufficient grasp of the English language, boasted about his blackouts and memory loss from excessive partying, and bragged about his propensity to snore away during his study hours in the Yale library. Entering public awareness partly through the efforts of the president himself, Bush's stupidity works propagandistically to consolidate his ideological power and his rhetorical platform around his insults to education and his antiintellectualism.

Much has been made of Bush's illiteracy. Mark Crispin Miller has deemed him the "most illiterate [president] in U.S. history":

> George W. Bush is so illiterate as to turn completely incoherent when he speaks without a script or unless he thinks his every statement through beforehand that the effort empties out his face[. . .] Without [. . .] hasty mental planning, Bush is likely to make statements that [. . .] don't mean anything ("I will have

foreign-handed foreign policy") or require unscrambling ("Families is where our nation finds hope, where wings take dream") or say the opposite of what he means ("Well, I think if you say you're going to do something and don't do it, that's trustworthiness") or are just dead wrong ("The legislature's job is to write law. It's the executive branch's job to interpret law"). (2001: 6)

Referring to the comedies and parodies of Bush's linguistic follies both during and after the campaign, Miller rightly notes that the widespread humor surrounding Bush's stupidity serves to deflect the much more serious failings of the administration, like his faulty business practices and, I would add, his propensity to fashion war discourse as though war itself were a video game. Think, for example, of the logic behind the argument for preemptive strike: we are told that the twenty-first century has brought with it the possibility of an attack that would kill millions; even though there's no evidence of this, nor is there any evidence that many nations besides the United States (e.g., Iraq) have the capacity to manufacture *and* transport such weapons, the United States must wipe out other nations, regardless of cost to human lives (exactly how it will be decided which nations are potentially dangerous in this way is not specified: agreeing to weapons inspections seemed at first to be one of the criteria, except that when Iraq agreed to weapons inspections, it remained on the list, while many other nations who have not agreed to weapons inspections have never made it on the list). The faulty logic exhibited here—with the absence of evidence, with various magical leaps in the argument, and with a fallback to faith rather than legitimating reason to justify power—would surely receive failing grades in any kind of assessment testing, but goes on to bolster a paranoid defense that one minute professes a faith in duct tape and plastic to save us from chemical and biological attacks and the next minute is forced to admit that duct tape and plastic are apt to cause suffocation and not guard us from toxins and infections but still should be purchased, just in case. Like Luna Lovegood, he will "only believe in things as long as there's no proof at all" (*Order of the Phoenix,* 262). While his utterances—like sympathetic magic—are supposed to make magically appear the substantive forms to which he alludes (e.g., WMD), the president's stupidity is shaping global power relations in its own image. "We'll use our technology to enhance uncertainties abroad," the president himself has promised. As Frankfurt School social philosopher Herbert Marcuse proclaimed and Dubya proves, the "sweeping rationality [of contemporary capitalism], which propels efficiency and growth, is itself irrational" (xlv).

Unfortunately, the president's stupidity is not restricted to the president's brain. As the president of the United States, he has the power to make the world stupid. The irrationality that guides policy-thinking crowns, as well, the making of the market. In Adam Smith's ideal market, participants made decisions based in a rational assessment of interests. The feeling now is that the market is erratic and undependable. As media critic Robert McChesney has remarked, "The mythology of the free market[. . .] submits that governments are inefficient institutions that should be limited so as not to hurt the magic of the natural 'laissez-faire' market" (13). As the stock market grinds downward, as corporate accounting corruption is revealed to be widespread, as people's retirement funds suffer landslide dips, the turns in the market exhibit a central unpredictability and violence, insinuating that rational planning was never anything more than a bad gamble, or rather, an irrational leap of faith. Even before the avalanche of corporate criminal allegations, with capital vying for deregulation, increased flexibility, the end of labor protections, and the privatization of securities, the magic of the market led to job losses, cuts in benefits, educational budget crunching, health care streamlining, a growing disparity between rich and poor, as well as a general loss of confidence that public institutions can offer basic protections. The existent ideology that the market offers magical remedies to many people's experiences of lost control is bolstered by a wide range of cultural messages, particularly in advertising, which, like consumption as a whole, is governed, as Jean Baudrillard once recognized, "by a form of magical *thinking*; daily life is governed by a mentality based on miraculous thinking, a primitive mentality, in so far as that has been defined as being based on a belief in the omnipotence of thoughts . . . [T]he blessings of consumption[. . .] are experienced as a *miracle*" (31). Erasing its limits and transcending its materiality, the all-powerful subject of consumption sees the world as a whole constructed as a replica and a playing field of its unbounded desire. The market provides the fantasy that the subject masters the world through the magic of its own entrepreneurial willfulness and craftiness.

This chapter focuses on the production of magical thought and irrational thinking in the Harry Potter book series for kids and some of its consequences for thinking about teaching. The Harry Potter series tells the story of Harry Potter who, at the age of one, is orphaned when Lord Voldemort, the evil which Must-Not-Be-Named, kills his parents. Harry is brought up by his mother's Muggle (or, nonwizard) huffy sister and her frequently fuming, bombastic husband who, despite the obvious wealth of Harry's parents, receive neither private payments nor public assistance for the baby Harry's child care.[1] He is kept in the closet under the stairs, deprived of birthday presents, condemned to the mediocrity of the working-class suburbs of Surrey (where J. K. Rowling is also from), and forced to bear the abuse of his spoiled, whiney, snotty-nosed, overfed cousin Dudley. When he is about to turn eleven, his aunt and uncle provide a smelly hand-me-down gray outfit for him to wear as he enters public school, whereas

Dudley has the fortune of wearing new orange knickerbockers and a maroon tailcoat to his private school. Harry learns he is a wizard when Hogwarts School for Witches and Wizards sends an emissary, Hagrid the games-keeper, to fetch him so that he can be schooled in wizadry and magic. The books, I argue, teach that magic can rescue us from hardships, misfor-tunes, cosmic threats, the breakup of the family, child abuse, or even prohi-bitions on candy and sweet drinks, and that magic can also rescue us from the aesthetic squalor which is all that is offered by public institutions. Like capital, Harry and his two cohort-friends Ron Weasley and Hermione Granger can escape the laws, public institutions, authority, and surveil-lance through a magical promise as they learn that the laws, public institu-tions, authority, and surveillance can only function as obstacles on the path to ultimate freedom. As Joan Acocella of *The New Yorker* indicates, "The subject of the Harry Potter series is power, an important matter for children, since they have so little of it. How does one acquire power?" (77). The fantasy that the novels offer is that kids can become magical like capital itself, that they can transport themselves just as capital does to wondrous dreamlands inaccessible to those stuck in the materiality of history, and that school can and should teach them how.

Meanwhile, as J. K. Rowlings, the author of the Harry Potter series, has become the richest novelist in history selling the dream of magic[2]—along with her agent, her publishers, and her publishers' stockholders (Smith, 206)—the magical market itself has been denying kids the hope of such power. As critical education theorist Henry Giroux has remarked,

> Childhood at the end of the twentieth century has [. . .] simply been trans-formed into a market strategy and a fashion aesthetic used to expand the con-sumer-based needs of privileged adults who live within a market culture that has little concern for ethical considerations, noncommercial spaces, or public responsibilities [. . .] [T]he notion of childhood innocence serves as a histori-cal and social referent for [adult society's] waning ability to offer children the social, cultural, and economic opportunities and resources they need to both survive and prosper in this society [. . .] The deteriorating state of America's children can be seen in the increased number of children living in poverty—20.5 percent of all children; the large number of children without affordable housing—more than 6.8 million; as well as the large number of American chil-dren who lack health insurance. According to a 1998 study by the *Children's Defense Report* all of these figures have increased since 1996. Not only are there twenty million children living in poverty in the United States, but the United States ranks in the lower half of the Western, industrialized countries in pro-viding family support services. (2000, 18–22)

The media industry's increasing consolidation throughout the 1990s, and especially after the 1996 Telecommunications bill followed by the one in 2003, has been accompanied by large-scale deregulation and public defunding. Procorporate, antifamily globalization policies like the 1996 abolishment of the AFDC, the development of welfare-to-work programs, cuts in food stamps, and cuts in Social Security income to the elderly and disabled have occurred alongside increased numbers of children living in extreme poverty in the United States and around the world (Mickelson, 24). "Child poverty in the wealthiest nations has worsened with real wages as national incomes have risen over the last half century."[3] As Heather Wokusch of the Common Dreams News Center summarizes, "Over 11 million American children live in poverty, 9.2 million have no health insurance, and 3.6 million suffer "worst-case" housing needs. While the US is the world leader in defense expenditures, it ranks only 17th in efforts to lift children out of poverty; while it is number one in health technology, it ranks 23rd in infant mortality." Cuts in public services have also formed part of structural adjustment programs in poorer countries: "According to UNICEF, in 1995 there were eight million abandoned children on the streets of Latin America. According to Human Rights Watch, in 1993 death squads linked to the police murdered six children a day in Colombia, four a day in Brazil" (Galeano, 2000: 18). With the curtailment of state-instituted equity measures and of social programs in the former Eastern Block countries and the Soviet Union, there has been a growth in the numbers of homeless kids, and as corporations search internationally for cheap labor niches, child labor is on the rise (Klees, Rizzini, and Dewees, 92). "Children, now part of the productivity process, are treated as [short-run] economic goods rather than society's future" (R. Wright, as cited in Klees, Rizzini, and Dewees, 92).

Most recently, the Bush administration has proposed massive cuts in social services that affect children. Aside from considerable reductions in education spending at both state and federal levels and the large-scale bursts in deficit spending, banking against the earnings of the next generation, the new budget contains: "$60.9 million cut from childcare, meaning access cut for 38,000 kids; $29 million cut from after-school programs; $13 million cut from programs that help abused and neglected children; $3 million cut from children's mental health funding; $42 million cut from substance abuse treatment programs" (Cockburn, 9). This domestic attack on kids has provided an ideological impetus for the dehumanization of other nations' citizens, leading to militarization and war, as, for example, then Secretary of State Madeleine Albright could announce on the 12 May 1996 program of *60 Minutes* that the half a million children killed under U.S.-enforced sanctions on Iraq (according to UNICEF) were worth the price, even as the sanctions were failing their stated intentions. With each month's worth of U.S. military spending equaling the amount it would take to stop kids' hunger worldwide for a year (Wokusch), the United States has gone to war against Iraq—a country of which 40 percent of the population is under the age of fourteen.

In the last twelve years, even as rates of youth delinquency are worsening and childhood poverty growing, children have been targeted by media corporations as the fastest growing consumer market. Scholastic, which bought the rights to distribution of the Harry Potter book series in the States for $100,000, has aggressively worked to build a youth market while projecting a noble image of their educational projects. Indeed, remarking how niche-building among youth creates brand loyalty for life, vice president Mark Evans has said, "More and more companies see education marketing as the most compelling, memorable and cost-effective way to build share of mind and market into the twenty-first century" (Molnar, 30–31), and certainly AOL/Time-Warner, the promoters of the films, would agree. Even before its merger with the largest Internet provider in the world, Time-Warner, one of the four combined entertainment and defense companies composing what media critic Mark Crispin Miller has identified as "a national entertainment state" (1997, 4), was the largest media company in the world, projecting revenue in 1997 at $25 billion, owning movie studios, theme parks, retail stores, a TV network, and its own news channel, CNN. Book publishing is no stranger to media conglomerates like Time-Warner, as profit targets among major commercial publishers and editorial salaries have risen, and public funding for schools and libraries has been radically cut, granting virtual distribution monopolies to large retail outlets like Barnes & Noble and Borders which, controlling 50 percent of all national sales, have been able to dictate much content production (Schiffrin, 80). The Harry Potter series has also generated an array of spin merchandising: toys, clothing, diaries, calendars, bookmarks, pillowcases, swim suits, baseball hats, hair bands, watches, candy, playing cards, and now the highest grossing video game ever, distributed by AOL to a potential audience of twenty-five million users (Smith, 205). Coca-Cola alone paid Warner Bros. $150,000 million for an exclusive partnership in the films' marketing, announcing, "It was tremendously important that we create a partnership that would have the ability to globally support the power and magic of Harry Potter" (Smith, 204).

Harry Potter's story is not, structurally, all that original or all that innovative. Congruent in many ways with Vladimir Propp's 1928 morphology of folktales, it starts with a "basic harm" (111) from where "the hero is given a task[. . .] accompanied by threats, should he fail, and promises, should he succeed" (104), giving rise, in turn, to the character of the displaced prince who, because of his inherent royalty, eventually—after trial, journey and adventure—recovers his proper place.[4] In fact, these elements of the folktale have even been incorporated into wizard lore, as Ursula K. Le Guin's 1968 fantasy classic about a wizard's education *A Wizard of Earthsea* follows this form. Orphaned, the protagonist of Le Guin's novel, the great voyager Sparrowhawk, discovers his magical powers at the age of eleven, the same age as Harry, when—popular myth, including psycho-analysis, tells us—little boys become sexually troubling and, Lacan theorizes, enter The Symbolic, and then become included in the fastest growing contemporary consumer market. During his education at a school for wizards, Sparrowhawk realizes his extraordinary powers, and, in a show of hubris, performs the enormous feat of calling out his own shadow from death. In his efforts to close the earth, he gets wounded, the scar from the original battle remaining afterward on his face. The shadow then constantly challenges him in the wizard sanctuary and beyond, trying through adversity—like Voldemort after him and Dr. Frankenstein's monster before him—to gain human form.

Many have lauded the Harry Potter books for their magical allure, celebrating the way fantasy and imagination, along with role-model heroes, are integral to children's intellectual and moral development. "In the Harry Potter books," Roni Natov observes, "magic calls attention to the awe and wonder of ordinary life. Rowling ingeniously enhances and amplifies the vitality of ordinary objects" (219). This has led some critics to deny the ideological content of the series, particularly of the magic itself, especially in light of the growing rates of children's literacy which have been attributed to the books' popularity. Critic Elizabeth Teare, for example, has seen in the Harry Potter books a "resistance to the consumerist pressures both children and adults face" (335) because wizardry is pretechnological, without considering that the concept of magic itself resembles the unfulfillable promise commodities and technology offer to transcend banality, labor, history, and material circumstance. The books themselves have acknowledged this connection: "*Ingenious,* really, how many ways Muggles have found of getting along without magic" (*Chamber,* 43), Mr. Weasley proclaims when Harry shows him how to use the telephone. This magic translates the very idea of a functional literacy into an identification with the more oppressive powers of capital. Collapsing the meaning of magic into identification with commodities and a transcendent subjective autonomous and mastering will, the Harry Potter series makes clear the shortcomings of a functional literacy which can be used only instrumentally to limit rather than to augment an active sense of participation in the building of a better future. As Brazilian educator Paulo Freire writes of the differences between critical literacy and functional literacy, "For the truly humanist educator and the authentic revolutionary, the object of action is the reality to be transformed by them together with other men[. . .]. The oppressors are the ones who act upon men to indoctrinate them and adjust them to a reality which must remain untouched" (1970: 83).

Others have considered the fantasy genre a license to parse the difference between realism and nonrealism, assuming that only as realist could the Harry Potter series actually be clearly political. Analyzing the parallels between wizarding culture and the legacy of Thatcherism in Britain, Karin E. Westman says that in *Goblet of Fire*, "Rowling heightens the existing realism of the previous books to make her clearest statement against a politics based on the body" (315), implying that fantasy would be a refuge from politics rather than its very mechanism. My contention is that the magical content operates to make the political even more powerful and meaningful, teaching kids that exciting options are possible if society is transformed by the magic of consumption and then hiding, behind this mask of magic, that it is doing any real teaching at all, or that there are any ethics or intentions behind the lessons.

Magic has also recently come to the attention of cultural studies theorists because it has offered a setting and a practice to think anew some of the definitional tenets of postmodernism. Simon During, for example, has focused on magic not only because it has historically functioned in an oppositional role to both reason and Enlightenment, but also because "once we fully recognize magic's role as a cultural agent, our sensitivity to the play of puzzlement, fictiveness, and contingency in modernity will be heightened[. . .] Thinking about secular magic reminds us then that we need to consider global modernity as having been shaped in part by tricks and fictions which are border posts at frontiers to a supernatural domain we can never map" (2). Among other things, During is interested in centralizing a cultural form that historically has been relegated to the margins of the mainstream and with historicizing the deconstructive play between the real, the essential, and the simulated. By aestheticizing magic as ritual and performance, During seems unaware of the ways magic has seeped into our cultural repository now to describe technology and capital in ways that place it at the hegemonic center of modern ideology, material distributions, and the politics of globalization, as the Harry Potter series demonstrates. In celebrating magic as a "new" paradigm or area for cultural studies' investigations, During is not noting how power currently does function, centrally and magically, by blurring the line between fiction and reality to such a degree that political discourse itself is endangered. This means that the president can base foreign policy on a science fiction of a possible future attack which suddenly is transformed into a very real resource war.

Far from marginal, magic has become the medium of liberalization and the new economic order, the ideological centerpiece of privatization initiatives, the means of demeaning the public sector, and the tool of imperialism. Magic is central to the construction of capital today, to politics, and therefore to how the opposition between reason and nonreason can be thought. For one, in myriad returns (including my own) to thinking about Modernism through magic realism, magic has been heralded as an aesthetics of defiance to Western principles of linearity, singularity, and the universal, as well as a particularizing marker of the postcolonial.[5] These types of analyses have set the tone for magic—and now children as well—to signify, in literary analysis, the reason of irrationality and the breaking of rules, notions central to "free market" liberalization that seems to escape a centralized authority even as the so-called free market itself works under a set of subsidies, incentives, and "anticompetitive" controls. As Robert McChesney among others have shown, the antiauthoritarian emphasis of neoliberal ideologists has meant, "they want and expect governments to funnel tax dollars to them, and to protect their markets for them from competition, but they want to assure that governments will not tax them or work supportively on behalf of non-business interests, especially on behalf of the poor and working class" (13).

Happily embracing political idealism at the expense of economic fairness, capital has incorporated magic to produce for itself an image of its healing and creative powers while shutting down the institutions that would allow healing and creativity to become more than just a trick-of-the-eye and a promise. Anthropologist Rosalind Morris, for example, has noted the parallels in the cultural anxiety surrounding the end of the "Asian economic miracle" in Thailand and a simultaneous desire for "transparency" in magical ritual. Morris traces a changing attitude in the mainstream media toward the tricks of a spirit medium called Chuchad as the public was demanding more accountability for the government's economic activities. In other words, Morris is remarking on how magic practices themselves are inflected within a broader economic culture, in this case challenging widespread public corruption and cronyism by asking for more authenticity in mystical communications with the dead. She concludes,

> The newspapers were full of stories about the new fetish of fiscal planning and market stabilization. And the transition from artificial stability to truer meaning seemed everywhere to incite dread and unease, but also the anticipation of relief[. . .] The means for mitigating this awful uncertainty took the form of a stabilization strategy that, on some levels, can be reduced to a single demand— disclosure[. . .] More than sixty of Thailand's lending institutions were closed within six months of the IMF plan on the basis of this strategy. Foreclosures, downsizing, unemployment, and reruralization became the symptoms of rationalization via disclosure. (207)

Magic is not just a familiar language that has uncanny resemblances to the languages of capital. As the Harry Potter books indicate, magic is also a material distribution of power favoring private will over public law, fiscal deregulation, and an ideological cover for instabilities caused by market reform.

The fact that the books, as tales of magic, target a readership of children has meant, for some, that the texts are innocent, as though the corporate media's products for children have, by osmosis, absorbed the sentimentalization of childhood that has made talking about the politics of children so difficult. The popular success of the novels among children "prove" their quality because, Amanda Cockrell maintains, "children do, in the lump, tend to know what is good" (17), as though children's tastes and experiences were pure and untouched, not affected by the media, class position, ideology, or the corporate desire to capture them as market-share. To address children, the novels often use bizarre situations and characters. Some of these characters say things which readers are clearly not supposed to take seriously, and this tone of friendly humor and cute irony often serves to blur and seemingly undercut any firm ideological content within characters' speech or the novels' narrative form, at least on the surface. For example, the character of Gilderoy Lockhart, the new Defense Against the Dark Arts teacher, first appears at the bookstore Flourish and Blotts doing a book signing and posing for newspaper pictures, the butt of continued ridicule throughout *The Chamber of Secrets* because of his excessive pomposity and vanity: "Gilderoy Lochart came slowly into view, seated at a table surrounded by large pictures of his own face, all winking and flashing dazzlingly white teeth at the crowd" (59). However, the possibility of reading in the book an ironic criticism of Lockhart collapses not only because "Lockhart's appearance prefigures the crowds that have grown around Rowling's [book signings]" (Teare, 335), but also because the series gives no alternative to mass production, commercialization, celebrity, insignificance, distortion, and self-promotion as the content-aim of books. Elizabeth Teare claims that through Harry himself, "Rowlings builds into her novels the possibility of resistance to celebrity book culture" (336). Yet: 1) Harry has not written a book, so Teare's position cannot account for the series' attitude toward the commercial appropriation of specifically intellectual content; and 2) it is very difficult to think of Harry Potter the character as working against celebrity appeal or representing a resistance to it even inside the novels when he appears on the cover of mainstream and entertainment magazines, on TV and the screen, and has a name that is most likely recognizable everywhere in the world. Lockhart feeds the ideology of celebrity and the commercialization of educational material more strongly because the irony which acts through his character makes the narration appear critical and disapproving of his self-celebration but yet his career seems the inevitable and even slightly adorable path for an author, particularly of books for school-age children.

Magic and the Market

> *"Never trust anything that can think for itself* if you can't see where it keeps its brain."
>
> —Mrs. Weasley referring to Tom Riddle's diary,
> *Harry Potter and the Chamber of Secrets*

The political economy of the media affects the way meanings are produced and provides an overall understanding of social options and relations which, like the Harry Potter series, erases the rational sensibility of social supports, including public education, in favor of an irrational faith in the magic of the market. The Harry Potter series does not only advertise brand names for its corporate sponsors; nor does it simply communicate consumer ideologies, though it performs both of these functions. Additionally, however, and most importantly, the Harry Potter series also participates in clearing the ground for private corporate management of the public as well as promoting an acceptance of the growth of private over public power that is marshaling in new markets and militarisms around the world. The prevailing common sense that the market magically heals has aided to create an atmosphere where it has become logical for the president to claim illogically that increased national investments in testing will improve schools and make them competitive even while class periods and summer school are being cut; music, art, physical education, and social studies reduced as the curriculum turns toward test preparation; richer schools are being turned into banks that loan money at interest to poorer schools; private educational companies are allowed to sue public schools for "unfair competition" under global management agreements like the FTAA; school closings will lead to the subcontracting of students to private tutors; teachers removed from classrooms due to budgetary constraints; supplies, library books, and technologies disinvested. Bush's educational reforms reflect a popular sense that schools need to gear themselves to skills and job training, and that the knowledge gained through such schools should be quantifiable, testable, accountable. In prognosticating the defunding or shutting down of schools—particularly disadvantaged schools, inner-city schools, and schools mostly servicing poor and nonwhite neighborhoods—for not sustaining standardized performance levels, such reforms envision knowledge precisely as irrational: if something you need is in disrepair, then make it compete for support and see if you can't make it succeed that way.

As Kenneth J. Saltman has compellingly argued, defining the goal of education in market terms—efficiency, competition, the failure of public education, accountability, privatization, and choice—"increases bureaucracy, increases costs, increases the potential for abuse and corruption, decreases public oversight, and decreases the stability and reliability of high quality services" (1) while standardizing racism and segregation and replacing the educational purposes of democracy, citizenry, and social value with the goals of preparing a globally competitive workforce. The media's intense promotion and celebration of the magical market accompanies policy initiatives that show the irrationality of the market as anything but magical as it sustains levels of public disinvestment through the work of corporate reason.

In place of social supports, the Bush administration has touted the line of school competition through high-stakes testing, emphasizing, as Stephen Metcalf of *The Nation* has indicated, "minimal competence along a narrow range of skills, with an eye toward satisfying the low end of the labor market." On the one hand, the conservative call for testing upholds censure over other remedies, with the administration advocating private parental choice—either through vouchers or some other initiative—which would allow students to use public funds for transfers to private or faith-based schools when public schools do not make the grade: "testing makes sense as a lone solution to school failure because, they [its conservative enthusiasts] insist, adequate resources are already in place, and only the threat of exposure and censure is necessary for schools to succeed[. . .] Liberal faddishness, not chronic underfunding of poorer schools or child poverty itself, is blamed for underachievement" (Metcalf). The 18 March 2003 episode of Fox's *Boston Public* illustrates some of what is at stake in the public dialogue about test assessment. The county is looking for a new vice principal for the high school. Everyone, especially the black principal, wants the black drama teacher Marla to win because she would be best for the job. However, the state assessment test is only three weeks away, and the state official says that the school could close if test scores do not go up. He encourages the white teacher who is also up for the job to make more of an effort, because the issue is not simply about making a difference, but actually about saving the school. Therefore, the white teacher, Ronnie, does not admit in front of the county commissioner that the tests are no measure of school excellence, the way Marla does, but rather says that the testing is here to stay and there is nothing anybody can do about it (this, despite the intensity of protests about assessment testing currently under way in Boston), so we might as well have a plan. Because the discussion revolves around whether to accommodate to the system, the competition for success seems to take for granted that everyone would agree on what makes this school successful, or what a "quality education" would look like, when this is exactly what is struggled over in the testing debates. Not only does the talk of testing here shut down dissent by insisting on the impossibility of change and the need to adapt to the system. But it also justifies denying the black teacher the economic equity that everybody admits she deserves, turning the politics of her position into the black teacher's unruly desire to earn more as more essential than her defense of public schooling, and showing that her desire for equity has been blocked because of her own political involvement and the clarity of her position (and so she deserves losing her bid for the job) rather than because of the mass redesigning of educational systems to accommodate privatization initiatives and other commonplace neoliberal practices. The TV program does not allow a glimpse of what may happen if the school does close: would it be bought by a company who would then run it according to the philosophy of the bottom line? Would the teachers be shuffled around to other failing schools? Would teachers' lessons then be scripted to adhere to the tests? Would the parents be given "choice," or vouchers to send the kids to religious schools?

As an underfunded federal mandate, the growth in high-stakes testing could mean huge profits—anywhere from $2.7 billion to 7 billion, according to the National Association of State Boards of Education—for testing and textbook companies. Among these companies sits predominantly McGraw-Hill, whose relationship with the Bushes goes back three generations and, according to *The Nation,* is comparable to the Bushes' entanglements with oil and energy firms, including Enron. Currently, his longtime political associate Harold McGraw III has advised Dubya to adopt phonics-based reading practices by citing scientific studies with faulty methods and with results distorted and falsified in reports to the public, as phonics-based teaching, like high-stakes testing, demands great textbook support while supplying little evidence for effectiveness in ending illiteracy. In other words, the "Education President" is not only ascribing to antiintellectualism through his public demeanor. But he is also enforcing it on kids through his policies designed, supposedly, for "global competitiveness," or rather, augmenting executive power at the expense of a functioning public school system while enhancing a low-end service-sector workforce for the benefit of high-end corporate cronies. With capital's deterministic access to power and decision, this market is far from magical. As professor of the dark arts Quirrell describes wizardry in *The Sorcerer's Stone,* "There is no good and evil, there is only power, and those too weak to seek it . . ." (291).

The ideology that says public rights need to prove "success" through competitive business models is currently extending from primary and secondary education into other spheres. The State of Florida, to start, is currently considering a plan to implement high-stakes assessment testing in public colleges and universities. On 7 February of 2003, at the American Association of Publishers School Division Annual meeting, Governor Jeb Bush met with representatives from Harcourt, Houghton Mifflin, Macmillan/McGraw Hill, Scott Foresman, and SRA/McGraw Hill and promised them contracts for local block grants, in the combined amount of $24.5 million, for implementing a Just Read, Florida! Initiative in grades K–3, as the Florida Department of Education proudly announced on its own Web site. Such assessment tests that have already been developed—Steve Uhlfelder, Bush appointed member of Florida's Board of Governors, mentions using the SAT as an exit test— would reduce what counts as learning to basic reading and math skills that can be quantitatively measured, effectively expunging most real learning that happens at the university level. The Department of Education boasts that the money would be used for, among other things, performing assessments and hiring reading coaches, in effect selling students to the highest corporate bidder while, like vouchers, "endors[ing] the transfer of state and federal dollars to private and religious schools" (Karp) and would be the first step in a series of similar future grants that would move beyond the K–3 level.

According to the information on Florida's Board of Education's Web site, the tests would be based on "reading research" that posits an "emphasis on phonemic awareness, phonics" even though, as Metcalf points out, such research was conducted under the auspices of then-governor of Texas George W. Bush, with the aid of consultants from McGraw-Hill. This panel concluded, as spokesperson Education Secretary Paige attested, that "scientific research" proved "phonemic awareness, [and] phonics" as "the most effective course of reading instruction." As Metcalf rejoins, "[T]o teach phonics you need a textbook and usually a series of items—worksheets, tests, teacher's editions—that constitute an elaborate purchase for a school district and a profitable product line for a publisher." Based on faulty research and "rife with errors," the report makes literacy into a technological procedure that can be cured by more textbook production rather than by confronting larger social issues like poverty; cuts in social services like health care, social services, and welfare; the gutting of urban supports as well as supports for children; and growing unemployment. Money that could be used to improve schools is instead being used to create reasons to shut them down while the corporate sector profits in the process of destroying children's lives. The *Palm Beach Post* estimates that the cost would equal the entire amount budgeted by the state to education (Jefferson).

Uhlfelder touts the plan in the *Tallahassee Democrat* as promising accountability in the face of public university tuition hikes and rising presidents' salaries, as he recently advocated post-tenure review (Uhlfelder). Recasting his argument in language popular among Floridians, Uhlfelder re-envisions education as a violent game of winners and losers: "What we are doing in higher education is tantamount to judging a football team by measuring attendance, the number of coaches, the size of the stadium and the amount of booster contributions, without keeping score on the field to see who actually wins the game." Uhlfelder's view, which equates sports performance with school success, is not so very different from a Hogwarts where a student's talent can be measured in winning at the wizard sport of Quidditch, nor is the call for accountability so far from the purported purpose of education expressed by Professor Umbridge, the temporary Ministry-appointed headmistress of Hogwarts. Though Umbridge is subsequently discredited because of her overzealous decrees, inspections, censorship, teaching to the test, cruel peer-observation reports, teacher firings, and outlawing of all student assembly including sports teams and study groups, the right and in fact the duty of the Ministry to impose standardized testing at Hogwarts remains firmly entrenched even after her demise into sickness and insanity. Though she is criticized for representing the Ministry's interference at Hogwarts (*Order of the Phoenix,* 214) as though public oversight was what was causing the imperative to accountability rather than tax cuts and budget crunches and the like, it is never clear that her end signifies the end to the "new era of openness, effectiveness, and accountability" (*Order of the Phoenix,* 213) that she announced during the welcome feast. At the conclusion the Ministry continues to select the head of the school as well as to administer the exams, and there is neither a question that these very processes should and would continue, nor is there any suggestion of alternative structural models outside of the personal benevolence of those the Ministry selects. Rowling never makes the connection between Umbridge's severely austere disciplinary practices and the rituals of testing which, outside of Hogwarts, have redesigned the ideology of schooling to make acceptable just such disciplinary practices as teacher firings and censorship as well as even more stringent ones like cuts in public support, as the Florida plan stipulates the intended result of the measure.

Florida education commissioner Jim Horne supports the tests as providing "proof of a return on investment" for the state (Kumar), while West Palm Beach regent Phil Lewis told the *Wall Street Journal,* "We need to make sure students are getting what they're paying for" (James), essentially rethinking schooling in the consumerist business model. Part of a broader corporate modeling of university administrations, this idea of education as an investment to be won or lost would go along with recent cuts in funding to public higher education in Florida and nationally, a political move that forces schools and teachers to seek out private funding sources as well as throwing the costs back onto the student by raising tuition. Additionally, it informs the growing disparity in pay between faculty and administrators as administrators are increasingly seen as corporate managers, and the growing quantification of instruction that instrumentalizes curricular knowledge and refashions the student body on a client-based principle as purchasers of disparate concrete goods. Such policies invigorate a trend to deskill teachers and professors, similar to the trends taking place through the technologization of the classroom, setting in place the possibility of mass-mediated commercial lessons managed by cheap technicians, on short-term individualized contracts, to be hired and fired on demand (Bousquet). One important thing that gets lost in such rote-learning exercises, or even in the more student-centered corporate-produced curricula,[6] is a political sense that the corporate-dominated global order can be criticized and changed; another is a sense that learning to understand and to interpret a literary or philosophical text is valuable, for instance, for probing the historical and cultural roots of ideas and beliefs, and cannot necessarily be subjected to quantification; another is that public rights like education should not be won or lost in competitions or high-stakes gambles.

Not so far different from the Bush ideal, the running of Hogwarts is based on competition, where the four different houses vie for points awarded for good behavior and subtracted punitively. In the school competition, even the teachers take sides. The ritualized competition over points extends into sports and classroom lessons, where students succeed and win points and status when they best can replicate the incantations of their masters. Harry hints that there might be ethical considerations outside of the point system when he faces down Voldemort in *The Sorcerer's Stone.* "Losing points doesn't matter anymore, can't you see?" he warns his friends. "D'you think he'll leave you and your families alone if Gryffindor wins the house cup?" (270). Yet, in the end Gryffindor does win the house cup because Harry defeats Voldemort, meaning that even the pursuit of ethical values can only make sense as a product of free competition. Developed as a system of cliques which often behave quite aggressively toward each other even to the point of injury (in the same vein as in Columbine High), the competition compels a consumer society which comprises status in the wizarding world, from who has the fastest and most agile broomstick, the newest on the market, to whose family can afford the sleekest dress robes, placing at the formative core of wizard identity the giant wizard shopping mall Diagon Alley with its snowy white bank filled with golden coins in individualized underground chambers and its colorful arrangements of desirable oddities on display, from bats' guts to eel eyes.

Tied to the point system, quizzes and exams at Hogwarts question the rote memorization of facts, for example, about new products like "batty old wizards who'd invented self-stirring cauldrons" (*Sorcerer's Stone*, 263), where points are awarded for correct answers like "my secret ambition is to rid the world of evil and market my own range of hair-care potions" (*Chamber*, 100). In the Harry Potter series, teaching is mostly made effective through fear, intimidation, and detention—"[H]ard work and pain are the best teachers if you ask me" (*Sorcerer's Stone*, 248), confesses Filch the caretaker while leading Harry into the Forbidden Forest for a night of hard and horror-filled detention labor which Malfoy calls "servant stuff" (250) and Hagrid sums up as "useful"—while tests and exams boost the competition among students. The knowledge that they acquire through such classes often ends up being immediately useful to them in their experiences and adventures, particularly for fighting evil, as when Hermione is able to rescue Harry and his friend Ron from the wriggling and flailing Devil's Snare because she remembered having learned in Herbology class that Devil's Snare liked the dark and damp and so could be defeated with fire (*Sorcerer's Stone*, 278)—the type of knowledge, in other words, that comes in handy for winning the competition both against the other houses and against the evil wizard Voldemort. The students' success, then, is understood as the ability to use independently the lessons learned in class, repeating them in narrowly defined tasks—as though the tasks had a one-on-one correspondence with Evil's particular challenge on that day—while immediately experiencing their usefulness in mastering things, nature, people, and other magical monsters: "[Hermione] raised her wand[. . .] His whole body rigid, [Nelville] swayed where he stood and then fell flat on his face, stiff as a board" (*Sorcerer's Stone*, 273). The point-system can be used to distinguish those who have the propensity to mastery from those who do not, while those who do not have the propensity lose the trophy or sometimes, as in fellow-student Nelville Longbottom's case, are, for their magical ineptitude, frozen out of the competition.

The Ministry

Understanding that the irrationality (like corporatism) in capitalism fed the rise of Fascism, Frankfurt School sociologists Max Horkheimer and Theodor Adorno were particularly concerned that the legacy of the Enlightenment did not overcome irrational practices like magic, but rather incorporated them. Describing capitalism's domination over nature where market fetishism and the ritualizing of production lead to fascism, Horkheimer and Adorno observed, as early as the 1940s, the market's parasitic relations to the irrational linked, in turn, to childhood regressions:

> The purpose of the Fascist formula, the ritual discipline, the uniforms, and the whole apparatus, which is at first sight irrational, is to allow mimetic behavior.

> The carefully thought out symbols ... the skulls and disguises, the barbaric
> drum beats, the monotonous repetition of words and gestures, are simply the
> organized imitation of magic practices [...]. Fascism is [...] totalitarian in
> that it seeks to make the rebellion of suppressed nature against domination
> directly useful to domination. (184–185)

Though clearly modeled on exclusive British boarding schools like Eton,
Hogwarts—run by the headmaster Albus Dumbledore, whom David Ansen
of *Newsweek* recognized as a "CEO"—operates under the jurisdiction of
the Ministry of Magic, the governing body of wizardry which, likened to a
board of trustees, can enforce mandates on issues ranging from faculty employment to curriculum, school security, sports events, and the kinds of
mythic beasts that are kept on the school grounds. Contingently, starting
from the school, wizard governance seeps out into other aspects of the life
of magic—setting the law, overseeing the bank, controlling trade, maintaining prisons—implying that wizard governance brings the entire witching
world under the magic of corporate management:

> A crowd of wizards, tightly packed and moving together with wands pointing
> straight upward, was marching slowly across the field. Harry squinted at them
> [...] High above them, floating along in midair, four struggling figures were
> being contorted into grotesque shapes[...] Then he realized that their heads
> were hooded and their faces masked. (*Goblet*, 119)

Projecting green-lighted skulls and dark shadows while chanting, the Ministry, dressed in hoods, is ritualistically torturing a family of Mudbloods,
half-wizard/half-Muggle.

Though there is an explicit critique of some of the more extreme racist
elements among the wizard elites called the Death Eaters (" 'That's sick,'
Ron muttered[...]" (*Goblet*, 120)), many of its features are borrowed into
the mainstream of magic. For example, even as the books seem to ridicule
these practices or condemn them as rituals of the dark forces, Harry's own
privileged wizard-birth justifies a hierarchical order of naturalized talent
based in blood and heredity, radically fraying the apparent critique of
white supremacist violence and also making him seem entitled to and worthy of the mountains of gold coins his parents left him in the underground
chambers of Gringotts Bank. At the age of one, Harry becomes famous
among wizards for vanquishing Voldemort, the lord of the dark forces,
when Voldemort murdered his parents, and since then, his extraordinary
precosiosity in sports, academics, magical know-how, and heroic battles
against evil has proven the worth of his birthright and class entitlement. As
well, Harry's dexterous feats of magic—when he is able to outsmart Voldemort again and again; when he excels in Quidditch, the wizard ballgame
played on broomsticks, and scores winning points for his team; when he
figures his way through murderous chess games, chases down flying keys,

defeats a dragon, vanquishes a giant spider, or sneaks by a fire-breathing three-headed dog to recapture the philosopher's stone and its promise of immortality—all confirm Harry's inbred talent inherited in his bloodline: "[Voldemort] didn't realize," the headmaster Dumbledore informs Harry, "that love as powerful as your mother's for you leaves its own mark" (*Sorcerer's Stone*, 299), and, in fact, the ghosts of his parents offer Harry protections and often allow his spells greater success as he crushes the enemy (*Goblet*, 667), even while Harry's father's excellence as a Quidditch player guarantees the son's stardom. Karin Westman has noted, "Far from Edwardian, the wizarding world struggles to negotiate a very contemporary problem in Britain: the legacy of a racial and class caste system that, though not entirely stable, is still looked upon by a minority of powerful individuals as the means to continued power and control[. . .] When Voldemort is thrown from power, the values of his dictatorship still ground the social organization of race and class."

Those not reaching the stature of heroism and assuming the criminal role of servants or assistants, like the murderer Peter Pettigrew, appear degenerate like the Nazi stereotype of a Jew, "something of the rat linger[ing] around his pointed nose and his very small, watery eyes" (*Prisoner*, 366), "weak" and "talentless" (*Prisoner*, 369) with "thin colorless hair" and a "shrunken appearance" (*Prisoner*, 366), or need to be tied up in the forest like the "uncivilized" giant who can only maybe turn "civilized" by learning English, as in the familiar colonialist tropes of savagery. Such adherence to heredity metaphors, combined with a widespread conviction that certain "cultures" have better "family values," humanistic feelings, and stronger physical features than others, have fostered racism and so have been used to explain such social phenomena as the deterioration of inner cities, drug addiction, imprisonment rates, and, indeed, school assessment rankings. As radical Brazilian educator Paulo Freire remarked in an interview with Donaldo Macedo, "[I]t is far more important to study the interrelationship between white supremacy and dehumanization than to spend time and energy to maintain white supremacy through the enactment of a pseudoscience that attempts to prove black inferiority dislodged from the sociocultural conditions that may, in fact, hinder normal intellectual development" (89).

Even as wizard governance takes on a quasi-Fascist structure, corporate culture takes over the world of magic as a whole. For example, in the fourth book, Percy Weasley, a recent graduate of Hogwarts, gets a job in the Ministry. His tasks include researching statistics on cauldron thickness because manufacturers have been unfairly cutting costs by exporting untested products. "We're trying to standardize cauldron thickness," explains Percy. "Some of these foreign imports are just a shade too thin—leakages have been increasing at a rate of almost three percent a year[. . .] Unless some sort of international law is imposed we might find the market flooded with flimsy, shallow-bottomed products that seriously endanger" (*Goblet*, 56). The other kids proceed to ridicule Percy, trivializing his work and suggesting that he is boring, marginal, pompous, and useless. "Ministry o' Magic messin' things up as usual" (*Sorcerer's Stone*, 64), Hagrid informs Harry. To Percy's critics, the absurd work of regulation and public administration here seems too mired in an excessive materialism.

The assault on any attempt to impose rules or restrictions on the use of magic for good business purposes translates into labor policy as well. The Ministry refuses to get involved in assuring labor fairness because the house-elves, for example, *like* to be treated as slaves, work without wages or vacations, wear cheap old sacks instead of clothes, and be subjected to extreme subservience, obedience, and punishment for minor infractions. Harry's friend Herminone's pathetic attempts to create a political movement to free the house-elves called "The House-Elf Liberation Front" only lead to contemptuous mockery. "Winky is properly ashamed of being freed!" (*Goblet*, 379) house-elf Winky herself counters. Hermione's political organizing in favor of labor protections is translated into an unwarranted act seeking to impose superfluous laws threatening the rights of slaves to self-determination. Slavery, Hermione learns, is what they want after all.

The point is not only that political protest is made to seem irritating, child's play, and against the interests of those for whom it advocates. After all, even if the other characters tease Hermione for her efforts on behalf of the house-elves, still remaining is the language of rights and freedom in which she frames the issue, including freedom of speech (*Goblet*, 378), as well as Dumbledore's benevolent approval, so the narrative voice itself is not necessarily confirming the characters' tease. The trivializing of Hermione's initiatives on behalf of labor, however, does perform two quite serious functions: 1) it makes political resistance seem ineffectual and unnecessary, because Hermione's organization is not what gives Dobby his freedom; its success is contingent on the backing of the management, as well as on a certain faith in the naturalized working of justice, rather than on a struggle against oppression; and 2) the only solution that the novels present for the house-elves is a type of patronizing service-oriented wage-labor, which does not appear to improve significantly their status or options. " 'But most wizards doesn't want a house-elf who wants paying, miss,' " Dobby tells Harry, Ron, and Hermione. " 'That's not the point of a house-elf,' they says, and they slammed the door in Dobby's face! Dobby likes work, but he wants to wear clothes and he wants to be paid[. . .] And so Dobby is a free elf, sir, and Dobby gets a Galleon a week and one day off a month![. . .] Dobby likes freedom, miss, but he isn't wanting too much, miss, he likes work better'" (*Goblet*, 378–79). The "self-determination" offered in corporate waged work parallels the "self-determination" of slavery.

Finally, with Voldemort's return in *Order of the Phoenix*, the possibility of political organization and opposition forms. There are three different trajectories through which politics are imagined. Yet, as the inept Ministry seems to have again been led astray by the influence of power brokers allied with the Dark Forces, all of these trajectories perform the identical role of defining politics as a defense of private interests from ineffectual, misdirected public manipulations. 1) The Order is originally fashioned through housekeeping rituals, where Mrs. Weasley ushers the kids through a series of cleanliness and cooking details to make the headquarters liveable. Other than this, it is not really clear what the operations of the Order entail, how its resistance is being implemented, or how its forces—a group of Harry's closest friends and their families, all bound by affiliation, school ties, and kinship—are to arrange recruitment, actions, alliances, planning, command, and defiance against both Voldemort's Dark Forces and their minions in the Ministry. Here, politics resembles a private family. 2) Ron's brothers, the twins Fred and George, stage some actions of resistance and diversions against the Ministry's new stringent policies by setting off, at school, demonstrations of the magical jokes they later plan to sell. After leaving school, the two wizard boys plan to start their own joke-shop business, at first raising the capital for this venture through their own initiative in games, blackmail, and gambling. Finally bankrolled with Harry's winnings from the Triwizard Tournament, the twins start to practice their commerce in the school, using first-year students as experimental guinea pigs for new untested products, plastering the bulletin boards with advertisements, using the hallways for spectacular displays, and turning students into clients. When Harry needs Professor Umbridge's attention to be diverted, the twins turn school corridors into swamps or set off fireworks that take on the shape of magical creatures, gaining in energy as they blast noisily through the classrooms, down the stairs, along the grounds. Here, politics resembles a private business. 3) With the administrative backing of Hermione, Harry starts to give secret lessons in Defense Against the Dark Arts. The Ministry has forbidden spells in the course, trying to cover up the evidence and apprehension of Voldemort's return, so Harry sets up a secret student society. This organization is kept even more under cover after Umbridge (coining for herself the title "High Inquisitor of Hogwarts") forbids, in the name of the Ministry, any meetings among students unless officially approved because "she's got some . . . some mad idea that Dumbledore could use the students in the school as a kind of private army. She thinks he'd mobilize us against the Ministry" (*Order of the Phoenix*, 344). Dumbledore later accepts this charge, claiming he wanted "[m]erely to see whether they would be interested in joining me" (*Order of the Phoenix,* 618). Here, politics resembles a private army.

The demeaning of politics as a privatized defense works alongside a more general disparagement of the public sector. Mr. Weasley's work as a low-level bureaucrat in the Ministry's office for Muggle Protection is seen as excessive, useless, cumbersome, meddlesome, and often wrong-headed, even absurd, while it keeps his family, embarrassingly, in poverty and hand-me-downs. Sarcasm and derision are directed at any of the Ministry's attempts to intervene in business practices except when it comes to discipline and security. It is strictly forbidden, for example, to perform magic in front of Muggles or to put charms on Muggle-made goods in case they end up back in a Muggle home and cause havoc, like when a jinxed teapot threw sugar tongs at an old man and left him hospitalized. However, wizards have various methods for circumventing these rules, from hiding hexed machinery in secret garages, to deprogramming the memories of witnesses, to stupefying the victims of magical tortures, or spreading false rumors in the Muggle press about certain events like mass death curses, for the Muggles' own benefit. Any attempts by the Ministry to put an end to such practices prove ineffectual, down to arrests and raids, which are often hexed or contravened by Experimental Charms or tricks. Harry himself often ventures outside the Ministry's would-be heavy hand and the school's micromanagement, just as wizard capitalism operates most fruit-ful without Percy's product liability inspections or the Ministry's absurd care for mere Muggles in trying to uphold, for example, an unenforceable embargo on flying carpet imports and other silly trade interferences. Em-ploying cunning and wit, Harry and the other kids at Hogwarts are also constantly venturing away from wizard laws, ducking out of school when he's not supposed to, wandering the corridors at night in defiance of the school code, hiding invisibly behind statues and bookstacks when teachers and supervisors prowl on the lookout, sneaking a suspected murderer away on a flying hippograph, even outsmarting the prison guards called Demen-tors invited by the Ministry's Board of Directors for purpose of policing and protecting both the school and the nearby village Hogsmeade.

The superhuman capacities of global capital to transcend the laws of the nation-state give it the feel of magic. Like magic, capital can maneuver through obstacles that ground production or expenses that limit con-sumption and jump over the barriers to human mobility, transporting and extending the speculating subject while alienating labor more fully for its territorial stagnancy and its rootedness in material need. For example, the Patriot Act, passed into law after the terrorist attacks of September 11, con-tained provisions to curtail national sovereignty: in particular, a section that would extend the use of U.S. courts to countries suing companies abroad for illegal commerce and tax evasion—with an eye to gauging money laundering, fraud, corporate smuggling, and terrorists' financial networks—was voted down in the House and only partially restored as a narrowed-down version in the Senate.[7] Severely restricting the nation-state's abilities to protect its public institutions and domestic production, this and other "free-trade" arrangements let corporate activity transcend the laws and responsibilities of a nation-state. Recently, these corporate protections have worked to allow the tobacco industry to avoid tariffs and taxes in foreign countries like Colombia, undersell local brands, and increase advertising without increasing legal imports, even as they, to a certain degree, protect the bank accounts of terrorist organizations. Like magic, capital can do things and go places and have experiences that are inaccessible to the ordinary human. Like growing up with the budding magic entrepreneurs Fred and George, growing up with capital means that "you sort of start thinking anything's possible if you've got enough nerve" (*Order of the Phoenix*, 655).

Hermione

The Harry Potter series composes two different but intersecting ideas about class. First, class works through a politics of the body where superiority shines out in exceptional talent and kindness. This perspective is in line with the returning prince scenario, where the lost character exhibits the behavior of a prince in order to show that he deserves the title. The Harry Potter books transform this fairy tale by racializing it in plots about blood and purity as does, for example, Mark Twain's 1894 novel *The Tragedy of Pudd'nhead Wilson and the Comedy of Those Extraordinary Twins,* where a white boy gets switched with a slave but finds his true place in part because of his undeniable nobility of character. As Farah Mendelsohn has summarized, "[A]ristocracy is allied with the country gentry in the care of the inferior; a High Toryism or modern liberalism where everyone is nice, and tolerant; where women are in the home and use their magic to speed the cooking and cleaning[. . .] and where differences are accepted but we all know who is inferior to whom and treat them nicely because they *are* inferior" (170). Second, class is self-made and self-determined, the product of hard work and ingenuity. This second formation characterizes Hermione, whose dedication to her studies is supposed to signify the hope of transcending her low Muggle birth. Hermione is able, through her dedicated and diligent library research, in *The Sorcerer's Stone* to discover the history and identity of the stone, in *The Chamber of Secrets* to find the clue that unlocks the chamber and reveals what is inside, and in *The Prisoner of Azkaban* to manipulate time so that she can attend two classes at once, doubling her course load in order to work even harder. She exhibits excellence through effort. Hermione's subjectivity appears in the accumulation of knowledge through practice, creativity, dedication, and experience, that is, through personal initiative. In female subjectivity arises the promise that hard work leads to a better position not defined through the gendered body but rather through service, in this case, service to Harry.

The novels position Hermione as the promise of class transcendence, that is, of self-construction, through service. Hermione's studiousness keeps her from descending to the status of Moaning Myrtle, also targeted as a Mudblood, who was caught unaware by the murderous stare of the Basilisk, King of the Serpents, and therefore remains perpetually as a ghost in the toilet where she was killed. Hermione learns in her library research that the Basilisk kills through staring directly at his victim, so she confronts the snake's gaze through a mirror. Hermione's ability to transcend class and race through turning her library learning into direct experience makes her seem a particularly good example of a feminism that formulates freedom through self-determination and focuses on building identity through self-construction and autonomy. Eliza Dresang, for example, has called "Hermione's propensity to 'wit and learning' " "signs of self-determination" even though she is "initially acting chiefly as Harry's agent" (227). Linked to the novels' broader depiction of a type of magic that transcends material obstacles, law, and history, the feminism read through Hermione's character imagines the market itself as marking the success of women's liberation, even though, contradictorily, Hermione's labor remains subordinated to Harry's greater purpose.

In fact, in today's political climate, women around the world are hardest hit by market reforms, even though, because of competitive labor markets, women's labor is ever more marketable because of its cheapened status. Since 1980, as the number of women participating in the global workforce has expanded,[8] women's poverty has increased, reaching 70 percent of the estimated one billion poor according to the United Nations. As Angela McRobbie notes, a feminism defining success in market terms—what she calls a "neo-liberal feminism"—creates a triumphalism around "wealth, financial independence from men, glamour and good looks" (362). At the same time, it does not "promise equality of income" (363) because "traditional disadvantages now combine with the downside effects of new and less predictable fluidities of opportunity" (364) produced by the mobilities of capital as well as by the insufficiencies of public support systems, particularly schooling. Examples would be in the Bush administration's welfare proposals, which harden requirements for recipients, insisting on a forty-hour work week while cutting child-care expenditures, or an "education president" submitting a budget with "40 times more money for tax cuts than for education" (Wokusch). Some definitional terms of this type of feminism—e.g., independence, autonomy, experience—have been twisted into an ideological imperative which fashions success and equality as unrestricted by power, patriarchy, and hierarchical subordination, parallel to fables about market freedom. Yet, the lifting of restrictions on capital through disinvesting the public has, in fact, curtailed the promise of open access or rising living standards for women worldwide.

The feminism expressed through Hermione positions intellectualism as a product of hard labor in which the payoff is a self new, improved, desirable, and presented, as Baudrillard says of the consumer object, "as *a harnessing of power*" (32). The hope this feminism offers is for an opening into the magic of class privilege, the ability to direct cosmic plots and reap rewards of personal fulfillment alongside Harry, a hope that is continually resurrected even faster than it can be nailed to the cross. Such an experience of knowledge would award the dream of material comfort and freedom from fear and uncertainty, what Baudrillard calls "[a] miraculous security" (34). Hermione's feminist bookishness parallels the self-construction and self-determinism offered in the market by products that offer fantasy lifestyles of the rich and famous, Michelob weekends, magical sunsets, and cozy cottages for those smart enough to choose such expressions of self and certainty, even though such dreams of freedom through plenty are not often available to those whose desire they capture. Through the feminization of knowledge, the Harry Potter series makes knowledge itself marketable as an illusory promise.

The subordinate status of the feminine and of the racially mixed Mudblood adds to this dream of security and class transcendence in the object of knowledge a tinge of insecurity, of possible failure, so that Hermione remains in service to and in need of Harry's transcendence and salvation as the dream is continually torn asunder and then mended. In fact, the precariousness of security offered in Hermione's miraculous abilities to acquire and accumulate knowledge works to bolster Harry as the ultimate guarantee of security in his naturalized superiority, thus determining knowledge as heterosexualizing even for Hermione. Because, in Hermione, female and nonwhite identities connect to book knowledge, they are more precarious, prone to assault and capture by the dark forces. As Baudrillard concludes about the magical object, "The violence and inhumanity of the outside world are needed[. . .] so that security may be experienced more deeply as security" (35). Hermione's second-class service status is subject to the waywardness of market value: Hermione's second-class status in racial terms is not always surmounted by her book knowledge and her ability to translate it directly into tasks, plots, and experience, as sometimes her trials fail, or the book lesson turns into a practical fiasco, like when she turns herself into a cat and needs to be hospitalized to get back to human form, or when the Basilisk paralyzes her through the mirror's gaze, meaning that the knowledge she has gained must serve Harry's survival and Harry's heroism as she is petrified and lies comatose in the infirmary, awaiting Harry's ultimate miraculous rescue. The books offer no critique of this outcome, inferring that Hermione's book knowledge is actually less secure than it promises. Significantly, the novels often refer to book knowledge as endangering security. "Some of the books the Ministry's confiscated," Ron explains, "[. . .]there was one that burned your eyes out. And everyone who read *Sonnets of a Sorcerer* spoke in limericks for the rest of their lives. And some old witch in Bath had a book that you could *never stop reading!* You just had to wander around with your nose in it, trying to do everything one-handed" (*Chamber,* 231). The antibook attitude culminates in the revenge of Tom Riddle's diary in *The Chamber of Secrets.* The diary seduces innocent Ginny Weasley into Voldemort's lair so that her body could be used as the life-source for Voldemort's return. The problem with Riddle's diary was not that the print and the history only became visible when the person whose name appeared on the cover, or the person whose hands it fell into, wrote into it, as it operates like a trans-historical telephone. Rather, the problem with the diary was that if the book got into the wrong hands—ultimately Ginny's—the knowledge it produced would be falsified, thus making all book knowledge suspicious. When stabbed by a snake's fang, the diary painfully bleeds out Riddle to his demise just as he is about to enter Ginny's body. The girl's body is the site where Riddle's knowledge of evil—his self-knowledge, his specious knowlege—threatens to come to life.

The Harry Potter books can acknowledge that reducing identity and knowledge to the personal can offer nothing else but the promise of a personal transcendence and security through inbred magical talent. Even as Dumbledore interprets Harry's battle against Riddle as proving "[i]t is our choices, Harry, that show what we truly are, far more than our abilities" (*Chamber,* 333), he concludes by insisting that Harry's true and authentic self was what allowed his victory. What saves Ginny from possession by Riddle's diary is not only Harry's distinctive bravery, but also a set of weapons that only respond personally to Harry's own faith, ability, and heredity, proving his might. There is no sense that anything could save Ginny except her savior's excelling in a ruthless competition of personal strength and ingenuity, replacing Riddle's self-constructed identity with Harry's better and stronger naturalized one. Feminism here is being used as marking the personal at the expense of the political. It is being used to justify competition and personal excellence as winning; its narratives are made to preclude imagining public interventions, public security, public safety nets, public deliberation, and, indeed, workable public schools; its promises are making work in a corporatized economy into the only locus of empowerment and self-fulfillment even as it tells women not to hope too hard or for too much.

Through the idea of girls' knowledge, Rowling continually raises the prospects of upward mobility but then transforms the dream of magical transcendence back into a proof of Harry's even more magical exceptionality, returning Hermione to her proper place where she will never be anything but a Mudblood and in service. The Harry Potter books profess a belief in the possibility of women's working hard and competing hard to get ahead (and their cosmic responsibility to do so), upholding the dream of magic—even anchoring it as the best hope for racial equality—while at the same time demolishing it, even turning its destruction into a heroic character. The connection between girls' knowledge and experience insinuated through Hermione's education makes girls' knowledge more precariously dependent on tales of acquisition, construction, and production than the more full-blooded, solid, naturalized, and secure wizard knowledge that Harry inherits.

Rowling's embrace of girls' identity as a product of the experience of knowledge and tasking grows out of her own career as a French teacher prior to being a millionaire novelist. As biographer Sean Smith describes them, Rowling's teaching methods developed out of a celebration of an antiauthoritarian, student-centered learning fashioned in accordance with a feminist concern to build political consciousness by teaching through experience. Simultaneous with Thatcherism and other moves to liberalize the market starting in the mid-1970s, the focus on feelings, confessions, and private life in feminist pedagogical theory arose in the wake of the 1970s feminist practice of consciousness-raising as it combined with Deweyian progressivism and the translation of Freirian thought into U.S. contexts. "Through consciousness-raising, women would pay close attention to their feelings as a way of understanding women's oppression" (Fisher, 30). Feminists were supposed to develop pedagogical practices that allowed students creatively and freely to define their identities through discussions of personal experience and self-affirmation: knowledge was supposed to be grasped by analyzing experience and finding common purpose through experience. For example, *Women's Ways of Knowing* asserts that the education that privileges propositions or general concepts absorbed from textbooks alienates women who prefer "to start from personal experience" (202) or "authentic voice" (209) or "the student's own rhythms" (210) or the kind of knowledge acquired from "adaptive responding" (201) picked up from practices of mothering. *The*

Feminist Classroom describes institutional knowledge as deflecting, alien-ating, and silencing the experiences of women and minorities and advises that particularly feminist forms of teaching should encourage, accommo-date, affirm, and celebrate confessions of "relevant personal experiences to shape a narrative of an emerging self" (18). As well, feminist educator Maxine Greene has talked about the imagination as restructuring experi-ence by restoring power to the personal. In the biography, Rowling adapts such theories by creating classroom activities around students' use of lan-guage in experience, but in card games and crosswords rather than toward analyzing oppressions. Indeed, the feminist pedagogical theory that guides Rowling's teaching and underlies her descriptions of learning in the novels lends itself to such avoidances because it isolates experience and the imagi-nation from broader historical currents and class struggle by restricting experience and imagination within chronologies of the developing, psy-chological self, the individual will to mastery, and entertainment.

According to Bernice Malka Fisher, opposition rose up within the femi-nist pedagogical movement at its inception, as some believed that personal experience would neither lead to the development of a general agenda for justice nor to a broad analysis of the social conditions of oppression. Oth-ers resented that the universalization of experience as the privileged cate-gory for political movements tended not to recognize racial, class, and sexual differences and so tended not to create bonds of common purpose. Indeed, Joan Scott's 1991 seminal feminist critique of experience warns against the return to essentialism in the trend to construct identities around experience. For Scott, experience implies that difference is estab-lished by fact, and so desubstantiates the histories through which differ-ences have been constructed or any analysis of the way power works through representation and the struggle over meaning: "They take as self-evident the identities of those whose experience is being documented and thus naturalize their difference. They locate resistance outside its discur-sive construction, and reify agency as an inherent attribute of individuals, thus decontextualizing it[. . .] But the project of making experience visi-ble precludes critical examination of the workings of the ideological sys-tem itself, its categories of representation[. . .], its premises about what these categories mean and how they operate, its notions of subjects, origin, and cause" (25). Even as student experience is central to classroom prac-tice, it must be thought of as part of broader histories and power structures and as the basis for a broader social analysis, whereas the feminist peda-gogical emphasis on liberation through self-construction often tends to forget the material and historical restrictions on agency, particularly on underclass agency, making agency instead seem psychologized as a magical projection of the will.

The isolation of experience as a pedagogical principle, in fact, often buttresses a pedagogical aspiration of confirming student experience regardless of how that experience has been structured through the multiple stimuli of a media-inflected culture, a market economy, and a racialized class system. Affirming the equal validity of all experiences serves, as Chandra Mohanty shows, to conceptualize "race and gender in terms of personal or individual experience" (1990: 194). Mohanty warns this privatization of social experience is frequently a way of neglecting the students' own interactions with history and power and undermining the significance of education "as a crucial form of resistance to the colonization of hearts and minds" (1990: 191), while Giroux has shown that privileging experience "often represents the endorsement of a particular way of life with a 'revenge' on those who do not share its attributes" (1988: 93). Any talk of experience must include an analysis of social power because it is impossible to think experience without it.

The Stupid Subject

The feminist pedagogical perspective that influences the construction of social power within the Harry Potter texts affirms that experience guarantees knowledge and empowerment because it is experience alone that shapes identity as an escape and refuge from power. However, even as the texts suggest that experience empowers identity and promises agency, they simultaneously undermine the sense that knowledge can guarantee self-determination, as it is likely not to protect you from capitulating to the dark forces, from losing in the final competition, or from succumbing because of inherent class, gender, or racial constitutional weaknesses comprising obstacles to magical transcendence. The idea that experiential knowledge is the source of empowered knowledge can be thought as part of a broader discourse that envisions power as operating strictly through repression and authoritarianism, and freedom as the possibility of stepping out of its controls through individual initiative, instead of seeing power, as Foucault taught, working productively to create identities, possibilities, and interactions. The celebration of experience participates in circumscribing a private space outside of power, as when Baudrillard described the magical sovereign subject of consumption as inhabiting "a marginal sector of indeterminacy where the Individual, elsewhere constantly constrained by social rules, might at last—being left to himself in the 'private' sphere—recover a margin of freedom and personal leeway" (81). Such a configuration has ramifications, as well, for more broadly considering how knowledge of the self—private knowledge—relates to public knowledge or wider and more generalizable fields of social intercourse as well as for thinking the politics of blame and who is responsible for economic deprivations, the need for discipline, and the success of the entrepreneur in an ideological setting where the private person is the locus of power.

Under neoliberalism, the contemporary exultation of the private, private feeling, and personal experience as fulfilling the promise of freedom grounds itself within values identified as feminine in both sexist and feminist depictions. The feminine that delineates the autonomy of the subject in the industrial economy, for example, the feminine that designates the housewife as the caregiver in socialization tales, like the feminine which fashions an independent subject for feminist empowerment, invokes the idea of freedom embedded in the popular concepts of privacy and the personal which presently mold the economics of globalization with its transfers of public power into the bolstering of consolidated private ownership. Standing in for the concept of the domestic, the privacy of femininity delineates the limits of public intervention or common need. As Judith Butler has noted in the case of feminism's appropriation of Antigone, femininity in its relation to kinship invokes prepolitics or antipolitics: "[K]inship is figured at the limit of what Hegel calls 'the ethical order,' the sphere of political participation but also of viable cultural norms" (2000: 3) as in Lacan, where the feminine figure separates the privacy of the family from the publicity of the Symbolic, politics, culture, the state. Using femininity—with its symbolic contingencies to family and private life—as a grand signifier for privacy, the personal, and the boundary of state action, such a symbolic system shores up corporate expansionism ideologically and materially by, for example, feminizing the corporatized service workforce, crushing unions, defending tax cuts on the basis of upholding the autonomy and free choice of families, and arguing for cutting educational funding and sex education under the guise that parents know best what is good for their own children.

Furthermore, within feminism as well as within other contemporary theories focusing on identity, the idea of the willful self, of the self whose self-knowledge leads directly into powerful action, of the self outside of constraints, of external power as dehumanizing and alienating—these positions and conditions of the contemporary autonomous self work alongside neoliberal philosophies in general to create a sense that power can only contain or stifle the free circulation of subjects. This sense erases the role that power, particularly corporate power, currently enjoys the ability to produce and defend the circulations of private capital: evading taxation, avoiding labor protections, replacing diplomacy with management agreements, rewriting law, inducing barriers to entry by reducing barriers to growth, mediating identity through commercialism, and leaving the free subject to circulate without recourse or defense, without, that is, the public institutions that have historically in democratic societies stood as the avenue for political action as well as for the redress of inequalities. The idea that power can only be repressive, however, is being widely adopted to define an oppositional politics in feminism, multiculturalism, and identity politics generally, and this serves to create a vision of democracy where freedom is identified as the avoidance of material obstruction, the magical freedom of capital. This configuration inflects various arenas of thinking politics and identity, including the construction of knowledge, subjectivity, and the growing celebration of private power.

Educational politics—where, in the name of standards, excellence, and flexibility, public funds are being moved into private and parochial educational businesses as well as commercial appropriations—must be thought, therefore, in combination with the current cultural distrust of reason in the philosophical tradition, in academia at large, in culture, and in politics: reason is becoming the standard signifier for repressive power. In particular, feminist pedagogical theories that explain student resistance and the failures of classroom communication through recourse to ideas about the split subject or the lack in the subject similarly separate the feminine, the empirical, and the magical as a liberatory escape from the oppressions of a rationality without history. Patti Lather, for example, has called for post-modernism to help her question "an excessive faith in the powers of the reasoning mind on the part of the subjects theorized as unified and capable of full consciousness" (1991: 137). In privileging the empirical as the dominant form of knowledge, and particularly of identity formation, Patti Lather among others restricts the possibilities of teaching students to critique and to protest power. Additionally, such a focus on self-construction translates social power into individual responsibility, a simple matter of trying hard enough.

Maxine Greene also takes her cue from psychoanalysis, where the Unconscious and the aesthetic disrupt the formation of identity, which is therefore never complete. Though she admits that "we cannot simply fantasize the disappearance of joblessness, homelessness, fatherlessness, disease" (18), she still believes that reading literature would grant a personal freedom to allow students to accommodate themselves to service jobs and the increasing technologization of the workplace: "How would it be possible to counter the dullness and banality of many service jobs by enabling the young to find fulfillments outside the world of work?" (1994: 89). As Greene defines freedom in the avoidance of work rather than in challenging the relations of work, learning culture allows the drift of the imagination away from work in order to make work easier and the individual adaptable to its repetitions. When Greene talks about how the experience of the imagination allows a questioning of things as they are and a positing of how things could be different, she is mostly referring to a personal transport into an elsewhere of vacation—a "breaking with the mundane" (1994: 77)—rather than a radical social transformation or a rethinking of institutional relations.

For Deborah Britzman as for Lather, what is wrong with education is that students are locked into an incomprehensible psychic difference whose experience can never be known by a teacher coming from a position of authority. Experience locks students into individuality and incomprehensibility. There is an imperative, in Britzman's theory, to recognize the inner desires of the student's Unconscious by inflating the "private into the subjective" (14). Feminist theorist Jacqueline Rose has brought this idea of the impossibility of communication and meaningful signification into the study of children's literature. Commenting on the twentieth-century history of children's fantasy literature, she has remarked, "Children's fiction is impossible, not in the sense that it cannot be written, but in that it hangs on an impossibility, one which it rarely ventures to speak. This is the impossible relation between adult and child" (58). As the linguistic sign is inadequate in determining its own outcome and reception, education is based on the individual's escape from parental authority, in misapprehension, fragmentation, subjective lack, and therefore in the irrational Unconscious.

Indeed, the "impossible relation" would cynically suggest that adults cannot teach children through language, that there can be no correspondence between children's fantasies and adult realities, the politics of everyday life, or, for example, the inequalities and hunger resulting from the decisions of powerful adults. Marcuse contends that the extreme focus on personal details in empiricism requires a blindness to broader social contexts, concepts, and theories that would point to the world beyond the experience and show how the experience becomes meaningful through reference to that world. In the absence of such transcendental thoughts, that world and its public, in turn, get steeped in allusions to mysticism, witchcraft, and magic to describe the insanity, incomprehensibility, and stupidity of the system. The isolation of the subject in such Kantian philosophies—where the subject can only gain knowledge through its own internal representations of itself and without access to outside reference, the material world being the limit of knowledge—envisions the subject as magically transcending and possessing the object world as this subject represents it to itself. As Adorno summarizes, "[T]he world upon which we may be said to depend appears to us [. . .] as if we were its masters [. . .] [A]s knowing subjects we know only ourselves. In this sense we are never able to get outside ourselves; we are imprisoned within ourselves" (137).

The empirical functions here to confirm the present; it indicates that describing what is tackles the question of what ought to be, and puts it to rest. As Marcuse remarks, "The individual and his behavior are analyzed in a therapeutic sense—adjustment to his society. Thought and expression, theory and practice are to be brought in line with the facts of his existence without leaving room for the conceptual critique of these facts" (107). Since the subject already contains what is there to be known, the subject can magically change the world by knowing differently, as all external norms and standards have been suspended. Marcuse has thoroughly exposed the dangers to political thought of overly privileging the empirical as personal experience:

> [The] larger context of experience, [the] real empirical world, today is still that of the gas chambers and concentration camps, of Hiroshima and Nagasaki, of American Cadillacs and German Mercedes, of the Pentagon and the Kremlin, of the nuclear cities and the Chinese communes, of Cuba, of brainwashing and massacres. But the real empirical world is also that in which all these things are taken for granted or forgotten or repressed or unknown, in which people are free. It is a world in which the broom in the corner or the taste of something like pineapple are quite important, in which the daily toil and the daily comforts are perhaps the only items that make up all experience. (180)

For Marcuse, what is at stake in the purely empirical is the collapse of the public into the private while what can be lost are the idea of difference, the possibility of principled, social abstraction, and the recognition that immediate experience is composed through layers of mediation:

> The idea of "inner freedom" here has its reality: it designates the private space in which man may become and remain "himself." Today this private space has been invaded and whittled down by technological reality. Mass production and mass distribution claim the *entire* individual, and industrial psychology has long since ceased to be confined to the factor[. . .] This immediate, automatic identification [. . .]is the product of a sophisticated, scientific management and organization. In this process, the "inner" dimension of the mind in which opposition to the status quo can take root is whittled down. The loss of this dimension in which[. . .] the critical power of Reason[. . .] is at home, is the ideological counterpart of the very material process in which advanced industrial society silences and reconciles the opposition. (10–11)

Marcuse goes on to analyze how the disappearance of the private into the public has changed the very structure of what counts as knowledge, making political communication itself "immune against the expression of protest and refusal" (90). Marcuse would tell us that the ideological production of privacy, leisure, and the bedroom as separate from "the media of mass communication" (19) on the one hand and from the "permanent mobilization for the defense of this universe" (18) on the other, would allow for a dissociation or nonidentification—the time for dream and reverie—to "develop into effective opposition, testing its strength and the validity of its objectives" (15). During industrialization, Marcuse observes (overly nostalgically), workers saw their interests as opposite to those of capital, but with the rise in the standard of living and the bait of commercialism, workers' desires have been absorbed by industrial production—"people recognize themselves in their commodities; they find their soul in their automobile" (9)—and so alienation has given way to ideological conformity: the inner, private life of the subject no longer resists, contradicts, subverts, evades and seeks to change the reality of Consciousness, as the Unconscious does in Freud. For Marcuse, language itself gets caught in "habits of thought," where facts are immediately identified with the truth of power, language becomes purely functional, definitions are set in place as descriptions, meaning is ossified in standard usage, concepts and principles are lost along with critical distance, and so "[m]agical, authoritarian and ritual elements permeate speech and language" (85) because "[i]t is the word that orders and organizes, that induces people to do, to buy, and to accept" (84).[9]

Social knowledge now appears as discrete, descriptive, operational facts seemingly without value, or pure empiricism, where the particular, the quantifiable, the immediate, the individual, and the direct substitute for the generality of thought, reason, the whole, the good, and the public. For example, researchers investigating worker complaints at the Hawthorne works electrical company ascertained that the language in which the complaints were formulated was "vague," and so they set out to translate the workers' statements about work conditions into particularlized statements about private individual problems: "[T]he statement 'the washrooms are unsanitary' was translated into 'on such and such occasion I went into this washroom, and the washbowl had some dirt in it.'[...] [A] worker B makes a general statement that the piece rates on the job are too low. The interview reveals that 'his wife is in the hospital and that he is worried about the doctor's bills'" (109–110). Simply a question of *that* little bit of dirt in *that* particular washroom, the imperative of the empirical chokes off the ethical referent, the historical situation, the critique of the systematicity of exploitation, the possibilities of abstracting a concept of justice, and the identification of unified oppressions which would help consolidate initiatives of workers movements, unions, protests, and the like.[10]

Today, the "private" is increasingly taking the place of the "public," or rather, the "public" is increasingly being organized as "private" through public appeals to privatization, personal initiative, private interests, and property as the guiding principles of public debate, while taxation, the public coffers, and the building of public institutions are being criticized, reconceived, and even cut on the justification that they obstruct the will of the individual to choose and determine how his/her own private earnings are spent. As legal and civil protections to rights of privacy have been narrowed under such policy initiatives as the Patriot Act and the War on

Terror, as the home is becoming increasingly a site of production, as tele-marketers and Internet providers are bringing the mall ever more indelibly into the home, as medical records are being publicly distributed for the benefit of large commercial pharmaceutical interests, the government it-self is hiding behind increasing cloaks of secrecy, and public responsibili-ties like welfare, schooling, and Social Security are being translated into private, familial, and volunteerist concerns. What is missing now is not pri-vate spaces and moments reserved for the irrational and private contem-plation, as Marcuse would argue, but rather a sense of the public, where general concepts and future visions can be elaborated. As the idea of privacy is restructured for a commercial public and for military mobilization, dreaming itself is reduced to the magical promises of willful mastery offered in advertisements.

The second-wave of feminism was initially concerned with releasing women from the servitude of the domestic and its financial dependence. Yet, it did not foresee the reorganization of social relations in the public sphere in the model of the private sphere—what Marcuse has called the "unification of opposites" (90), where dependence is seen as a moral stigma because it draws on public assistance rather than private accumula-tion, thereby making visible the limits to the logic of the market. The pri-vatization of public life is also wielded to criticize compassionate state functions, as when the governor of Florida, for instance, can claim marital love to be the answer to the state's fiscal crisis, since governments cannot love, calling for an end to "big government" by demanding a revote on the class-size amendment—passed by 52 percent in a state-wide election in 2002—which would limit the number of students in public school classes (Governor Bush has claimed in the past that there is "no evidence" that smaller class sizes mean better education). Clichés about the sanctity of the private home justify government cutbacks. The private family substitutes for government action, as femininity denotes an escape into love and sov-ereignty, outside of rationalized public controls like support for education.

The privacy now forming the ideological underpinnings of the impera-tive to women's independence and individualism in the market is standard-ized as a dominant code for signifying freedom and often appropriated as an ideological tool for deepening exploitation in the name of market freedom. The assault on the public sphere initiated in the name of free mar-ket liberalization has led to what John Gray has identified as a "fragility and decline of the traditional family" (29) (particularly, in this case, under Thatcherism): "In those British cities in which Thatcherite policies of labour market deregulation were most successful in lowering rates of un-employment, rates of divorce and family breakdown were correspondingly highest" (30). As the power brokers call for an increasing governance by the private family, the family itself is losing its own stability and leverage.

By shoring up an ideal of privacy outside of power, the discursive linking of women to the empirical, the irrational, and the private—as is happening in some theories of teaching—continues to bolster a neoliberalism dependent on service labor. In *Closing the Gender Gap*, Madeleine Arnot, Miriam David, and Gaby Weiner have shown how Margaret Thatcher and the conservatives encouraged a return to such Victorian values of the family in order to formulate a "cult of individualism," which would bolster market liberalization at the expense of social programs, even as she herself was clearly not at home taking care of her twins. "[T]he push to privatization [in public social services] was both towards the implementation of business forms of organization of the private or commercial sector and towards allotting responsibility for social welfare and education to the private family" (87). As the family itself was falling into disarray, the appeal to the family on the part of power was used to fashion "a framework[. . .] within which the free market[. . .] would be self-regulating" (Gray, 28–29). Meanwhile, the same neoliberal policies that were professed to be protecting women were actually, in England as globally, aggravating the segregation of men and women in the workplace while ghettoizing women in low-paying service sector jobs. At the same time, as demonstrated in such stories as feminist pedagogical "empowerment," such policies placed the public responsibility for poverty, for family dissolution, and for unemployment onto women as mothers and as motherly teachers who should be encouraging children to transcend economic obstacles through inherent strength and personal initiative.

In addition, the displacing of public responsibilities onto the family and the individual—eliding women's work into the private and the unregulated—builds into a distrust of public interventions and assistance. As Angela McRobbie observes, "The Thatcher years saw a shift of responsibility for young people from the state back to the privatized sphere of the family[. . .] Benefit changes, and the removal of access to housing subsidy, have pushed disadvantaged young people if not onto the streets then noticeably into poverty" (364). The ideological remodeling of the public in the image of the family does not create stories of emancipation and empowerment, nor does it support the goals of feminism to build equality in the workplace, nor does it secure autonomy for women. Rather, it presently feeds privatization initiatives that undermine the power of the public and diminish the economic power and autonomy of women.

World-Class Woman

The idea that the public, the law, and the political only serve repressive functions and impede wizards' abilities to practice the fullest extent of their strengths and talents is, in fact, the very premise on which the book series itself is marketed. Rowling's story tells that through her own dedication, adventurous imagination, and ingenuity, much like Harry's, she was able to rise above the hardship of being a single mother, riding the wave of her talent to fame and riches. "I made a superhuman effort," she confesses to her biographer. "I would put Jessica in her pushchair, take her to the park and try to tire her out. When she fell asleep I'd rush to a café and write" (Fraser, 44). Rowling professes a Horatio Algers fortitude, catapulted, by sheer force of will and desire, beyond any need for public assistance or family services and making the very idea of any public supports seem obsolete, an admission of lack of inbred talent, intelligence, and inspiration, and an espousal of Muggle-like mediocrity. "Joanne's health visitor," tells her biographer Sean Smith, "—a compulsory extra for a single mother on benefits—brought round a few second-hand toys for Jessica: a grubby old teddy bear, a little plastic house and a telephone that you pulled along with a piece of string. Joanne was so humiliated by this act of genuine kindness that she stuffed the toys into a black rubbish bag and left it on the street for the refuse collection" (124).

Angela McRobbie has discerned a focus on women in the political rhetoric of meritocracy, where, in what she calls a "magical reversal" (360), girls—"their bodies, their labour power, and their social behaviour" (361)—now embody the worries over changing market requirements and consumer conditions. "[E]ven though the majority of young women do not have these opportunities to become high wage earners" (365), the growing number of independent and "top-earning" women signify the success of free market enterprise. For McRobbie, there is a definitive link between "a generation of women whose commitment to earning a living and accumulating assets is taken for granted" (362) and women "from extremely disadvantaged communities which have been experiencing for some time the impact of joblessness" (368). The feminism which advantaged women are identifying as dictating economic independence from men is also soliciting a moral condemnation of women who, at the lower ends of the social hierarchy, cannot make it in the marketplace. As Angela McRobbie has remarked, "[S]liding into place almost unnoticed[. . .] is a New Right vocabulary which celebrates female success in the marketplace, which punished failure as individual weakness, and which boldly advocates competitive individualism as the mark of modern young womanhood" (371). For example, in John Stockwell's 2002 film *Blue Crush,* the lead character, played by Kate Bosworth, is a hotel maid who worries about making rent every month, particularly after she gets fired from her job. Her goal is to win a particularly treacherous surfing contest so that she will become an advertisement for surfing products and a covergirl for the magazines. As she trains, she meets an NFL superstar quarterback who gives her emotional support as she makes a bid to get the attention of the commercial promoters. As superstar femininity is tied into marketable talent or rather what McRobbie calls the wish for becoming the "TV blond," Bosworth's character gets the money, the job, and the guy. Shadowing the romance here and condemned to poverty because she is not glib, beautiful, and enterprising is the suggested possibility of a base foil: a ghostly and despicable hotel maid who is unjustly fired from her job yet does not act savvy, smart, and sexy enough to woo the filthy rich football hero nor to ride the waves to glory, wealth, love, celebrity, and a lucrative career.

In the United States as in Britain, Rowling's promotion tells a successful story of self-help in an economy of unmitigated desire: she manages to go from welfare to work quite successfully without buckling under the difficulties that many low-income parents have experienced under such programs, like insurance cuts and disappearing applications for day care and food stamps due to overloaded state bureaucratic systems (Houppert, 11–31). "[J]ust six years before she had been a newly divorced mother of a young baby," writes Smith, "caught in a benefits trap, stuck in poor housing and unable to improve her situation without endangering the essential payments needed to live[. . .] If the Harry Potter phenomenon had not come along [. . .], she would still have escaped the stigma of single motherhood by determination and hard work" (10–11). "The majority of the submitted scripts would go straight into the reject basket," narrates Smith at the point when the first Harry Potter manuscript arrived at the Christopher Little Literary Agency. "I fished it out to take a look" (131), confesses Bryony Evens, the office manager whose job it was to sort through submissions, like the Sorting Hat, which can read through students' thoughts and decide in which of the four Houses in Hogwarts they belong—"Some sort of test, I think" (Sorcerer's Stone, 115), Ron tells Harry. Evens never ended up earning a share of the huge sums that the agency takes in, but the Harry Potter manuscript magically rises to the top of the pile because of its distinction, and the rest is history.

Rowling's story sets her apart from the standard stereotype of single motherhood: the dependent, often black, welfare mom. Indeed, this mother-made-good works to falsify any claims that corporatization has led to a shrinking of state supports and a contingent impoverishment of the living conditions of low-income people, the increasing obstacles to better standards of living, and a growing worldwide culture of racism as the "Third World" is turned into a labor force increasingly cheapening to accommodate the flights of capital with increasingly invisible borders. In fact, the black welfare mom is one of the dominant stereotypes that cultural historian Robin Kelley has identified as producing a racism focused on culture and behavior over biology, where "black people and the 'inner city'" are constituted as inherited "social problems," adding up "to a merciless attack on black mothers specifically, and black families more generally" (4). In the case of Harry Potter, the successes of Harry and of

J. K. Rowling herself "prove" that the background figure of the black welfare mom is, if not deserving of the kind of treatment dealt out by the Death Eaters, at the very least culturally deficient because she lacks the drive, competence, diligence, and the inbred talent that have given moms like Rowling a better chance. The irony here is that even as women in the marketing of the Harry Potter books are representing the freedom of pure capitalism and the miracles of freedom of opportunity, women worldwide are the hardest hit by such magic, and that rather than flourishing under the ghostly protections of sacrificing mothers, children are suffering and even starving as a result of women's strangulation in economic lassitude, wage depressions, educational impoverishment, austerity measures, and lack of public assistance. The corporate initiative to win kids' support while driving down the institutions that support them cannot be understood outside of the parallel assault on and scapegoating of motherhood.

The identification of Rowling's life with Harry's own has been remarked on in biographies: "You can see really that the books emanate from her childhood" (100), Sean Smith reports one of Rowling's neighbors as saying. This emphasis, in the marketing, on the nearly perfect correspondence between Harry Potter's fiction and J. K. Rowling's reality means that Harry broadens the discourse of the welfare mother to include a much vaster condemnation of political institutions, including schools, and the public sphere more generally. The specters of blackness and poverty do not end with narratives about inheritance, excellence, and natural talent, which the market—like standardized tests and magical hats—immediately and magically recognizes. As well, when a murderer escapes from prison, the directors of Hogwarts invite over the high-security prison guards called Dementors to police the grounds. "Standing in the doorway, illuminated by the shivering flames[. . .], was a cloaked figured that towered to the ceiling. Its face was completely hidden beneath its hood. Harry's eyes darted downward, and what he saw made his stomach contract. There was a hand protruding from the cloak and it was glistening, grayish, slimy-looking, and scabbed, like something dead that had decayed in water" (*Prisoner*, 83). Once used for punishing criminals and now transferred to disciplining students in the name of security, this treacherous creature painfully sucks out the soul of transgressors, clamping his jaws over the mouth of victims to remove the memory and sense of self, leaving only an empty shell, and the victim, Harry says (though tentatively), usually deserves it (*Prisoner*, 247).

> Dementors are among the foulest creatures that walk this earth. They infest the darkest, filthiest places, they glory in decay and despair, they drain peace, hope, and happiness out of the air around them[. . .] Get too near a dementor and every good feeling, every happy memory will be sucked out of you. If it can, the dementor will feed on you long enough to reduce you to something like itself . . .

soulless and evil. You'll be left with nothing but the worst experiences of your life. (*Prisoner,* 187)

Fortunately, when the mystery gets solved and the murderer is no longer dangerously at large, the Dementors return to the prison, and the students are freed from their threatening surveillance and the fear of being caught by their torturing kiss.

In the United States, with two million people in prison and 6.6 million in the criminal justice system as a whole,

> [t]he vast majority of those behind bars are poor; 40 percent of state prisoners can't even read; and 67 percent of prison inmates did not have full-time employment when they were arrested. The per capita incarceration rate among blacks is seven times that among whites. African Americans make up about 12 percent of the general population, but more than half of the prison population. They serve longer sentences, have higher arrest and conviction rates, face higher bail amounts, and are more often the victims of police use of deadly force than white citizens. (Cole, 4)

Lurking just below the surface of Harry Potter's safety is not only the possibility of Harry's own punishment if his magical talent and wisdom do not succeed in saving him from the Dementors' aggressions or from the predations of criminals. Also invoked is the increasing use of "physical constraint as a remedy to the problem of public schooling" (82). As Kenneth J. Saltman has shown, "This trend is exemplified in schools by the imposition of surveillance cameras, metal detectors, drug tests, solitary confinement punishments and other behaviorist control tactics, mandatory uniforms, police presence, and the hiring of military personnel as instructors and administrators at all levels of education" (2000: 82). Harry's expertise in getting around and escaping the Dementors through cunning and wit demonstrate that the Dementors belong elsewhere, wherever it might be that wizards and witches deserve to have their souls taken from them because they have allied with the dark forces, or where they have already been turned into empty shells and left with nothing but despair.

The Dementors function, then, to evoke school discipline as the reality for those less endowed with the talent and ingenuity to solve the mystery, return to safety, and restore the conditions of happiness. In fact, the presence of the Dementors recalls the unhappy moment when Harry almost was sent to public school and that his aunt and uncle, embarrassed by Harry's difference, still boast to their friends and relatives that Harry is attending a school for uncurable criminals. In other words, the Dementors separate a place of bourgeois spirit and profitability as undeserving of pain, punishment, and containment from the nonproductive sectors from which Harry is to be saved, sectors defined here as human waste, or rather, public schools that make their students soulless and stupid. The Dementors suggest the hazards of public interventions in the affairs of private business by insinuating the narrative double of Harry's life: what would have happened if he were a needy orphan not endowed with the superiority of his birth and his estate nor saved by magic? The representation of the need for discipline in public places, particularly schools, feeds a conservative logic that blames public institutions and the individuals who are bereft enough to need them for all social ills, from crime to inefficiency, and ultimately puts the pressure of reform onto racially stigmatized and economically disadvantaged groups. As Saltman puts it, "The focus on discipline wrongly suggests that the problems of education stem from the failures of individuals—students, teachers, and administrators—to conform to a fundamentally fair system" (83) when, he goes on to say, it is the social context and an ideological faith in the healing powers of the market that have produced inadequate schooling.

Clearly, student experience needs to be taken into account in pedagogy. Yet the kinds of personal experience that are often talked about in teaching theory serve to void the political by focusing exclusively and morally on the private. Such methods privilege the private to such a degree that the possibility of public life or workable public institutions gets denied, turning thinking into an individual irrational dreamspace that gets identified as the only recognizable politics. In turn, this disregard of public politics enforces a widespread faith in privatization initiatives that are producing increasing poverty and inequality as well as more easily exploitable work conditions that enhance corporate power. Additionally, it allows education to individualize suffering and oppression while encouraging the imagination to function, as in advertising, to promise personal escape rather than social alternatives. The personal is, indeed, political, but not at the expense of the public. If education wants to focus on personal experience, it should also indicate how this experience can lead to a much more wide-ranging critique of the institutional context in which it is set along with the ideological mechanisms which orient it, or rather, the broad organization of public understanding and concepts of justice which allows experience to generate meaning.

The terms of a liberal feminism which premised itself on financial independence, personal choice, and equal representation are now being used against its own goals; female financial independence was redesigned in neoliberal philosophy to denounce and scapegoat public institutions and thereby blame poor people for social, economic, and cultural inequalities instituted by the unfair distribution of public resources demanded by the pundits and profiteers of corporatism and privatization. This has led to a depoliticization of feminist issues, where some have claimed feminism over because more women enjoy positions of economic power while others have concluded that feminism is obsolete because it has already accomplished what it set out to accomplish, letting women acquire greater wealth and consumer access. Feminism needs now to be vitally retheorized under the assumption that the current state of capitalism is incompatible with equality; that feminism needs to work against rather than for the private accumulation of things, people, nature, and experience for the benefit of consolidated power; and that right now, the shrinking of public power is inducing a backlash and a crisis that feminism needs to face.

CHAPTER 3

A Time for Flying Horses

Oil Education and the Future of Literature

A Learning Company

In 1984, Keri Hulme's Maori novel *The Bone People* won the Pegasus Prize for Literature established by Mobil Corporation. Since then, *The Bone People* has been frequently read in college courses on postcolonial and/or multicultural literature, and its appeal in the classroom and in lists of required reading for doctoral qualification is only seconded by its promotion, even today, in major bookstores, where, for example, a multiplex Barnes & Noble in Manhattan's Union Square included it in its recommended readings for Christmas 2000. Started in 1977, the Pegasus Prize is awarded, the publishers remark on the back cover, "to distinguished works from countries whose literature too rarely receives international recognition," and is chosen by a group of scholars, reportedly outside of Mobil's oversight, in a country first selected by elite members of the U.S. literary establishment like Paul Engle (then-director of the celebrated Iowa Writers' Workshop) and William Jay Smith (former chair of Columbia University's writers' program), among others.[1]

Mobil's stated cause here is to promote multiculturalism on a global scale. "Mobil has long been interested in celebrating the art and cultures of many countries where it does business," announced Joel H. Maness, president of Mobil de Venezuela, host of the 1998 Pegasus Prize granted to Ana Teresa Torres for the novel *Doña Inez Vs. Oblivion*, the first woman writer to receive the prize since Keri Hulme.[2] As Mobil's promotion states,

> [The Pegasus Prize] was designed[. . .] to make sure all voices are heard in the global chorus of ideas[. . .] Mobil strives to demonstrate that business can enrich international understanding by helping to illuminate and communicate

the best values of the world's cultures[. . .] "We created and support the Pegasus Prize because as a global company with operations in more than 125 nations, Mobil's interest lies in bringing people together—culturally as well as economically," says Lucio A. Noto, Chairman and Chief Executive Officer of Mobil Corporation. "And the Prize helps us demonstrate to foreign leaders and publics that we're a unique kind of business partner." (Mobil)

In the eyes of its corporate promoters, *The Bone People* presents an opportunity for English-speaking readers to learn what is valuable about Maori culture and what Maori culture can contribute to a universal human spirit, in order to "recognize" and give dignity to a historically marginalized and, indeed, colonized ethnic population.[3] Mobil has become, as *New York Times* correspondent Thomas Friedman has said of Chevron in his widely acclaimed best-seller about globalism, "not an oil company, it's a learning company" (176).

Praising Mobil as the third largest corporate sponsor of the arts and humanities (probably ascending on this list after its merger with Exxon which is also a major contributor), the Taft group documents that "Mobil Corp. and the Mobil Foundation disbursed grants totaling $9,879,000 in grants to arts and cultural organizations. Supporting a variety of arts disciplines, Mobil encourages mixing cultures, customs, and ideas through sponsorship of painting, theater, music, literature, sculpture, weaving, and numerous other cultural activities: PBS for Mobil Masterpiece Theater, the Mobil Pegasus Prize for Literature, and art exhibitions are some of the programs being sponsored by Mobil" (Taft Group). Corporate involvement in education certainly reforms curricular content as corporate intent, as when an "environmental curriculum video was produced by Shell Oil,[. . .] offering students pearls of wisdom like, "You can't get to nature without gasoline or cars" or when an Exxon-produced video "praises the company's role in restoring the ecology of Prince William Sound while avoiding any discussion of what (or who) caused the Alaska oil spill in the first place" (Manning, 17). Large investments in education and culture by large corporations in general—and oil, communications, transportation, and aerodynamic firms in particular—indicate that consolidation is backed by massive distributions of ideological messages that advance and sell corporatist worldviews as a whole. Fredric Jameson has argued that the GATT and NAFTA agreements have been necessarily accompanied by innovative types of cultural production and consumable forms of cultural diversity where "freedom of ideas is important because the ideas are private property and designed to be sold in great and profitable quantities" (1998: 61). Picking up on the discussions in earlier chapters about the privatization of identity, this chapter considers how certain constructions of ethnic identity are ideologically fueling a shrinking of the public sphere as it is remade for corporate identifications. I look at Keri Hulme's novel *The Bone People* as it constructs a relationship between the private and the public spheres of power that all but shreds imagining a possible politics of public interventions in private production.

Brand Maori

The Bone People is the story of Kerewin, an independently wealthy artist (she won the lottery, and then invested the surplus) who isolated herself in a tower, cutting off connections with both family and friends in order to pursue freely her creative work. When the novel opens, her creative spirit is blocked. Enter Simon. Simon is a mute boy, an angelic prodigy, who suddenly and mysteriously appears in the tower and ends up winning over her heart. Kerewin next meets Joe, who is Simon's ostensible father (it is only later that Joe tells of how Simon was washed up on the beach after a shipwreck and how Joe and his wife adopted him before his wife and child died of the flu). As the story develops in a series of fishing trips and nights of drinking, these three characters play out a cycle of violence and forgiveness. Kerewin soon discovers that Joe is beating Simon and tries to stop the abuse but only ends up identifying with Joe's frustrations and hitting Simon herself. The three are split up when Joe bashes Simon's head in, causing a serious concussion and permanent cerebral damage, which lands Simon in the hospital. But because of his love and devotion to his adopted family, Simon only dreams of bringing the three of them back together, defying both doctors' orders and the better judgment of state social workers who intend, most maliciously, to keep Simon away from his tormentors forever. In the last section of the novel, all three characters, broken, go on pilgrimages, encountering figures of Maori foundational mythology. Joe becomes the keeper of the lost Maori canoe which brought the Maori people to the island of New Zealand; Kerewin has her stomach cancer healed through the interventions of an ancestral Maori phantasm; and at last the three happily meet again as the guardians of the sacred canoe, reuniting for a harmonious feast in a moment of renewal preordained in the Maori mythical return to the homeland.

While a text such as *The Bone People* is open to different interpretive frameworks, interpretations are hardly endlessly open-ended. Rather, they are shaped and limited by broader discourses in the cultural field that are historically and materially struggled over. *The Bone People* needs to be read in a way that shows how it affirms rather than challenges the activities of multinational oil companies such as MobilExxon that make corporate values into human values. This chapter discusses how *The Bone People* takes up, as defining ethnic identity, some of the thematic contents of privacy identified in prior chapters as attributes of women, childhood socialization, and the family. So why would Mobil Corporation want to promote this version of Maori culture under their own trademark? Setting aside for now the hard-to-swallow idea of benevolent and forgivable child abusers, one might remark, to start, on the novel's constant invocations of a pristine and unsullied environment on both land and sea, on the complete absence of any kind of labor problems or organizations even though Joe works in a factory, and on the elimination of any state role except for the rather stupid and ineffectual social workers who treat Simon, the useless schools, which are not able to discipline his eruptive spirit, and the health care system, which is neglectful, in for example the case of Joe's wife and child, of preventing death from a perfectly treatable disease.

"Compassionate" Corporatism

The Maori certainly do have just cause to criticize and even vilify the state, not only because of the state's role in implementing a colonial government which, among other abuses, took away much of their territory, but also as the current state continues to cause deprivation among the Maori. However, the curtailment of state powers in New Zealand, as capital is deregulated and consolidated, has not effectively brought equality and justice to the Maori, but rather the opposite. Underfunding of Maori education and health care, welfare cuts, and assimilation policies have caused, according to Donna Awatere, decreased birth rates among the Maori, increasing poverty and a growing culture of white supremacy affecting hiring practices, justice claims, salaries, and incarceration rates. "Any Maori child is four times more likely than a white child to appear before a Children's Court" (Awatere, 15). "In 1976 and 81[. . .] there were three-and-a-half times more Maoris unemployed than whites" (Awatere, 15). "In 1976[. . .] six more whites earned $10,000 and over compared to Maoris, yet every Maori wage had to support 2.2 people (compared to 1.5 for whites)" (Awatere, 17).

As the compassionate public function of nation-states declines, the growth of corporate power has meant, for many people around the world, the literal annihilation of democratic possibilities and civil protections. At the time that *The Bone People* was published in New Zealand, New Zealand was considering new laws for transportation, commerce, licensing, and energy that would seriously effect Mobil's operations on the North Island where the events in the novel take place. In the 1930s, New Zealand's labor laws restricted the distance goods could be transported away from the railway lines to thirty miles, favoring the interests of domestic workers and state-supported infrastructure. In the 1980s, new legislation would be passed that would ease Mobil's abilities to exploit oil for export by lifting these restrictions and deregulating transportation. Additionally, in the late 1970s, after years of oil companies' vying for the rights, New Zealand's Liquid Fuels Trust Board approved Mobil's controversial methanol-to-gas processing plant projected for construction on the North Island in 1985.

The Bone People's publication happens simultaneously, then, with a concerted effort by corporations—and by oil and transportation in particular—to transform public power into private power and to introduce new neoliberalist policies oriented against the protection of labor and domestic production and toward a globalist, outward-looking focus for the economy. A reading of *The Bone People* must therefore consider how the very act of dismantling these corporate values requires a revitalized notion of civil society, public life, and public institutions to offset corporate controls and the consequent end of democratic citizenship. As Gayatri Spivak elaborates,

> Some commonly understood arenas such as health, education, welfare, and social security, and the civil as opposed to penal or criminal legal code, fall within the purview of civil society[. . .] When increasingly privatized, as in the New World Order, the priorities of the civil society are shifted from services to the citizen to capital maximization[. . .] [T]ransnationality is shrinking the possibility of an operative civil society in developing nations. ("Diasporas Old and New," 5–6)

The shrinking of civil societies throughout the world has led to a severe diminution of a politics of the public, reducing most oppositional political action to motivations defined by narrowly defined private interests or identity-based claims to rights. Among other institutional supports of the public, education needs to counter such imaging of corporate citizenship as depicted in *The Bone People* in order to establish itself as a viable public sphere for democratic deliberation, learning, thinking, and action. The New Zealand governments of the 1970s and 1980s were instrumental in furthering the interests of international capital at the expense of the public. New Zealand's 1984 election responded to a critique of the welfare state starting, under a Conservative administration, in the 1970s and ushered in a period of austerity, cuts in social spending, deregulated exchange rates, tariff cuts, incentives for foreign investment, and antilabor policies. Such a reconfiguration of economic relations, of course, eased Mobil's position within the New Zealand economy on the one hand, but, on the other hand, spurred economic trouble in New Zealand as the external debt quadrupled, rates of productivity growth for the next eight years fell to 0.9 percent, while rates of unemployment and poverty increased (Herman and McChesney, 179).

Even as new legislation was limiting federal democratizing interventions into the economy, the government itself was spinning tales of new democratic openings.[4] A 1997 report from New Zealand's Ministry of Commerce, for instance, evaluated the deregulation initiatives of the mid-1980s as advancing democratic access to the economy by removing barriers to entry. Because of the reduction of environmental protectionist laws and the agencies to enforce them, the report claims, it is less costly for smaller companies to compete in the industry, resulting in more services available to consumers even if they are at higher prices.

> Lowering these unnecessary costs[. . .] would at least make it easier and more profitable to undertake investments which might otherwise be inhibited[. . .] Because there are no barriers to entry into the New Zealand petrol market, government action to facilitate entry is not required[. . .] Any intervention to facilitate entry would therefore introduce inefficiencies into the market. For example, policies designed to break down horizontal arrangements or force participation in horizontal arrangements by incumbents[. . .] could be expected to increase costs of suppl[y]ing petrol in New Zealand. (ACIL Economics, Policy and Strategy Consultants)

Omitted from this analysis are the ways that the current consolidation of capital has resulted in mergers, buyouts, and takeovers, allowing large companies to price out small companies by outsourcing parts of the production process to satellites, or to control markets by becoming the only buyers of a particular stage of the production process. Unmentioned as well is the history of oil which, as William Greider has shown, has never been on a free-market course, but rather managed by governments.[5] In other words, the oil industry's consolidation has led to oligapolization touted as democratic freedom, while democratic freedom is being refashioned as the "unfettering" of markets in the name of profits and consumer rights, even if labor, environmental, and democratic decision-making and access get thwarted, and even if "unfettering" is exactly what such deregulation policies are not accomplishing. As in *The Bone People,* the good citizen appears as the independent investor, free of labor and controls, unconcerned about human connections, living in an unworrisome environment, surrounded by a mythically crystalline sea.[6]

Like the government's own self-reporting, *The Bone People* provides a benevolent image of a deregulated society full of private initiative. It also develops a sense of autonomous individuals who are completely free, sovereign masters of their own choice in a landscape open and available to their wanderings even as it falls under a system of private ownership: Simon is a trespasser in Kerewin's tower, for instance: "[I]n case no-one ever told you before, people's houses are private and sacrosanct" (20), she tells him, but he makes himself welcome and Kerewin would never restrict his access. Contingently, all public institutions are demonized because they restrict this freedom: Simon is scared of doctors and panics in hospitals, and at school (which he frequently avoids, to nobody's real consternation) he comes in for a lot of "petty bullying and shitslinging[. . .] because he's a bit of an outlaw" (49), where school confines Simon's self-expression by restricting his wayward explorations in the wild. *The Bone People* operates within a certain logic where 1) reading produces identifications with capitalist power and capitalist values; and 2) relations of power and human values which support capitalist expansions and appropriations are made to seem natural and common sense.

The Pegasus Novels

This is not to say that Keri Hulme is to blame, or that she intentionally supported a promotional campaign where she single-handedly built exploitative practices into the economy, or that her aim is to advertise oil. Neither is the argument here about how Hulme should be condemned or castigated for not drawing attention to how multinational corporations are destroying environments in other countries, unjustly bypassing local laws and ethical considerations about local land tenure systems and economic rights, or making life conditions more and more miserable for larger numbers of people, particularly indigenous peoples, by deregulating labor protections. The purpose here is not to target individuals but rather to show how corporations and the institutions that support them—the system of global capitalism itself—have succeeded in limiting possibilities for what can be expressed, configuring human value as only conceivable within neoliberal productive relations.

In general, the Pegasus novels do not overtly pontificate the values of corporatism nor expound on the benefits of oil-based energy. Rather, they create and sell a social vision in which corporate globalization seems logical, natural, wholesome, necessary, and good, while the faultlines and destructive capacities of capitalist growth and greed become illogical, invisible, and even unthinkable, and the very idea of public democratic organization seems out of sync with ethnic identity. As a whole, the novels share certain ideas about the relationship between characters and their social environments: 1) the novels are primarily psychological, introspective, and sometimes existential, emphasizing the isolated, individual, psychological subject; 2) the characters are wanderers, often using the globe itself as plane on which to explore and discover the psychological self. "A Person born of honest Folk who in foreign Lands doth wander, findeth that [in] his Travel[. . .] many a time against his own Will is he beset by unforeseen Hardship and Misfortune and doth require Money and other Necessities of Life, and so he desireth, and in Truth he hath but this Choice, to set out upon Land and Sea," begins, for example, *Dollar Road*; 3) the novels are experimental, dressing themselves up as "the new" without ever invoking newness or change in terms of the social relations of production; 4) the novels often present multicultural encounters, as in *And the War Is Over,* the recipient of the 1984 prize, which tells of Dutch prisoners of war in an Indonesian camp during the Japanese occupation, or *Rituals,* which concludes in a Japanese tea ceremony taking place in the Netherlands; 5) labor is considered an affront to the humanity of the subject as well as an oppression forced by the state, whereas speculative investment indicates freedom of thought and expression; 6) there is a natural movement of history toward capitalist progress, so large-scale capitalist production is never at fault for destruction, alienation, or hardship but rather destruction, alienation, and hardship figure as just a natural, though sad refuse to a much grander, even inevitable historical project. "On the day that Inni Wintrop committed suicide," begins, for example, Cess Nooteboom's *Rituals,* a Dutch novel and winner of the 1982 Pegasus Prize, "Philips shares stood at 149.60. The Amersterdam Bank closing rate was 375, and Shipping Union had slipped to 141.50" (1). In this novel, the main character, Inni, expelled from school, works in an office (he does not say what he does) until he receives an inheritance from a long-lost aunt. Though, until now, "he had never become anything[. . .] There was no central thought, such as a career, an ambition. He simply existed[. . .]" (32–33), he received the inheritance because "that job of yours is pointless, that is obvious. You should spend a year reading or traveling. You are not suited to be a subordinate" (34). In fact, Inni's psychological search is so tied up with finance and investment that desire operates only through the free flow of money: sex with his wife is described as "[t]he squaring of accounts" (15), as they "play prostitute" and exchange cash in foreplay.

Travel continues as an important motif in the Pegasus novels, linking the journeys of capital to the free movement of the consuming, desiring subject. For example, the 1992 Pegasus Prize winner, Martin M. Simecka's Slovakian novel *The Year of the Frog*—introduced by former playwright, political theorist, and president of the Czech Republic, Václav Havel—tells the story of a former prize-winning runner who is searching for the meaning of existence during the waning years of the Communist regime in Prague. When the Communist police track him down and threaten arrest, he is forced to work in various state-run enterprises: first a cancer ward, then a hardware store, and finally a birthing clinic, which does just as many messy, grotesque, even tragic abortions. The pressures put on him by the police and by his work schedule severely limit his wanderings through the city, his running, his love, his home life, and his art (he is also a writer). Describing how globalization creates new class hierarchies based on relations of space, Zygmunt Bauman has explained how movement indicates consumption on the one hand and, on the other, a lack of responsibility for local communities as capital freely relocates. In contrast, the state is seen as restricting, constraining, and policing movement: "Today's existence," he forewarns, "is stretched along the hierarchy of the global and the local, with global freedom of movement signalling social promotion, advancement and success, and immobility exuding the repugnant odour of defeat, failed life and being left behind[. . .] Life ambitions are more often than not expressed in terms of mobility, the free choice of place, travelling, seeing the world; life fears, on the contrary, are talked about in terms of confinement, lack of change, being barred from places which others traverse easily, explore and enjoy" (1998: 121). This ideological configuration of globalization underlies the logic of *The Year of the Frog*, as freedom of movement is associated with Western consumption: "how beautiful life is when you can just walk into a store and buy a pair of Marathon running shoes the first time you go in" (6). In the places where the protagonist works for the Communist state, however, he confronts only graphic scenes of death, sickness, desperation, corruption, and shortage. In fact, the novel begins with a condemnation of, precisely, a state-run refinery that is condemned first for ill-treating labor ("I've lost thirty pounds in the last three months," says the old man the protagonist meets at the payroll office [1]) and then for polluting ("It's the gas, my boy, the gas that's leaking from the pipes" [1]). Death and disease, the stopping-up of thought and expression, are linked to the stagnancy of a state-controlled heavy-industry and production-oriented capital that cannot move. This is opposed to speculation or investment capital, which runs unrestrictedly across natural borders like the rugged terrain, the bridges, tree roots, and icy passages crossed by the narrator.

The movements of capital do not just control consciousness, desire, and freedom in the Pegasus novels, but also politics, nature, happiness, and history. "In a plain, indisputable way," writes Kjartan Fløgstad in the Norwegian novel *Dollar Road*, winner of the 1988 Pegasus Prize, "Selmer Høysand sensed the mysterious power that finds its statistical expression in the capitalistic logic of daily stock-market prices" (8). *Dollar Road* chronicles the family history of a father, his son, and his nephew as a Scandinavian region passes from agriculture to industry and then to global entrepreneurship, shipping, militarism, adventurism, and the like. Though industrialization is clearly ruining the landscape, even ruining traditional ways of life as it forces people away from their homes, there is no sense of any alternative to the factory, which offers the only possibility of lucrative work for the failing farmers. Neither is there any sense of connection between the coming of the factory and the laying waste of the fields, except that the factory absorbs the surplus labor as the farms become economically unviable. Just as politics does not seem to matter except as it registers the historical rhythms of change in the stock market,[7] so pollution seems to touch only surfaces and then wash away, its victims moving from industrial smoke-inhalation to global environmental catastrophes. "The oil tank exploded!" Rasmus Høysand, the nephew, woke up one night to discover. "The oil tank!![. . .] Oil was thick in his mouth, black before his eyes, plugging his ears. Everywhere. Now for a match! A spark! Now for the Apocalypse!" (159). The spill was caused by a natural disaster, a tropical hurricane, rather than by corporate mismanagement or faulty equipment, and the rig itself seems to belong to no one in particular. The next day, he woke up on a raft, floating on the sea, with "oil stains over his entire bare body" (160), only to be rescued by a friendly ship bringing raw aluminum from Jamaica back to Europe. Here, there is no outside, no respite or rescue from the tragedies of capital, and capital is not, the text suggests, wreaking as much havoc as you would think. The oil is no sooner spilled than forgotten as new and profitable adventures await.

In fact, the progress of capitalism brings justice by allowing for multicultural kinship, but what kind of justice is it, who gets to define it, and who benefits from its outcomes? *Doña Inez vs. Oblivion* narrates the story of a land dispute starting in colonial Venezuela and resolved in the present. The plantation owner Alejandro Martínez de Villegas y Blanco promised a portion of his land to his illegitimate mulatto son, Juan del Rosario Villegas, born by one of his slaves. When Juan del Rosario formed a community of runaway and freed slaves on the fallow plantation lands, Alejandro's surviving wife, Doña Inés Villegas y Solórzano, initiated a series of legal claims questioning her former houseboy's titles, escalating it to the point where the ex-slaves even petition and win an audience with the king of Spain. Throughout the next four hundred years of Venezuelan history, Doña Inés' deceased voice tells of governments and their laws that rise and fall, wars that are waged, new political philosophies that gain prominence, waves of migrants that overtake the cities, and technology that changes the ways people live on the land and the types of production they perform. Yet, in the end, the authenticity of the original title is "justly" reinstated as Doña Inéz' descendants, in trusting partnership with the community of inheritors of Juan de Rosario's tract, turn the plantation into a multinational tourist haven by the sea. In a manner of speaking, property itself takes on the role of "character" in the novel as different propertied positions enter into conflict and then resolve their differences, while Doña Inés' "voice" is developed through her various claims to ownership.[8]

Furthermore, this image of a new, peaceful future of a Venezuela full of multicultural comraderie in the name of business is guaranteed in Venezuela's redemption as an oil-producing nation: "this is a poor, backward country," says Salbic the jeweler, a small-business owner who eventually gets run out by the multiplex businesses that arise on all sides, "—but you'll see, the oil business will change it completely. Keep in mind what I'm telling you; a few years from now, everything's going to be different" (149). In Venezuela, however, this type of multicultural corporate harmony has been thoroughly unraveled in the oil industry's campaign to subordinate the powers of the public sector. The national oil enterprise PDVSA in conjunction with the Confederation of Venezuelan workers (*Confederación de Trabajadores de Venezuela*, or CTC) staged a walkout to protest President Hugo Chavez's[9] attempts to include his own party affiliates on the oil company's board of directors in 2002. The street protests resulted in a shoot-out, with over 100 people injured and at least 10 people killed[10] as well as a military coup which lasted for a day and received the tacit approval of Condoleeza Rice and the U.S. government, who only condemned the temporary overthrow once Chavez had been restored as head of state. The event shows that rather than a friendly partnership between democratic populism and private consumerist industry as *Doña Inéz* envisions, the oil company's defense of privatization is waged at the expense of democratic governance, labor rights, public redistribution, and the right to assembly, and can only be implemented through recourse to militarism.

The Pegasus novels are not simply promotional materials exhibiting a brand name on an uplifting cultural product, but rather they provide an image of corporatist logic that determines the ways economic, cultural, and social relations can be thought by erasing the politics of the public sphere. For example, as a laborer, Joe in *The Bone People* accepts without dissenting, organizing, or resisting his "being a puppet in someone else's play. Not having any say" (Hulme, 89). *The Bone People* depicts labor as, succinctly, nonpolitical by relegating it purely to the aesthetics of poetic self-representation, using his position as laborer to define Joe as a citizen without political opinions. Though this might have provided an opening for considering Joe's abuse of Simon in relation to alienation and economic oppression, Joe's resolution to labor dissatisfaction is, instead, to write poetry and to go on vacation: "I'd dearly like to take a decent holiday," he says (89), cutting off any suggestion that political action or change would be the necessary antidote, not a few days off. Joe, Kerewin, and Simon then go to Kerewin's ancestral home for fishing, feasting, and quiet healing. Like the novel's project of cultural retrieval, the implication here is that a culturalist escape will soothe the pain of economic hardships and exploitation rather than providing a way of thinking of cultural discrimination in the workplace as imbricated in systematic economic injustices or in the reason that Joe's working conditions are so egregious. In other words, *The Bone People* constructs Maori culture as a way of avoiding confrontation and finding therapeutic solace within an oppressive system, rather than to ask the important questions that Nancy Fraser has asked: "Under what circumstances can a politics of recognition help support a politics of redistribution? And when it is more likely to undermine it? Which of the many varieties of identity politics best synergize with struggles for social equality? And which tend to interfere with the latter?" (1997: 12).

Expressions of Difference: Gender Roles

The criticism on *The Bone People* focuses on two major ways the novel supposedly succeeds in its political project and its empowering expressions of difference: one, in its feminist statement; and two, in its multiculturalist support of cultural recognition, diversity, and inclusion. *The Bone People* gets interpreted as feminist because it supposedly dismantles traditional ways of thinking about gender and family. As Chris Prentice writes, "In *The Bone People[. . .]* Hulme has created physically and, from a traditional perspective, behaviourally ambiguous characters[. . .] Stereotypical literary portrayals of femininity are rejected[. . .] Kerewin, Simon and Joe are all unstable mixtures of passivity and activity, control and aggression, nurturance and selfishness" (Prentice, 71). While Joe is not aggressively male and is content to wait patiently for Kerewin's attentions to turn toward him, Kerewin is asexual, androgynous, and can fight. "All right, woman, you think you can fight a man?" Hulme begins her description of Kerewin's "manly" warrior skills, "and strikes for Kerewin's face[. . .]. Kerewin kicks him [Joe] in the side and dances around Simon . . . She slips past the flailing hands and hits him on the mouth with the side of her hand. It feels like being hit with a board. He staggers, is spun round and kicked viciously in the back[. . .]. [S]he whacks his face again and then steps sideways and drives her knuckles across his midriff . . . " (191). This form of androgyny, an identification with power and violence, is what these feminist critics have indicated as a feminist answer to oppressive gender typing. In addition to being liberated through these physical traits of masculinity, Kerewin is independent both financially and emotionally, and her independence is frequently interpreted as evidence of the novel's emancipatory intentions.

As Keri Hulme describes the publication process in the introduction, a feminist collective saved the novel from falling into relative obscurity. Three other publishers that considered the novel first rejected it. However, the Spiral Collective noticed the talents that these other companies failed to see, and appreciated the novel for the very eccentricities for which it had been faulted. Here is a story of an independently thinking artist working in isolation, an artist whose genius is innovation and who, because of her in-novations, almost ends up as a beleaguered pariah. Despite the attacks from institutions of power, however, this genius-artist persisted in her in-dividualistic idiosyncrasies and private efforts until a small, upstart, revo-lutionary, entrepreneurial group recognized her virtues and, by this miraculous stroke of luck, her talents were finally recognized, and she sin-gle-handedly, by sheer force of endurance, managed to work her way from rags to riches, hitting the limelight.

What is left out of this glorious story, however, is that the other three publishers that Hulme solicited with *The Bone People* had, actually, a much more radical agenda than the Spiral Collective's. As C. K. Stead remarks,

> For the record let it be said first that of the three who were offered the novel before Spiral saw it, one was a feminist publisher who thought it insufficiently feminist for her list[. . .]. It should also be said that Spiral received a govern-ment grant which made the publication possible, and that this was on the recom-mendation of the Literary Fund Advisory Committee, consisting at that time of five men and one woman. (Stead, 102)

Perhaps what makes so many critics see *The Bone People* as feminist has to do with how it exposes that a female who challenges gender roles in her androgyny and independence is still relegated to a maternal role through the inevitable closure of the family cycle and the sanctity of the private sphere, and, despite herself, falls under the sway of her maternal instinct. This is why, for instance, Suzette Henke, who can see that "Keri Hulme deliberately reconstructs and redistributes traditional sex-roles" (136), concludes that "Who but a female hero could rescue this battered goblin-soul [Simon]?" (140). *The Bone People* conforms to what Edward Herman and Robert McChesney have portrayed as the narrowing of media and ide-ological content resulting from the increasing alliance and centralization of corporate interests in what they call "oligopolistic markets[. . .] [and] loosely knit cartels" (187) all but locking out dissent and public debate: "A supportive environment [for selling goods] does not challenge materialis-tic values and is not set in grim circumstances; it shows people who spend and gain status by acquisition and consumption, displayed in surround-ings of wealth[. . .], favoring consumption as the solution to human hap-piness[. . .] [P]lots regularly honor the family-oriented" (140). As Nancy Fraser and others have pointed out, the ideal of the nuclear family is the main avenue through which contemporary capitalism justifies its policies of unequal economic distributions, including cuts in social welfare spend-ing,[11] as responsibility for social hardships and inequalities is transferred from public institutions to the private family or, more particularly, to the mother. What *The Bone People* does is to repeat the status quo, to use

Kerewin as proof of the entrenchability of gender, class, and the natural-ness of the nuclear family, and then to gloss it over by labeling this reac-tionary attitude as a subversive gesture.

Nancy Fraser has argued that celebrating women's sexual and economic independence as an emancipatory project is tantamount to equating human worth with wage-labor. For Fraser, the critique of women's depen-dence currently shapes popular dismissals of the public welfare state: "the condition of poor women with children who maintain their families with neither a male breadwinner nor an adequate wage and who rely for eco-nomic support on a stingy and politically unpopular government pro-gram" (123). Taking the next step, *The Bone People* upholds speculation as the basis for conceiving the liberated, autonomous subject. Kerewin's propensity to resist the role of reproduction to which women in the nu-clear family are often reduced is therefore set in place by a nonproductive economic structure, an idea of wealth promising low-growth and low so-cial investiture while historically assuring high profits for highly corpora-tized economic sectors like telecommunications and oil.[12] The idea of "feminism" in the novel serves as a backhanded critique of government's redistributive interventions in the economy, claiming that freedom only arises through economic self-motivation, regulatory autonomy, and free-dom from public interventions. The connotation here is that oppositional feminism can only appear as material comfort.

Expressions of Difference: Authenticity

The second major concern of the criticism is about whether or not Hulme's novel is an adequate or authentic representation of Maori culture, especially, such critics assert, when Hulme herself is only one-eighth Maori and is writing in English. In contrast, the point in this paper is not to argue that Keri Hulme is or is not authentically Maori, or that *The Bone People* is or is not an authentically Maori text. Rather, the point here is to ask under what political conditions does the very question of cultural authenticity get mobilized, and toward what ends.

Much criticism of *The Bone People* insists that the novel's intent is to revive community "and make human beings one family" (Hulme, 199). In-deed, the coming together of the threesome and their respective families in the final drunken feast is definitely a feel-good, even salvational moment after the hardship of their separation. Says, for example, Christine Hamelin, "[. . .] despite Kerewin's remarkable self-sufficiency, the concept of individualism is subverted and replaced with the notion of commensal-ism[. . .] Kerewin's new view of the artist is linked to the gradual replace-ment of her controlling voice with the polyphonous voices which rise up at the end" (110). In *The Bone People,* therefore, the overconsumption of alcohol and related violence appears as a recognition (for multiculturalists outside of New Zealand) of the Maori[13] and, particularly, of the Maori rituals of commensualism. Alienation and alcoholism are reframed as positive values: cultural expression, rituals, family bonding events, and customary practices fill the novel with constant excuses for prideful drunkeness: "knots of happy people, chattering people, singing-tired and weeping-drunk people" (Hulme, 441). Even bringing kids into bars is lauded as a type of family bonding: "Nobody minds a kiddie being in the bar," asserts the bartender, "provided someone's looking after it. Better that than leave them at home uncared for, or stuck out by themselves in a car, isn't it?" (245). Here, the narration assumes drinking is necessary and inevitable for the building of cultural community, so kids must be accommodated around it, rather than the parents participating in events that would benefit, educate, or simply amuse the kids. Meanwhile, Hulme depicts the carpenter who opposes Simon's presence in the bar as brutish, threatening, and mean, justifying Kerewin's drunken show of force. The family ritual of Maori commensualism reframes negative effects of addictive consumption into cultural assets: affective bonding and parental protection.

Yet, for the most part, criticism of *The Bone People* uncritically celebrates the novel as subversive in its compassionate embrace of "Otherness" and/or cultural "hybridity": claims, for example, Graham Huggan, as he explores the implications of Hulme's Modernist influences, "[Hulme] hints at the emergence of an emancipated post-colonial voice containing within it the contradictions of and hybrid elements in post-colonial cultures which perceive their creolized status in terms other than those of self-deprecatory assimilation or self-glorifying recuperations" (35). *The Bone People* creates a feel-good sentiment around globalization. Like the other Pegasus novels, it uses images of multicultural love to sweeten globalization even as it seems to recognize cultures of difference. Omitted here is any possibility of recognition for ethnicities in places where Mobil might not do business or any sense that the public should be formed through any institutional structure other than the private, ethnic family with its bonds of love. Instead, as in liberal notions of equal and exchangeable representational identities, *The Bone People* treats difference as relegated purely to the private realms of family, sentiment, artistic inspiration, affiliative bonding, mystical practices, religion, leisure, and expression.

Many advocates for multiculturalism profess that the mere recognition of other cultures outside the West is a counter-hegemonic action, undermining the reification of identities and representations, denaturalizing racist categories, fragmenting universalisms, and radically challenging presuppositions of power granted, institutionally, to some over others. For example, Maryanne Dever contends that *The Bone People* "offers an alternative voice, one that enfranchises multiplicity and undermines the authority of imperialism's homogenizing linguistic imperative" (25). By simply adding on more differences and more features, such inclusionists claim, more equality can be achieved, so that justice becomes merely a matter of refining realist methods with a greater and more abundant attention to empirical form and detail, and a clearer and more precise focus on the way things get named. Culture becomes a matter of aesthetics, and therefore immaterial and private, leaving aside issues of economic redistribution or equitable reorganization.

Such views also uncritically celebrate love—and in particular family love—as the basis for getting along across cultural borders. However, they are not able to consider at the same time how this vision of multicultural love supports power, and that this power is not necessarily going to allow an optimistic or utopian future for everybody, where, as in the denouement, everybody has their "arms round each other's necks all good cheers and covered tears and matey friendship" (Hulme, 443). Not only do these assertions of multiculturalism tend to romanticize Maori culture, but they also tend to force Maori culture to express the ideals of peace and love which are lost and needed for the redemption of a poetically beleaguered Western soul too much immersed in commerce and technology. Such a re-creation of Maori culture only offers an easy, symbolic redemption. As Donaldo Macedo and Lilia I. Bartolomé acknowledge, "[M]any white liberals willingly call and work for cultural tolerance but are reluctant to confront issues of inequality, power, ethics, race, and ethnicity in a way that could actually led to social transformation that would make society more democratic and humane and less racist and discriminatory" (14). C. K. Stead's contention against Mobil's granting of the Pegasus Prize to Hulme was that the novel allows Maori culture to be re-created through its identification with white culture, allowing for such "affirmative action" initiatives by multinational corporations to seem as though they are helping oppressed cultures.

In *The Bone People,* a Maori "cultural authenticity" appears as a type of internalized artistic expression, but such expression is not just a pure surge of ancestral spirit emanating from a connection with the Maori community and landscape, as the criticism would have it. Christine Hamelin, for example, writes, "Kerewin's notion of the artist shifts as she becomes an active individual, involved in the community, open to emotions, prepared to accept the fragmentation of life and to lend an unencumbering pattern to it. The artist must also be joined to the land[. . .]" (117). Cultural equality is here reduced to a type of freedom of expression with an emphasis on autonomy based in the privacy of feeling. The image of Maori "cultural authenticity" and expression that the novel presents does not, however, talk about how the Maori myth of the canoe was drawn from several European colonialist and settler accounts and has tended, in recent land reform movements, to give favor to the most powerful and influential among the Maori tribes.[14] Anne Maxwell has discussed how in 1985 the Labour Government in New Zealand instituted an official policy of biculturalism to enforce original land contracts, made under Queen Victorian, between the Maoris and the British Crown. There was subsequently an upsurge in interest in university Maori studies as well as in Maori literature and Maori language, and this interest served to create a binary concept of New Zealand culture, which excluded those Maoris who did not fit under the homogenizing definition offered in these official versions. These official and exclusionary versions, like *The Bone People*, concentrated on the Maori canoe mythologies.[15] Kerewin's version of Maori "cultural authenticity" allows for the making of art, the private and inspired autonomy of the artist, and most importantly, the freedom from productive labor.

This is all not to say that all multiculturalism must therefore be dismissed as just another phase of imperialism or racism. Clearly, multiculturalism does not necessarily always feed cultural differences into a corporate, colonialist mill, but, still, it is worth both noting that multiculturalism sits comfortably as a product of globalization and thinking about the reasons why.[16] Contingently, multicultualism can only provide a counterhegemonic imperative if it contributes a sharp critique of the way contemporary global power works as well as ideas about ways to organize against it. One needs to ask of *The Bone People* how and when multiculturalism actually supports the growth of market cultures around the globe, not only by commodifying exotic goods and spectacles, but also by producing a sense that there can be no alternative to the authority of the market, private power, and global capital devoid of public controls.

The Environment

In its rhapsodic celebrations of the Maori experience of nature, *The Bone People* is unable to envision history, context, politics, ethics, or economic distributions in terms of the ways these forces already affect nature's possibilities. For Kerewin to rejuvenate her creative spirit, she needs to reintegrate herself aesthetically and emotionally within the Maori culture from which she has become alienated. What is left out here is any kind of consideration that systems of capital flow are what have alienated her from Maori culture in the first place. *The Bone People*'s "Maori culture" includes ritualistic practices, family relations, and diet, but also a sensibility and respect toward nature, an emotional and even religious connection to both land and sea. "Tears come to my eyes whenever I hear a gull keen," Kerewin laments, "or watch a shag pass on whistling wings. O land, you're too deep in my heart and mind. O sea, you're the blood of me" (166). Kerewin cannot bear to see living creatures get hurt, so she throws fish that are not good to eat back into the crystalline waters.

These images of nature reveal Maori "cultural authenticity" as proof of an idyllic natural abundance and environmental sustainability. In *The Bone People*, cancer is a product of a loss of faith rather than of noxious industrial emissions. There is no mention here of industrial pollutants, contaminants, environmental destruction. There are no plants or animals sickly or dying from exposure to poisons and toxins. There is no sense that Maori ways of life have been seriously threatened by oil spills, nor that the reason that the fish might not survive has to do more with waste products of multinational manufacturing than with individual fisherpeople making catches with fishing rods and canoes. There is no description here which relates to other testimonies of regions where multinationals have excavated oil, as in the Oriente of the Ecuadorian Amazon where Texaco has drilled 1.4 billion gallons of crude oil since the 1970s while disregarding international laws protecting the environment and human rights. There, as a correspondent from *The Nation* writes, "everything was eerily still, the fish and birds nowhere in sight and the vegetation stained black with petroleum residue" (Press, 11). The extreme environmental devastation in this region has caused death and disease among indigenous peoples, revealing that oil companies are not in the service of defending human values but rather, in systematically rooting out obstacles to production. "[T]he poisoning of streams and rivers has amounted to[. . .] nothing short of ethnocide" (Press, 12). Yet, the benevolent way which Kerewin, through her Maori-ness, has learned to treat nature makes invisible the processes through which capitalism has already changed the terrain, how increased corporatism promises even more widespread damage, and that everything might not appear quite so green upon Kerewin's arrival the next time, through no fault of her own. Kerewin and her "authentic Maori culture" might not have such complete control over maintaining nature in a state of purity, cleanliness, health, and abundance as the novel wants to suggest.[17]

Speculation

By focusing on Maori "authentic culture" as a spirit-force necessary for the production of art, Hulme is able to erase the way both culture and nature are configured through power struggles while disallowing any sincere and engaged critique about how the construction of "authentic Maori culture" serves philosophies of deregulation. Indeed, *The Bone People*'s realization of Maori "authentic culture" is provisioned on support from Kerewin's international investments. "Once," she admits,

> I had to work at horrible jobs to earn enough money to buy food to eat it in order to live to work at horrible jobs to earn enough[. . .]. I hated that life[. . .]. So I quit. I did what my heart told me and painted for my living[. . .]. Money was the only problem[. . .] then it all changed. I won a lottery. I invested it. I earned a fortune by fast talking. (28)

Not only has stock ownership been concentrated among an ever narrowing circle of the very rich,[18] but, too, as Gayatri Spivak has noted, the rise of multiculturalism in pedagogical practice happened simultaneously with the opening up of financial and currency markets to transnationalism in the early 1970s.[19] Kerewin's story shows how this same process was then internationalized so that individuals, even in developing countries, could buy bonds on foreign state debt, ensuring themselves that private efforts can reduce losses due to public failings like the depletion of Social Security or commitments like requiring the provision of employee benefits.[20]

Violence and the Politics of Recognition

The most wrenching, difficult, and appalling feature of what *The Bone People* counts as Maori "cultural authenticity" is purely and simply the acceptability of extreme violence. Joe's treatment of Simon is defined as quite simply a casualty of love. Simon is impetuous, does not attend school when he should, does not follow Joe's directives all the time, sometimes steals, is strong-willed, stubborn, mischievous, at times destructive. During the last beating, he even attacks and seriously wounds Joe by cutting into his stomach with a piece of jaded glass. So, as Kerewin herself observes, Simon deserves it, and even benefits from it: "[I]t all shows you cared deeply. In a negative way, so does the fact that you beat him. At least, you worried enough about what you considered was his wrongdoing to try and correct it" (325). In the logic of *The Bone People*, causing severe pain is what people do when they care.

The critics concur. Elizabeth Webby, for example, writes, "The horror of Keri Hulme's portrait of the child as victim, of well-meaning even more than not well-meaning adults, would be unbearable if she had not created in Simon such a tough little nut of a character" (20). Georges-Goulven Le Cam even goes so far as to say that the abuse turns Simon into a Christ figure on which the redemption of the world depends: "Right till the end, the boy shows amazing *forgiveness* for Joe, his "torturer," and keeps loving the man with a vengeance. His "sacrifice"—the ultimate bashing-cum-crucifixation, which sends him into a coma—is necessary to *redeem* the threesome, and beyond the threesome, to redeem New Zealand. The Kingdom has come and things can start healing again" (74). Yet, the brutality of Joe's attacks on Simon is not easily dismissable as good parenting or the prerogative of a father to punish severely a wayward child:

> He is aching, he is breaking apart with pain. The agony is everywhere, hands, body, legs, head. He is shaking so badly he cannot stand. The hard wood keeps griding past him[. . .] The first punch hit his head. His head slammed back into the door frame. The punches keep coming. Again. Again. And again[. . .]. The blood pours from everywhere. He can feel it spilling from his mouth, his ears, his eyes, and his nose. (308–309)

The culmination of a long series of similar outbursts, this time Simon loses his eyesight and the doctors speculate that the brain damage will be permanent. *The Bone People* presents Maori "cultural authenticity" as naturally violent, violent in the blood, inheriting a legacy of cannibalism and precolonial warfare which resurfaces as the core of identity.[21] Pain and injustice are redefined as cultural recognition. Unexplainable acts of aggression on the part of private power lead to peace, understanding, empowerment, learning, and love. Multiculturalism's politics of inclusion and Maori "cultural authenticity" are here being used as an alibi, an excuse for a politics of violence.[22]

Charles Taylor defines multiculturalism as the "politics of recognition," in other words, an acknowledgment that "cultures that have provided the horizon of meaning for large numbers of human beings[. . .] are almost certain to have something that deserves our admiration and respect" (101). Yet, in commending the obviously beneficial values that multiculturalism contributes to education, to the Enlightenment's values of universal humanity and universal human freedom, critics like Taylor must also consider what it means that one compelling example of multicultural recognition and inclusion was when, for example, from one week to the next, most U.S. citizens learned and recognized that there was a place called Kosovo, for example—one providing "the horizon of meaning for large numbers of human beings"—because bombers were being sent to wreck it. The violence in *The Bone People* must be read as not simply a study in the multiple meanings of violence nor as a complex look at violence from different points of view nor as a nuanced analysis of psychological motivation nor as a tableau of private human sentiment revealing a deeper comprehension of human action and suffering. Instead, it must be read alongside the other ways that understandings of violence, and particularly corporate violence, influence meaning, power, and justice within geopolitical and ideological struggles. Just as the news coverage on Kosovo produced identifications with U.S. military power, *The Bone People* allows an "understanding" of the psychology of child abusers and a resultant sympathy with the traumas and frustrations that might have caused their recourse to extreme brutality, thus incapacitating either a critique or an outright condemnation of violence against the less powerful. One must distinguish between the multiculturalism that has been successful in disrupting and decentering the power structure of canon, allowing for a greater equality and justice, and another multiculturalism, which has been successful in strengthening the power of capital to exploit the globe, supporting a racist corporate agenda and, ultimately, establishing canonical Western values as undeniably right in their very mighty genocidal abilities to recognize others.

The Future of Literature

There is nothing new in power's use of culture for the purposes of domination of the less powerful. As various theorists of colonialism—from Franz Fanon to Paulo Freire, Edward Said, Homi Bhabha, and so on—have demonstrated, colonialism is a pedagogical practice because it teaches meanings, assigns values, relegates consciousness, redirects social signification, and consolidates hierarchies of oppression. In fact, education has historically supported the enforcement of colonial regulation and production. As Gauri Viswanathan has shown in the case of nineteenth-century India,

> The history of education in British India shows that certain humanistic functions traditionally associated with literature—for example, the shaping of character or the development of the aesthetic sense or the disciplines of ethical thinking—were considered essential to the processes of sociopolitical control by the guardians of the same tradition[. . .]. Indeed, once such importance is conceded to the educational function, it is easier to see that values assigned to literature—such as the proper development of character or the shaping of critical thought or the formation of aesthetic judgment—are only problematically located there and are more obviously serviceable to the dynamic of power relations between the educator and those who are to be educated. (3–4)

Viswanathan discusses how, in colonial India, literature replaced military power as the primary enforcer of morality and respect for the law, as the Indians were taught that assimilation into the ranks of the colonial administration required the ability to absorb the lessons of literary eclecticism. Jacqui Alexander and Chandra Mohanty have pointed out that, in colonialist situations, the ruling classes propagate " 'myths'[. . .] to preserve the capitalist status-quo." These myths "are[. . .] propositions about 'Democracy' within a liberal, capitalist culture" (xxxiii). "Together," Alexander and Mohanty continue, "these myths constitute a rhetoric of freedom and equality that consolidates the very oppressive practices and values of capitalist domination" (xxxiii).

The values and lessons propagated in the service of private power and profit, however, are not fixed in meaning, but rather are negotiated. The

myths that Alexander and Mohanty have identified as furthering colonialist expansion can and must therefore be unlearned for new emancipatory
social relations and governing systems to form: "Decolonization has a fundamentally pedagogical dimension—an imperative to understand, to reflect, and to transform relations of objectification and dehumanization,
and to pass this knowledge along to future generations" (xxviii–xxix). As
corporations and corporate messages infiltrate school curricula, it is more
important than ever to revitalize a notion of education as vital to the
expansion of public knowledge and public power and the consequent production of meaning in the service of civil society and democracy for citizens rather than only for corporations.

Mobil's support of *The Bone People* makes indelibly clear the role that
literary studies must play in dismantling a popular imagination geared
more and more into a corporate mantle, setting up, in its stead, the possibility of alternatives. However, in her 1998 Presidential Address to the
Modern Language Association, Elaine Showalter actually concedes that literary scholarship is too far removed from the economic-assimilation aims
to which higher education has been reduced. The downsizing of the university, the diminishing importance of the humanities in general and, particularly, the shrinking of literary departments in higher education—all
these tendencies seem to Showalter an invitation to encourage graduate
students to use their literary knowledge to pursue corporate careers:

> [A]nother way to increase the commodity value of humanities Ph.D.s is to give
> them mobility and choices. As Bob Weisbuch writes[. . .], "On the day when
> the year's most gifted graduate in, say, comparative literature decides to forego
> an assistant professorship at Stanford for a beginning position with the *Wash-
> ington Post* or the Ford Foundation or the McDonald's Corporation, the status
> of the Humanities is revolutionized." [. . .]I would add that the humanities
> will be even more revolutionized when a mid-level graduate student can
> choose among teaching at a college perhaps very different from the sort of
> place he or she originally aspired to, going into academic administration, or
> joining the corporate world[. . .]. As Paula Backscheider asserted as long ago
> as 1981, "[. . .]Should we not be as proud of the Ph. D. who begins as a '*com-
> munications manager*' at Gulf Oil as we are of the one who starts out as an assis-
> tant professor?" (325; emphasis mine)

Showalter admits to a crisis in the academic job market but does not admit
that part of this crisis is due to corporate infiltration in higher education in
the form of long-distance learning and other curriculum restructuring,
the redefining of the goals of education as purely a matter of job assimilation and economic mobility, the turning of university administrations into
investment portfolio management systems, the attack on tenure, and the
like. She also does not admit that constructing literary training as corporate training would inevitably lead to an emptying out of the public value

of education as well as a curtailment of the possibilities of imagining social relations differently from corporate models. Like the *kaumatua*, Joe's spirit guide, Showalter seems to think that "[a]ll we can do is look after the precious matters which are our heritage, and wait, and hope" (Hulme, 371), accepting passively the overwhelming cultural domination of "development schemes" which are creating such a "mess" (Hulme, 371). She does not, rather, identify the current humanities crisis as a sign of a much larger crisis in economic distribution and as a call to take action. Reducing all career options as well as ethics to the lowest common denominator of universal exchangeability, Showalter does not argue the need for literary studies to discuss how they got to seem marginal or even negligible to the management of the contemporary economy, the ideological configuration of global capital, and the deification of corporate culture. In her view, what is important is solely determined by students' free consumer choice: unfettered fashion trends, pleasures, and taste rather than by questions of power, ideological manipulation, and funding. Showalter should know from her renowned contributions to feminist literary studies that denying the politics of literature, pedagogy, and other cultural work affirms power, oppression, and the credibility of violence and hinders the possibilities for constructing a democratic, global civil society for the future.

CHAPTER 4

The Triumphant but Tragic
Wealth of the Poor

*Buchi Emecheta Meets Hernando De Soto's
Informal Markets*

Utopia in the Market

The Mystery of Capital, Hernando De Soto's empirical study on the global informal economy, contends that poverty is an illusion.

> [I]n Asia, Africa, the Middle East, and Latin America, . . . most of the poor already possess the assets they need to make a success of capitalism . . . The value of savings among the poor is, in fact, immense—forty times all the foreign aid received throughout the world since 1945. In Egypt, for instance, the wealth that the poor have accumulated is worth fifty-five times as much as the sum of all direct foreign investment ever recorded there, including the Suez Canal and the Aswan Dam. In Haiti, the poorest nation in Latin America, the total assets of the poor are more than one hundred fifty times greater than all the foreign investment received since Haiti's independence from France in 1804. If the United States were to hike its foreign aid budget to the level recommended by the United Nations—0.7 percent of national income—it would take the richest country on earth more than 150 years to transfer to the world's poor resources equal to those they already possess (5).

From a series of interviews and case studies of unlicensed local trade and vendors, De Soto concludes that poor people already have a substantial amount of assets, more even than the values of the stock exchange and international financial institutions combined.[1] However, non-Western peoples have been unable to use their assets—mostly labor and resources—to the fullest efficiency because of government regulations such as fees, permits, oversight, and licensing, which curtail capital investment incentives by limiting access.[2] Insisting that the problem of poverty is caused by too much public control, De Soto's main contention is that developing nations need an integrated property system that standardizes representations of value and minimizes the public's role in "fine-tuning" the economy, thus allowing all people equally and democratically to realize the potential of their capital.

Picking up on the thematization of privacy as freedom in prior chapters—and what this has meant for women, politics, and the public—this chapter shows how De Soto's empirical research on informal markets fails to account for the economic problems of the poor caused by neoliberal economic reforms, deregulation, privatization, private labor contracting, and power. By reading Buchi Emecheta's 1979 novel *The Joys of Motherhood,* this chapter explores how the poor are losing assets through neoliberalization, in particular, through the privatization of public interests which has strengthened imperialism. In the words of Kenyan novelist, playwright, political dissident, and cultural theorist Ngugi Wa Thiong'o:

> There are other absurdities. Mobuto of Zaire, in an act of supreme African authenticity, had ceded a whole territory many times the size of New Zealand to a West German rocket company. A group of African leaders recently begged France to send troops to Chad to protect French legitimate interests, threatened by "imperialist" Libya. Moi of Kenya has given military bases to U.S.A. without a debate in parliament, with Kenyans only later learning about the "secret" deal through a debate in U.S. Congress. One could quote other even more incredible episodes, of the callous massacre of children, of the equally callous genocide of part of a population and all by native leaders on behalf of imperialism. (80)

The commodification of knowledge which De Soto invites as the solution to world poverty contributes, in Emecheta's assessment, to deepening hardships among Third World workers due to depletions in public resources and protections and is implemented only through institutionalized violence, corporate and military alliances, and the militarization of civil society. Based in nineteenth- and early twentieth-century ideas of the subject as constituted through primitive desires, De Soto formulates a conception of market freedom as a naturalized sphere of production devoid of the controls that Freud attributed to maturity and civilization, while democracy is brought into play as unmediated, infantile consumer desire bubbling up beneath the authoritarian paternal prohibition instituted by public oversight. In other words, democracy appears as the Id of consumer desire held in tow by the Super-Ego of the nation-state. De Soto's solution to poverty by instituting internal property law reforms and human labor commodification does not take into account important changes in national and international power, capital consolidation, public disinvestiture, ideological manipulation, labor exploitation, and global warfare.

This chapter builds on the premise of the last two chapters that literature projects values that serve to construct, frame, and instruct people about future possibilities, identifications, affiliations, agency, action, and belief systems. Responding to the same informal economies that inform De Soto's work, and like De Soto describing the new labor conditions and relations of production in the global economy, Emecheta's literature, like De Soto's economics, is currently participating in imagining social actors, interactions, and mobilized identities within new global relations of capital and of power. Unlike in De Soto's market/utopic call for deregulation and procedural regularity, Emecheta, however, shows how new regimes of global power have incapacitated ordinary people from satisfying basic needs, let alone acquiring assets. Indicating that literature answers the call to identity heard in capital's needs for labor and resources, Emecheta demonstrates the tragic outcomes to the poor when public assets like education are reconfigured according to the rules of the market,[3] that is, through the logics of privatization, contracting, decentralization, antiauthoritarianism, competition, flexibility, autonomous agency, and militarization.[4] Emecheta shows how De Soto's plan for the privatization of labor—turning laboring people into private companies to be hired on a contract or piece basis for broader flexibility—actually limits the possibility of accumulation for the poor.

Many critics have praised *The Joys of Motherhood* as exemplary of an African woman's experience of and resistance to patriarchal power and/or of the construction of a strategic ethnic identity to counter imperialism. "Emecheta's reputation in world letters as a major voice in African women's liberation," writes, for example, Marie Umeh in the introduction to a collection of critical essays on Emecheta's work, "rests on her protest against the victimization of women in Ibuza society and, by extension, in all societies" (xxiv). "[I]n the works of Emecheta . . . and others," Florence Stratton argues, "it is frequently within the writer's adaptive integration into her text of such elements as myth, rites, and social practices that the defining features of a distinctively female literary tradition lie" (144). Critics generally place Emecheta's work within a literary tradition started by Flora Nwapa with her 1966 novel *Efuru*. A response to Chinua Achebe's 1959 classic *Things Fall Apart*, *Efuru*, like *The Joys of Motherhood*, explores women's role in traditional Igbo life still ordered around seasonal agriculture, small-time trade, and ritualized kin and community relations. Moreover, critics often trace this body of writing back to the 1929 Igbo Aba

Women's War, *Ogu Umunwanyi,* when women organized in markets and mobilized against native courts, women's taxation, and British colonial presence. Susan Andrade, for example, sees the *Efuru* tradition, like the Aba Women's War, as women's "self-inscription into history" because it "interrogates the imperialist authority that Hegel symbolizes" and thus disrupts power by dialoguing with it (97).

It is important to stop treating the speaking and recognizing of identity on aesthetic and cultural terms alone as a force strong enough to fend off imperialism, patriarchy, and consolidated power, and to start thinking anew the relationships between literary production, state power, and the retreat of the nation-state before the rise of global corporate visions.[5] As Patrick Hogan emphasizes, the Women's War was a response to the ways women "were rapidly losing out in the new economic structure" (176). The focus of Nnu Ego's plight in *Joys of Motherhood* is not only on how she constructs an autonomous identity through giving representation to an oppressed gender and ethnic minority heretofore neglected, but also, and perhaps more fundamentally in global terms, on how she gradually loses an autonomous identity through colonial and then postcolonial De Soto-like market reforms. As Hogan points out, when Nigeria was integrated into the world economy, "[W]omen lost the considerable security and independence they enjoyed in traditional culture[. . . T]raditionally, women had often substantial wealth" (174). *The Joys of Motherhood* centers on how Nnu Ego loses her identity during a time of national transition into a wage economy set up to keep labor costs low and public obligations minimal in order to ensure profitability for foreign investments and war.

Understanding cultural analysis as a continual recognition of proliferating differences responds to a liberal desire to see globalization as happening through an accumulation of cultures rather than as an increasing privatization of public functions which *The Joys of Motherhood* and Emecheta's other works document. This chapter follows on prior chapters' criticism of how certain liberal constructions of identity depend on a type of privacy which—by reducing difference to culture devoid of structural economies—holds representation as the key to the global advancement of equality much in the same way as does *The Mystery of Capital.* This position assumes that everybody is equal before the aesthetic and the law just as they are assumed to be equal before the object of consumption. The waning of public power which De Soto advocates for the sake of underclass political autonomy becomes the very wedge through which such autonomy becomes an impossibility for Nnu Ego.

Under neoliberal regimes, right-wing pundits like De Soto have appropriated and frequently monopolized discourses of hope. Wendy Brown states it well:

> Throughout that decade [of the 1980s], "freedom" was deployed by the Right
> to justify thuggish mercenaries in Central America, the expenditure of billions
> on cold war defense, the deregulation of toxic enterprise, the destruction of
> unions with "right to work" protection, the importance of saluting—and the
> blasphemy of burning—the flag[. . .] In the contemporary popular refrain,
> freedom other than free enterprise was cast as selfish, infantile, or killing [as in
> the "sexual emancipation" that, in such perspectives, led to the AIDS crisis],
> and placed in ignominious counterpoise to commitment, maturity, discipline,
> sacrifice, and sobriety[. . .] Contemporary disorientation about freedom also
> appears consequent to the Right's programmatic attack on the welfare state
> since the mid-1970s[. . .] Thus, as the Right promulgated an increasingly nar-
> row and predominantly economic formulation of freedom and claimed free-
> dom's ground as its own, liberals and leftists lined up behind an equally narrow
> and predominantly economic formulation of equality. (9–10)

The move of "freedom" to the right has meant the reformulation of freedom from a democratic principle to a false promise of economic mobility. As Peter McLaren elaborates, "The very meaning of freedom has come
to denote the freedom to structure the distribution of wealth and to exploit
workers more easily across national boundaries by driving down wages
to their lowest common denominator and by eviscerating social programs
designed to assist laboring humanity. Territories that were once linked to
national interests have given way to networks inscribed within world markets independent of major national political constraints" (32). The eco-
nomism or economic reductionism with which Marxist theory is charged
dwarfs in comparison to the economistic turn in such right-wing free-
market prophecies. The formulation of political struggle around "the
desire to participate in shaping the conditions and terms of life" (4) has
been translated into a widespread belief that access to commodities should
secure democratic freedom because commodities grant rights to self-
determination, so that the commodity actually holds freedom within it.
Emecheta's biting appraisal of liberalization provides a language of critique that could be used to reclaim, for the left, a politics based in public
rather than private notions of freedom.

Patrick Hogan has recognized that this faith in ultimate freedom
through the acquisition of Western commodities mobilizes sentiment
about the Third World, where Western knowledge is said to offer an egali-
tarian escape from the oppressions of indigenous traditions and customs.
If only, such logics claim, Western practices of economic autonomy and independence were adopted as counters to patriarchal tribal systems, then
not only would fundamentalism disappear, but women would also at last
be free. This is the kind of rationale, for example, behind the U.S. invasion
of Afghanistan, and the rush to "liberate" Iraq and bring "freedom" to the
Iraqi people, and then the "surprise"—expressed by the military and the

press alike—that the Iraqis did not flock into the streets to cheer the advancement of the Marines as their "liberators," and that some even resisted. As Hogan elaborates,

> [C]olonized women in regions of high intensity contact are unlikely to be freed from indigenous patriarchal oppression, except in very limited ways and in very limited circumstances. Indeed, European intervention seems, on the whole, more likely to worsen this oppression than to ameliorate it, for it often leads to reactionary rigidification and in some cases blocks indigenous efforts at reform. In addition to living with the continuing and perhaps even worsened effects of indigenous patriarchy—often without the corresponding rights and institutional support of traditional women's communities—the colonized woman in the region of contact is likely to find herself burdened by European constraints as well. (179)

Emecheta, argues Hogan, foregrounds how the usual way that market culture is organized inhibits and restricts women's "ability to earn and to sustain themselves and their children through productive labor" (183), reducing gender to an exchange value—a mere representation without identity—often pushing women into slavery to patriarchy and imperialism, and devastating both mobility and freedom.

Having formed a research institute—*Instituto Libertad y Democracia*—to study Peru's informal economy in the 1980s, De Soto wrote a book called *The Other Path (El otro sendero)*, which claimed to have found a path to freedom for the poor different and more expedient than the solutions offered at the time by Peru's Maoist guerrillas Sendero Luminoso or by the socialist-based APRA party (*Alianza Popular Revolucionaria Americana*, or the American Popular Revolutionary Party) then in power under Peruvian president Alan Garcia.[6] De Soto sent out researchers into poor, urban communities, asking how long it would take and how much money it would require to turn a house or a business into a capital good, which could generate profits or secure investments. He collected statistics documenting that it often took generations to complete all the steps for legalization. For example, just for the initial expenses of doing business, it took ten months and $1036.60 to complete the bureaucratic process to establish an industry, eighty-three months to get permits for building, twenty-eight months to get approvals for land development, and additional costs, too, for developing transportation, starting markets, and building stores. If the state itself were the principle owner, the proceedings took even longer, since the cost of state abjudication was estimated at $526,019. Remaining informal cost less but at the expense of accumulating inventory, long-term planning, and infrastructural investments (*The Other Path*, 132–146). De Soto's suggestions for neoliberal economic reform through easing legalization, dismantling public interventions, denationalizing industries and banking, and privatization in the name of self-determination later became the platform for Mario Vargas Llosa's campaign for presidency[7] (Vargas Llosa wrote the introduction to *The Other Path*) and still later became the ideological lever of what Peruvians have called "Fuji-Shock," or rather Alberto Fujimori's lifting of price ceilings overnight, when prices escalated to the point where there was a night of national crying, as Peruvians described it. Endorsed by the likes of Margaret Thatcher, Milton Friedman, Francis Fukuyama, Javier Perez de Cuellar, Bill Bradley, William Buckley Jr., and Jeanne Kirkpatrick, *The Mystery of Capital* is meant to extend De Soto's Peruvian researches globally, perhaps even to extend his model for the "economic miracle" which has increased destitution in much of Peru and delegitimated Fujimori's government until the point where it collapsed in scandal in 2000.

De Soto's premises also underlie U.S. president George W. Bush's claims, as he rallies, with bipartisan support, for global market expansion and domestic school "choice",[8] that free markets and trade liberalization are the only way for the poor to lift themselves out of poverty. This domestic agenda often furnishes the rationale for foreign policy. As he was going off to meet with the G8 leaders in Genoa, Italy, in 2001, Bush said, against compelling evidence, that protestors against globalization were no friends to the poor but free trade would end poverty. Going further than even Adam Smith, who believed that the excesses of the market needed to be countered by public checks and balances,[9] these fans of free trade are insisting that the market can cure all social ills.

In fact, however, while corporate news media heralded economic boom at the millennium's turn, disparities in wealth under neoliberal governance have reached greater proportions than during the Great Depression,[10] with the world's richest three hundred individuals possessing more wealth than the world's poorest forty-eight countries combined, and the richest fifteen having a greater fortune than the total product of sub-Saharan Africa (Bauman, *The Individualized Society,* 115). As well, austerity measures imposed by world trade organizations such as the World Bank, the World Trade Organization, and the International Monetary Fund in the name of expanding free trade ensure that poor nations stay poor by imposing "fiscal discipline" and public disinvestiture, while no such discipline applies to entire industries such as defense, entertainment, transportation, and corporate agriculture that are heavily subsidized by the public sector in the United States and many other advanced-industrial countries. As formerly New Right advocate and Thatcherite John Gray has pointed out,

> According to the Thatcherite understanding of the role of the state, its task was to supply a framework of rules and regulations within which the free market—including, crucially, the labour market—would be self-regulating[...] The contemporary model that informed these changes throughout was the American labour market, with its high levels of mobility, downward flexibility of wages and low cost for employers. Partly as a result of these policies, there was an explosive increase in part-time and contract work[...] The innermost contradiction of the free market is that it works to weaken the traditional social institutions on which it has depended in the past[...] Many low-skill workers earned less than the minimum needed to support a family. (2000: 28–29)

De Soto based his model of informal markets and extralegality on a particular reading of U.S. history and property law, where, he says, the wilderness was joyfully colonized by the incorporation of extralegal social contracts into the legal framework (De Soto, of course, does not acknowledge that the settlers' contracts on the land did not often include, either legally or extralegally, its original inhabitants):

> Americans had been settling—and improving—the land extralegally for decades. Their politicians gradually modified the law to integrate this reality into the official legal system and won some political points in the bargain. Having thus changed their laws to accommodate existing extralegal arrangements, U.S. officials left the assets of the American settlers and miners primed to be converted into capital[... I]t is "experience" that gives life to the law demonstrating[...] that the law must be compatible with how people actually arrange their lives. The way law stays alive is by keeping in touch with social contract pieced together among real people on the ground. (2000: 108)

As Carlos Lozada has stated in a review which infers *The Mystery* is foreshadowing De Soto's bid for the presidency of Peru, De Soto "[i]gnores the likelihood that many illegally occupied lands presumably are owned by someone—publicly or privately—and that trying to meld legal and extralegal property systems likely would result in endless court challenges."

Liberalized trade policy has not led to greater equality or an alleviation of poverty but rather to a growth in the disparity between rich and poor, an undermining of labor, civil, and environmental rights, a weakening of job security and public protections for much of the world, and an intensifying exploitation of the poor as work is compensated increasingly by the piece rather than by the hour. Additionally, the world financial and commerce establishments' attack on domestic state functions, and particularly public oversight in the Third World, has further strangulated these struggling economies. As Immanuel Wallerstein points out, mercentalists from the economic core countries are able to employ strong state formations to protect their interests at home while weakening the state formations in peripheral countries in order to protect the core's hegemonic controls.

De Soto's vision of a Third World exemplar of a self-regulating market is not a new cry for freedom but rather an old practice of world systems integration under global capitalist management.

Knowledge and Representation

The Joys of Motherhood tells the story of Nnu Ego when she moves from her rural, ancestral village into the capital city of Lagos at the time when the British colonialists were beginning to pull out of Nigeria in the 1940s. Having first married a local farmer chosen by her chieftan father, she does not conceive until he rejects her for not bearing children and she moves to the city to marry her father's second choice. The novel then narrates Nnu Ego's struggles to find solvency for herself and her family against a harsh new urban marketplace that prohibits her from establishing a steady trade. The trajectory from Nnu Ego's mother's rural girlhood to her own and then to her married life, her move to the city, and, finally, to motherhood thereby corresponds to Nigeria's historical movement as it was integrated into new relations of global financial management, urban industrialization, wartime culture, and economic adjustment.

One of the ways that *The Joys of Motherhood* critiques neoliberal capitalism is by, like in *The Mystery of Capital,* linking the accumulation of surplus to the acquisition of knowledge. De Soto wants to equalize property by creating a system of representation where the economy can be marked through units of universal exchangeability, expunging from these representations—as in liberal theories of governance—the differences that would not, in principle, accord. This idea of representation as an equalizer assumes knowledge as a commodity in order to turn people into capital. Whereas in *The Joys of Motherhood* Emecheta denounces the difficulties of access to schooling in a wage market, De Soto lauds the abilities of a market-based economy to provide universal access to knowledge as capital as well as universal exchangeability. In other words, Emecheta critiques the idea, so prevalent in De Soto's work, that privatizing public goods like education would be preferable to, as he puts it, allowing governments to compete with private interests (2000: 86–87).

De Soto claims that capital, like knowledge and consciousness, contains a latent content; like knowledge, capital needs to be represented in its most natural form in order to be accessed and in order for its virtual value to be realized:

> For thousands of years our wisest men [*sic*] have been telling us that life has different degrees of reality, many of them invisible, and that it is only by constructing representational devices that we will be able to access them[. . .] [C]ivilization has worked hard to fashion representational systems to access

and grasp the part of our reality that is virtual and to represent it in terms we can understand[. . .] Unlike tigers and wolves, who bare their teeth to protect their territory, man [*sic*], physically a much weaker animal, has used his mind to create a legal environment—property—to protect his territory. Without anyone fully realizing it, the representational system the West created to settle territorial claims took on a life of its own, providing the knowledge base and rules necessary to fix and realize capital. (220–221)

In other words, knowledge is property, and property is metaphysical, like God. Knowledge operates like property because it gives returns, expansive returns whose growth is reliant on uniform procedures of description specifying uniform rules for extracting potential values. The quest for profit here appears as the search for the invisible truth—value—in representation, and a successful search for truth requires true and unfettered experience just as wild animals have. In order for knowledge to become transparent as profits on property, it depends on the ability of individuals to operate freely within a field governed by a set of rules or regular laws of nature. These laws of nature guarantee that the returns on human activity are contradictorily both predictable and unrestricted. The idea that free, natural experience leads to progress comes out of the nineteenth-century sciences of recapitulation, where, as Gail Bederman has shown, children were supposed to be encouraged to play freely in the wilderness like their primitive ancestors in order to develop properly into civilized adulthood.[11] In De Soto's view, the proper market would resemble the free play of children, primitive people, naive emotions, and wild beasts. Representing children, primitive people, naive emotions, and wild beasts as prelinguistic, prerepresentational, and therefore free (as did Freud, among others) feeds imperialist ideologies where Third World nations are seen as needing Western forms of knowledge and organization in the absence of their own political systems and sovereignty. Legalized markets co-opt the freedom of free desire, organize it, and run with it.

The Mystery

De Soto's ideas about the benefits of neoliberalism to the world's poor are based in his conviction that everything can be turned into capital. In other words, all possessions can and should be converted into equatable representations of market value which can circulate through exchange. Though he never specifies what counts as an asset, he continually asserts that what poor people have can be turned into one by a reformulation of property law. Uniform and standard categories to describe the productive elements of an object would promise that those elements could be made "fungible," or rather productive of "surplus value," "able to be fashioned to suit practically any transaction" (56): "One of the most important things a formal property system does is transform assets from a less accessible condition to a more accessible condition, so that they can do additional work" (56). This theory relies on the collapse between labor and capital where De Soto assumes capital itself catalyzes the production process, performs the "work," and becomes the force behind its own growth in value: "Clearly much of today's surplus value in the West has originated not in scandalously expropriated labor time but in the way that property has given minds the mechanisms with which to extract additional work from commodities" (217). In other words, focusing purely on speculation, De Soto takes the human element out of Marx's theory of labor.

De Soto assumes that everyone can own and run his or her own business, so his theory cannot account for conflicts between proprietors and the ones who work for them, or rather, any theory of labor or unequal power. Since everyone is equal before the act of speculation, there is no sense that, in capitalism, owning the means of production gives one advantages, clout, and authority to decide and shape the social field. It is not likely, for example, that an upstart hamburger vender operating out of a cart would be able to assemble a community of public interests to open highway stops to small-time competitors. Notes Samir Amin,

> The active army of labour exists here and may continue its progression. But it will never, as far into the future as we can see, be able to absorb the reserve from the rural and informal economies—both because global competitiveness now requires techniques of production that make such absorbtion impossible, and because the safety-valve of mass emigration is not available. As for the non-industrial and/or non-competitive peripheral countries of Africa and the Arab world, the situation is still more dramatic: the active army barely exists at all, virtually the whole nation being a reserve in world terms. (1997: ix)

De Soto chooses not to understand that productive businesses presently require technology and management systems that are not cheap or simple and that therefore put in place barriers to entry. As well, the restriction of public protections which De Soto advocates would benefit large corporations more than small proprietors, because it removes obstacles to unlimited corporate growth, obstacles like taxes, community provisions, or the cost of applying labor and environmental laws, even as it does not take into account how most large corporations have developed through public subsidies or contracts of some sort or another. De Soto's call to informalize labor markets turns labor into buyable contracts, each one exchangeable on an open market. In other words, the reforms that De Soto deems necessary to alleviate poverty would aid more in turning sidewalk vendors into cheap, exploitable, and unprotected labor for large industry and manufacturing enterprises than in turning them into business owners.

De Soto's ideas about standardizing representation of informal markets imply that freedom results from more capitalism divided up into exchangeable property units: independent contractors and small business enterprises serving as outsourced production sites that take on a piece of a larger corporate process. This way of thinking, however, is not restricted to right-wing justifications for fiscally conservative policy and labor deregulation. It has, additionally, seeped into left-leaning liberal analysis. In *The End of Capitalism (As We Knew It): A Feminist Critique of Political Economy,* J. K. Gibson-Graham,[12] for example, argues that the reason that it is so difficult to think alternatives to capitalism is that capitalism, like the Phallus under patriarchy, has become a universal, hegemonic, and dominating signifier unquestionably at the ideological center of all social relations. This type of representation has become performative rather than descriptive, actually producing a capitalism that seeps into the very margins of social existence. What is needed instead, she says, is a more fluid and deconstructable concept of capitalism—like the de-essentialized concepts of sexual and gender identity promoted by post-structural feminist theorizing—where the question might be asked "what a hybridized and nomadic 'economic identity' might be" (12). Gibson-Graham believes that there are plenty of instances of noncapitalist relations within the current social organization, and that these examples of economic difference can demonstrate the limits to capitalist hegemony as well as its complexities, rifts, multiple references, overdeterminizations, and contradictions.

So far, so good; but in order to situate capitalism as a certain instance of a much broader tableau of social experience, Gibson-Graham has to narrow what she means by capitalism to an adjectival form, where it appears most of the time as a certain act or as a singularized exploitative relationship between a manager and a laborer. Rejecting any important differences in representations of the economy between the right and the left, Gibson-Graham understands capitalism as "the image of two classes locked in struggle" (9ff) defined through exploitation and domination and degrees of ownership and possession, "from managing director to production supervisor to laborer" (50), as seen in the labor process. Noncapitalism, then, is constituted in spaces which are free of direct managerial control or the extraction of surplus value for the profit and accumulation of owners of the particular means of production where this extraction happens: "Noncapitalism is found in the household, the place of woman, related to capitalism through service and complementarity. Noncapitalism is the before or the after of capitalism: it appears as a precapitalist mode of production (identified by its fate of inevitable supersession); it appears as socialism, for which capitalism is both the negative and the positive precondition" (7). What is missing from this formulation is the way that capitalist outsourcing to private household industries and sweatshops has not produced greater freedom from exploitation, as both Gibson-Graham and De Soto contend, but rather a cheapening of labor and an intensification of exploitation between different levels of capitalist production systems, and particularly of Third World and female labor. "[C]apitalism," as Immanuel Wallerstein indicates in "The Rise and Demise of the Capitalist System", "involves not only appropriation of surplus-value by an owner from a laborer, but an appropriation of surplus of the whole world-economy by core areas" (86). Household industry is not outside of capitalism, but rather, as I argue in the next chapter, the central component of its advanced, global stage.

The examples given show that Gibson-Graham, like De Soto, can only think of capitalism as the direct extraction of surplus from hired labor in conventional industrial situations, so much of what passes as labor under capitalism now—temporary or contract labor, piecelabor, outsourced labor—falls outside of capitalist relations in her descriptions. Like De Soto again, she seems to disregard the fact that these newly proliferating forms of labor create an intensified polarization between those who own the means of production on a world scale and those without assets, between First World economic dominance and Third World poverty:

> Recent developments in the international semiconductor industry indicate that the penetration of Asia by foreign MNCs [multinational corporations] has borne unexpected fruit. Both upstream suppliers and downstream users of semiconductors have sprung up in a regional complex of indigenous firms in south-east Asia, including technical training facilities, centered in Thailand. This development counters the image of the sterile branch plant in poor countries, which repatriates profits and contributes only to underdevelopment rather than industrial growth. (130–131)

In this view, multinational corporations are "unwittingly generative" because they create satellite enterprises on the margins of industrial production which decrease the costs of production by lessening the costs of in-house labor for those corporations—including the costs of benefits and labor negotiations of any sort—as do all informalizations of labor markets. Furthermore, the situation described by Gibson-Graham could have given rise to the liquidity crisis that caused the collapse of Thailand's bubble economy in 1997, the year after the book was published, alongside the vast unemployment that followed and the closing of many of the small businesses that Gibson-Graham lauds. Again:

> Perhaps we might see the proliferation of credit and deregulation of financial markets as creating opportunities for the growth of noncapitalist class relations as well as capitalist ones. The huge expansion of consumer credit (including credit-card financing with large maximum limits, home equity loans, and a

variety of other instruments almost forced upon "consumers") is often assumed to promote personal indebtedness associated with a culture of consumption. Yet, given the growth in self-employment and of home-based
industries—some of which is associated with the downsizing and streamlining
of capitalist firms—it is clear that much of what is seen as consumer credit is
actually (or also) producer credit, in other words it is used to buy means of
production (including computers and other equipment) and other inputs into
the production process of self-employed workers. (138)

While household debt has been increasing steadily since the 1950s, there
has been, since the 1970s, an increase in the proportion of household income to household debt from under 12 percent to over 14 percent
(Campell) along with an increase in the amount of personal bankruptcies
by five times (until the time when bankruptcy attainability itself was made
legally bankrupt) (Ellis) and an increase in the number of indebted low-
income families from 45 percent in 1983 to 54 percent in 1992 and rising.
In 1999, the Federal Reserve reported an average of $4,000 in consumer
debt for every adult and child in the U.S., leading to higher interest rates,
and more people filed for bankruptcy in the U.S. than graduated from college (Mann). As for the idea that consumer debt helps to make people
more lucrative by giving them the means of starting their own small businesses, one would need only to look at the monumental increase in debt
for the poor instituted by small, short-term payday loans, often reissued in
a series of rollovers to as much as 2000 percent interest: "Critics counter
that poor working people, disproportionately people of color, are the primary users of payday loans. The Woodstock study found that 19 percent of
payday loan customers make less than $15,000 a year, and another 38 per-
cent make between $15,000 and $25,000. The Woodstock study also says
that borrowers in predominantly minority neighborhoods had an average
of 13.8 rollovers, 37 percent higher than in predominantly white neighborhoods" (Lyderson). It is difficult to elevate this debt system to the principle
behind a noncapitalist resolution to the problem of capitalist oppression,
or to an escape from the capitalist system of profit accumulation through
exploitation.

Fungibility and the Marketing of Genius

De Soto's notion of fungibility draws from the principles behind the creation of Wall Street felon Michael Milken's junk-bond empire.[13] Michael
Milken built his fortune by popularizing the buying and selling of junk
bonds, or rather, the practice of issuing high-yield public bonds on failing
companies that were below investment grade. This meant that dead capital
and unproductive businesses, and later failing schools—or "junk"—could
be turned into speculative profit. Though Milken was convicted on charges

of insider trading and fraud—as William Adler shows, "the bidding process was about as genuine as Milken's hairpiece" (243)—De Soto still upholds him as the hero of the poor and of the Third World: "the great practitioners of capitalism, from the creators of integrated title systems and corporate stock to Michael Milken, were able to reveal and extract capital where others saw only junk by devising new ways to represent the invisible potential that is locked up in the assets we accumulate" (7). In other words, the poor would be saved if they could turn their garbage into assets and thus into investment opportunities: there should be no limit to marketability; anything can be capital. The idea behind De Soto's model is that Third World vendors are the same as devastated businesses: mere junk.

For De Soto as for Milken, market experience converts, through representation, into assets: the market itself becomes the basis for producing knowledge as profit potential for everyone. "Formal property," he writes, "is more than just ownership . . . [I]t has to be viewed as the indispensable process that provides people with the tools to focus their thinking on those aspects of their resources from which they can extract capital . . . [I]t is an instrument of thought" (218). In other words, thought itself needs to be structured according to expanded property law, so that all thought which cannot be, for instance, patented needs to be represented in ways to make it patentable, or rather, worthy of investment and speculative profit. This would mean representing natural or customary experience, in other words, what people in the informal market already practice. There is, however, no explanation here of how thought can be turned into an asset, of how that might change the very nature of thought, or of what the difference might be between thought that can be converted into an exchangeable asset and thought that cannot, or what might become of thought that would thereby be excluded from representation because it does not function only as a tool for extracting capital. De Soto makes it clear that the mind itself is most useful when its products are made fungible—extracting the latent meaning—that is, when it can generate stock profits, as when Bill Gates's "personal genius" translates into "deals and long-term projects" based on "enforceable contracts," "liability systems and insurance policies" (224) (De Soto somehow neglects to mention here that Bill Gates's "personal genius" perhaps turned a profit precisely because Microsoft *violated* property rights law). For Emecheta on the other hand, the informal market substitutes for formal schooling: the informal market works in ways that make knowledge inaccessible and advancement into a formal market system impossible. This is especially the case for women, and in particular for Third World women, who, despite De Soto's idealism about the market's pledge of equality, are not equal within the present wage-labor system.

Nnu Ego works her whole life to provide for her children and give them an education. She hopes they will earn enough to support her in her old age. Yet, even nearing the end of her life, "[s]he could not afford the rent and she had no courage to start struggling all over again" (220). Nnu Ego is not "rich" (223), as the lorry driver teases her during her final return to Ibuza. The driver teases her as rich because he learns she has lots of children and one son studying in America. Emecheta here ironically foreshadows, within the lorry driver's false impressions, the destitution that leads to her character's demise: "one night, Nnu Ego lay down by the roadside, thinking that she had arrived home. She died quietly there, with no child to hold her hand and no friend to talk to her. She had never really made many friends, so busy had she been building up her joys as a mother" (224). Nnu Ego's wish to give her children profitable knowledge collapses. "What help can one give with only twelve pounds a month?" Oshia inquires begrudgingly. "That is what they pay now, even with a good Cambridge school-leaving certificate" (191). The market does not turn her experience of struggle or her children's education into assets to be converted, through representation, into profit, speculative potential, or secure investments. Though some of her children—notably, the boys—do get sporadic schooling, the novel ends with Nnu Ego's death, before the children come back offering either earnings or development projects, and so the economic promise is left indefinitely unfulfilled. As John Gray concludes, "The natural counterpart of a free market economy is a politics of insecurity. If 'capitalism' means 'the free market,' then no view is more deluded than the belief that the future lies with 'democratic capitalism'" (17). De Soto's faith in the possibilities of capitalizing fruitfully on market access contrasts sharply with Emecheta's ideas about how people are impoverished when capitalism reduces their experience to the market, offering the insufficient assurance of turning an eventual profit on it or using it as an asset. Not blaming Nigerian depravity simply on a deficient legal structure, Emecheta makes clear, rather, that such trade liberalization policies as allowing for unrestricted market extensions only invite foreign investments to replace public supports, thereby ensuring the continuation of poverty.

Emecheta's skepticism about defining labor as free enterprise needs to be looked at in relation to De Soto's market idealism. De Soto's vision of Western capitalism's success story reduces the role of the state to the background and then erases any public presence besides state repression (but only economic repression). In other words, the ideal Western state appears as a set of rules before which everyone is equal and autonomous, "a view of society as a fair system of cooperation between free and equal persons" (Mouffe, 44), whereas the corrupt Third World State—a site of contention between various interests, corruption, arbitrary authority, beaurocracies, and unequal application of the law—operates as an obstacle to development[14] and to knowledge. This view denies the very important play of politics, other roles that the state performs besides creating obstacles for business (e.g., redistributive functions, functions of justice, etc.), the ways that international market integration redefines the extensions and potentials of state power, and mitigating social inequalities produced by the market. De Soto does not take into account political theorist Chantal Mouffe's criticisms of this model of liberal government where "there could never be, in a modern democracy, a final agreement on a single set of principles of justice" (52). Instead, because his idea of politics fits within the singular functioning of an economically repressive state, De Soto assumes that a consensus could be reached about the rules of representing capital as property, forgetting the kinds of differences that must be washed out if everything is given value only through interchangeable representational structure. He does not, therefore, consider antagonisms and power struggles within the democratic political process or "the bargaining advantages that could affect the process of decision and distort the result" (Mouffe, 44), in other words, as Orwell might say, that some ways of representing property are more equal than others. Nor does he indicate that representation itself is subject to interpretive frameworks that exist as the result of struggles over power. As educational theorist Henry Giroux contends, "Representations are always produced within cultural limits and theoretical borders, and as such are necessarily implicated in particular economies of truth, value, and power" (1992: 219). De Soto's theory could only be logical and workable either if power were absolute or *if there were no such thing as power*, in other words, if power could be routed out.

De Soto's idea that decentralized representation removes power and thereby produces freedom conforms to the many right-wing ideologues who use the same justification to consider the "triumph" of the global market. *New York Times* foreign correspondent Thomas Friedman here quotes a Merrill Lynch advertisement to portray the golden promise of interconnectiveness and access under neoliberalism: "Many world markets are only recently freed, governed for the first time by the emotions of the people rather than the fists of the state[. . .] The spread of free markets and democracy around the world is permitting more people everywhere to turn their aspirations into achievements. And technology, properly harnessed and liberally distributed, has the power to erase not just geographical borders but also human ones" (xiii–xiv). Full of peace, love, harmony, fast food, easy travel, intense commodification, and ultimately skyrocketing productivity, the world that Friedman describes provides enough for everybody, as long as all anybody wants is American products or Japanese robotics, and fulfills everyone's desires, even when it has to kill a few people along the way because they are too slow or maybe too uncivil to be grateful for all that Taco Bell has done for them. Like De Soto, Friedman sees current globalization schemes as a utopia formed through the removal of power, as power only can operate through authoritarian repression, and particularly in this case, the repression of the natural, primitive, vital energy and consumer desire of the people, or what Friedman calls democracy.

As with Structural Adjustment Programs demanded by the IMF, the World Trade Organization, and the World Bank in much of the Third World, De Soto envisions the public sector as a tyrannical cap on individual creativity, innovative experience, and economic maximization, but a cap that can be removed to release choice freedom and prosperity. De Soto can only imagine power as public, public power as State power, and public power as therefore repressive, like Freud's dominating Ego Ideal: it is only public power that needs to be legally circumscribed and set within limits. Describing the success of capitalist development in post-Renaissance Europe, De Soto talks about a historical conflict between the market and the state where the market, in the end, was triumphant, establishing freedom:

> European governments were gradually forced to retreat in the face of growing extralegality—as governments in developing and former communists (*sic*) countries are doing today[. . .] In England, the state was forced to recognize that new industries were developing primarily in places where there were no guilds or legal restrictions[. . .] Moreover, the extralegal industries were more efficient and successful[. . .] The extralegals' numbers, persistence, and success began to undermine the very foundations of the mercantilist order. Whatever success they had, it was won in spite of the state, and they were bound to view the authorities as their enemies. In those countries where the state outlawed and prosecuted extralegal entrepreneurs instead of adjusting the system to absorb their enterprise, not only was economic progress delayed, but unrest increased, spilling into violence. The best-known manifestations were the French and Russian revolutions. (2000: 99)

In other words, the market works best and guarantees freedom only when devoid of politics, as though markets themselves are not constantly constituted through struggles in political arenas as these very examples demonstrate. As John Gray has elaborated, "In reality a *laissez-faire* economy—that is to say, an economy in which markets are deregulated and put beyond the possibility of political or social control—cannot be reinvented. Even in its heyday it was a misnomer. It was created by state coercion, and depended at every point in its workings on the power of government[. . . W]ithout diminishing the size of the state or reinstating the social institutions that supported the free market in its Victorian heyday, free market policies have encouraged new inequalities in income, wealth, access to work and quality of life that rival those found in the vastly poorer world of the mid-nineteenth century" (5).

An example of the same economistic, utopian logic of freedom as consumer desire that is found in Friedman's and De Soto's work appears as well in a recent MSN article about reactions against Coca-Cola in the Middle East. The article laments the good old days of imperialist expansion when Russians welcomed McDonald's into their midst and says that now, during the war with Iraq, Arabs are rejecting U.S. products, choosing European Colas instead with names like Zamzam Cola (after a holy spring in Mecca) and Mecca-Cola, with some of the profits going to local charities. The article goes on to claim that the political motivation behind alternative colas is actually detrimental to local economies: "In the Middle East, however, a successful boycott [of Coke and Pepsi] could be harmful to the boycotters, not the targeted companies. Western fast-food restaurants are locally owned franchises; their employees, naturally, are also local[. . .] In Palestine, Coke, which is the region's second-largest investor, and their Palestinian bottling company offer steady work, loans, and business training. In Egypt, Procter & Gamble, the company that supposedly named its products after Ariel Sharon, has spent $97 million on factories and community projects; it has built schools and paid for pilgrims to go to Mecca" (Fasman). What is missing here is any kind of questions about why Palestine needs Coke and Pepsi to build its schools in the first place (could it be because U.S.-sponsored and U.S.-armed Israeli incursions have closed down most Palestinian schools?) or why they would resist contract labor or why there are not local industries to employ local labor (could it have anything to do with the way the tax base in some of these countries is depleted through corporate incentive schemes?) or why people might not see Coca-Cola as the best employer. Also, the article assumes that people should want this unhealthy product, which tastes like soap, and that buying it rather than not buying it constitutes their freedom, so that the only alternative to corporate imperialist dominance is expanded corporate imperialist dominance. Like MSN and Friedman, De Soto idealistically assumes that removing politics, state interventions, and political barriers to trade will assure the democratization of capital guided by consumer desire and insists that "choice," "taste," and "desire" will be the agents unfolding the global future. He suggests that the role of the state and therefore the public should be reduced to regularizing bureaucratic procedures for commerce and equalizing capital's potential for expansion by instituting a uniform property system that treats everyone the same.

De Soto fails to consider here the insights of the dependency theorists who were able to demonstrate how Third World markets arise in a disadvantaged position within integrated world systems. Nor does De Soto take into account how advanced nations developed through state-subsidized industry rather than by "laissez-faire" (Chomsky). Uruguayan political theorist Eduardo Galeano analyzed succinctly the historical recurrence of imperial relations within capitalism. According to Galeano in *The Open Veins of Latin America*, the modern nation developed as part of an ongoing class struggle where some nations provided raw materials and labor for other countries' enrichment, and some nations' economies were formed to exist "at the service of others' needs": "The division of labor among nations," he states, "is that some specialize in winning and others in losing" (1973: 11). What is missing from De Soto's argument are the relational aspects of underdevelopment. De Soto fails to recognize, for example, how not only custom, but predominantly power influences the formation of laws, so that, for example, tax laws in many of these countries favor foreign corporate investment over local industries in the name of creating jobs, even when these jobs do not provide adequate subsistence, fair treatment, labor organizing, environmental equity, or optimal satisfaction for the local populations and even when these jobs do not ever materialize. Attempts to change structural economic imbalances legally have led to various reprisals, from economic squeezing, loan disqualification, economic sanctions, and capital flight to, for example, the outright military invasion and presidential coup in Guatemala in 1954 by the combined forces of United Fruit and the CIA.[15]

The Joys

In contrast to *The Mystery*, in *The Joys of Motherhood*, Emecheta includes ideas about how power works not only as repression, but also to support the interests of the powerful, through force if necessary, and to produce a market that distributes freedoms unequally for imperialist profit. "If they allowed us to develop the production of our own gin, who would buy theirs?" asks Nnu Ego's second husband Naife when Nnu Ego questions why the British outlawed local whisky production (111). Unlike De Soto's contentions, Emecheta's work suggests that the waning of state and public involvement does not produce freedom, since the power of the state only wanes—as De Soto's recommendations suggest—when it comes to support for the poor.

When Nnu Ego first arrives in Lagos, her husband-to-be Nnaife works as a clothes launderer for the British master Dr. Meers. Though steady, his salary is not enough to provide for a growing family, so Nnu Ego learns from her Igbo women neighbors how to acquire tins of cigarettes and matches and sell them for a slight profit. Within six months, Nnu Ego is able to complete a purchase of an entire new outfit complete with matching head tie, while her remaining meager surplus is exhausted in paying for the naming ceremony of her first child (who dies not long afterward). Throughout the novel, Nnu Ego is engaged in various small commercial enterprises from selling cigarettes, to collecting fallen timber to sell as firewood, to selling the nearly rotten vegetables she grows in her yard—precisely, her "junk"—but without ever being able to acquire, set aside, or accumulate savings or assets, even in the complete absence of any kind of repressive public action.

When the public sector did intervene, the vicissitudes of income stabilized, wages regularized, and futures became more secure. "Nnaife was among the lucky few who found work with the government," Emecheta narrates when Nnu Ego's husband finds work as a grass cutter with the national Railroad. "Thus employed, one could hardly be sacked and could rest assured the morning would never come when one was told that there was no more work to be done. On top of that, if one stayed in government service long enough, one was sure of a small pension, something still quite new to most Ibos" (141). This pension, however, is eventually taken away not because, as De Soto would have it, public power acts arbitrarily to limit the economic potential of free citizens, but rather because private financial power is able to gain control over public institutions. This happened after Nnaife attacked a private Yoruba business with a cutlass[16] for violating Igbo customary law (the butcher's son was going to marry his daughter Kehinde without paying the bride-price) during a time when the Yoruba were rising politically because of their economic ties with Britain. The promise of Nnaife's pension founders. "He [the lawyer] told her [Nnu Ego] that there was some likelihood of Nnaife being released from prison after serving only three months, because some "important" people had decided that he had not been responsible for his actions . . . He would lose a great part of his gratuity, but they would give him a small pension" (220).

Although De Soto might attribute Nnaife's loss of pension to public corruption or to the lack of limitations on public authority, Emecheta is demonstrating, rather, how the conditions and provisions of poverty worsen with the weakening of public supports and that public supports in the Third World are weakened because foreign economic interests undermine state power, as to augment their own accumulation and decrease local competition: After all, economically powerful nations become economically powerful through a system of state supports denied to developing economies. Nnu Ego and Nnaife cannot acquire assets because those making decisions about crime, discipline, work conditions, and benefits to the poor are serving different interests and different agendas which clash with the public's social welfare: "[most of] the jury . . . were Europeans." In contrast to the faith De Soto has in the market itself as an equalizer in the interests of everybody, Emecheta shows how the market allows private power to influence the implementation of the law. The public system of accountability to employees and citizens here translates into the maintenance of colonial power, foreign investment, the exploitation of cheap labor, and the turning of the poor themselves into assets for the profits of the rich. "The British own us, just like God does, and just like God they are free to take any of us when they wish" (148).

Like De Soto, Nnu Ego sees the promise of fortune in the marketability of knowledge: "when he finishes his education," she says confidently of her first son, Oshia, "then we will all be better off" (191). Yet throughout the novel the demands of the market block the regularity of her children's schooling, either because Nnu Ego cannot meet the payments of school fees, or because she needs her children to help her with her trade, or because she needs to use her small allowance to buy, for example, a sewing machine that would enhance her sales by giving her a skill if she could only find the time to learn and develop it, or even because the necessity of eating must compete with schooling: " 'I had thought Oshia would be going to school, starting after Christmas. Now we have little money to buy even food,' Nnu Ego despaired" (85). "[L]earn as much as you can from school," she later tells Oshia, "because when they demand the next school fees, I don't think I shall be able to pay" (173). Sometimes, she is able to scrounge together enough funds to get her kids private tutors when the regular school fees get too steep, even while acknowledging that the option of private education makes lessons sporadic and less rigorous: "So at the beginning of the next term Oshia and his brother Adim attended a private class at Adam Street, where the teacher taught them how to write neatly and do some sums. All the other complicated subjects were forgotten. Oshia knew that the arrangement was nothing compared to a 'real school' but there was nothing he could do about it" (174). Emecheta also makes it clear that the rich are not subject to the same delays, insecurities, discontinuities, and downright threats to the promise of education when Nnu Ego announces that Oshia's friends the Folorunsho do not have to leave school because they "own Lagos" (173). Emecheta is pointing out that public education is here failing because it is structured as an unregulated, privatized market, which does not promise equal freedom for everybody.

The constant butting-up against need and desperation affects the girls' education more than the boys', as the twins Kehinde and Taiwo, forced to leave school, end up partially illiterate: "The twins will have to leave and help me in running the house and in my trade," Nnu Ego confesses. "They don't need to stay long in school—only a year or two" (174).[17] "We have Adim and Nnamdio to think of and, with Oshia's big school fees, we cannot afford fees for the twins . . . ," Nnu Ego confesses later when her co-wife Adaku questions her about the twins' lack of schooling and illiteracy. "I personally do not regret it. They will be married in a few years. They can earn an added income by trading" (189). Nnu Ego here considers school to be a rare public asset for which her children compete, while the ones that win the not-so-fair-competition are set, at the start, with patriarchal privilege. Without recourse to eduction, the girls are forced into the informal economy as unskilled laborers.

Indeed, there seem very few other options for the twins besides prostitution or teaching, though Nnu Ego's co-wife Adaku suggests hopefully, tentatively, even if unconvincingly that "there may be a future for educated women" (189). Adaku left the house because, as the second wife and as a mother only of girls, she felt disadvantaged and disrespected. She opened her own market stall, though it is understood that her large profits came when she sold her sex. With this, she paid for her daughters' education. *The Joys of Motherhood* illustrates the limitations of a model of knowledge-acquisition based on the market by indicating the inherent inequalities produced in a market that can only maintain itself by undercutting public institutions and providing cheap labor to attract foreign private investments. Thus the novel criticizes the idea—just below the surface of De Soto's arguments and Milken's practices—that schools should turn children into capital.

Nnu Ego was not, indeed, better off when Oshia finished his education. Oshia's education kept taking him farther and farther afield as he procrastinated the time of his return to help out his family, to pay for his brothers' and sisters' education, and to work for his country's development. "Adim knew, after talking to his brother during the holidays when he was home, that though he would like to help his parents, that help was going to be a very long time in coming" (191). Finally, Oshia won a scholarship to study in the United States. The implication is that Nigeria's investments in national education are inadequate for future national development. Education becomes another institution of foreign control, turning Third World children into opportunities for foreign investment.

In many of Emecheta's books, she talks about the transformative promises of education, and how the inherent conflict between education and the market crushes these possibilities. In *A Second Class Citizen* (1974), for example, the main character, Adah, hopes that her education will give her an advantage in potential earnings, and even open up opportunities for herself and her children as she decides to continue her education in London. In the end, though, Adah is disappointed, as the hardships of the market force her constantly into difficult work situations, intensified by persistent racism in hiring practices, the absence of public supports for child care, health and housing, and the inadequacies of public protections against her husband's abuses, so that her intellectual pursuits remain constantly thwarted.

In *The Joys of Motherhood,* education at first seems not only the answer to individual ambitions but also the hope of postcolonial nationhood: "People agreed that it was worth the trouble one had to go through to train children in a difficult place like Lagos. 'But things are changing fast,' said Ubani [one of the neighbors] . . . 'They say that in the not-too-distant future we shall be ruling ourselves, making our own laws' " (199). Oshia, in fact, contends that his education will lead to a future of self-governance. Speaking of the educated classes, "[The new Nigerians] will do [the job of ruling ourselves, being District Officer or Reverend Father] even better, because this is their country. They have never been given the chance before. Now things are changing and Nigerian politicians are springing up and demanding our rights" (199).

However, the Nigerian educated classes, like Oshia, did not return to govern with respect for people's rights to self-determination, nor did Nigerian self-governance favor the working poor in terms of formalizing their assets, capitalizing their savings, or offering them control over the means of production and thus the conditions of their working and non-working lives. Instead, the return of the postcolonial technocrats and the foreign-educated has revealed that foreign education did not lead to Nigerian enrichment but to the continued disparity between rich and poor as well as to the continued profiting, from Nnu Ego's cheap labor, by an established elite. As a 1996 update in *The Economist* reports:

> anger is palpable just below the surface. People complain fiercely, even by Nigerian standards, that their wealth and their future have been stolen . . . The prices of staple food and transport, the two that matter to the urban poor, are rising fast. Health care has slipped backward. Education, the only honest way out of poverty, is a disaster: schools are without books, teachers unpaid and universities on strike (again).

Hardly a bastion of radical thought, *The Economist* recounts that the deregulation of banking has permitted the educated elites to get wealthy off of foreign exchange, and this in turn has allowed for the despoilment of public resources as the financiers linked to foreign interests get rich and massive public monies disappear (around $60 million, according to *The Economist*). The top arm of the supposedly civilian government had earmarked certain oil revenues for the development of public highways, but the military, profiting from oil looting, was unlikely to go along. Because of the growth in military power bolstered by the oil industry, "[m]ost Nigerians lived better before the 1973–74 oil-price rise," Pat Utomi, an economist at the Lagos Business School, says. Clearly, Emecheta's informal markets of the urban poor will not be able to get their interests represented against this kind of militarized, multinational control of national income, nor would representing their property and assets free up their access to these types of controlled markets or make them competitive.

Emecheta is aware that reducing education to the market will foster a growth in militarism, or rather, that markets and militarism go together.[18] To show this, she parallels Oshia's scholarship in the United States to the tactics of the British colonialist army. Just as Naife was taken from his home and family and forced to work for British shipping or to defend

British interests in Burma during World War II, Oshia is sent abroad to train as a scientist-technician in the new economic administration of his country. Oshia even started school with Naife's earnings from his "slave pay" on the ship; this "slave pay," at least at the beginning, covered the costs of Oshia's khaki school uniform as well as his fees (112). Just as Naife promised to send a salary that ended up arriving too late or not at all and never was enough to provide for the family, Oshia's lucrative return is also constantly delayed. Though Oshia, indeed, consents to go abroad and learn to work for the implementation of colonialist law whereas Naife is coerced, Oshia's education to be a technician for the new global economy—in Nigeria, most likely in the service of the oil companies or the military or both— appears here as repeating the colonialist practice of exploitation, violence, and forced conscription of nationals for foreign interests.

War

The Joys of Motherhood chronicles how the new corporate imperialisms have manged to fracture the public supports for labor and education in the Third World. In fact, the imperialist assault on Nigeria's public sphere was aggressively carried forth by a violent public intervention to force in the kind of market reforms that De Soto advocates. In the time between *Efuru* and *The Joys of Motherhood*, the Igbos were involved in a brutal civil war in which potentially one million Igbos were starved to death. In 1966, there were massacres of Igbos in the northern part of Nigeria (an estimated 10,000 deaths, with substantial evidence that the army contributed, most likely with the knowledge, if not the consent, of the regime in Lagos), followed by a massive migration of Igbos from the northern to the eastern part where Igbos dominated, and then the succession of eastern Nigeria, renamed Biafra. The ensuing war lasted three years.

> Lagos's strategy in the civil war consisted of blockading Biafra and trying to starve it into submission. Such a strategy, of course, made civilians the primary victims of the war. Nigerian officials acknowledged as much: "I want to prevent even one Ibo having one piece to eat before their capitulation," proclaimed the Nigerian military commander on the southern front. And Lagos's highest ranking civilian declared, "All is fair in war and starvation is one of the weapons of war." (Shalom)

Biafra had large deposits of oil. Under the contention that their former colonialist status granted the right to intervene in another sovereign nation's internal affairs, Britain backed the cruel efforts on the part of the Lagos government to end the succession. The United States, wanting Britain's continued support in their own war against Vietnam, also backed Lagos, suspending aid to eastern Nigeria while continuing it in other parts (private relief organizations continued to provide food but had trouble

144 • World, Class, Women

getting it into Biafra because of Nigerian control of transportation networks). As Nnu Ego asks in *The Joys of Motherhood,* "Are we not all slaves to the white men, in a way?[. . .] If they permit us to eat, then we will eat. If they say we will not, then where will we get the food?" (117). Both Britain and the United States heavily armed Nigeria's increasing militarization by endorsing and provisioning a war with ethically unsound claims against the rights of a people to self-determination and self-protection against genocide.

Emecheta is aware that market liberalization was enforced through military means and not, as De Soto would interpret, as a result of the people's democratic desire for self-determination. Emecheta's novel about Biafra called *Destination Biafra* (1982) tells the story of an elite Ibo girl Debbie who, having been educated in Britain, returns and joins the Nigerian military. When the massacres occur and the war breaks out, her father is one of the first Ibo politicians killed. She is then solicited by the Nigerian government to travel to Biafra and ask the new president of the Biafran government, Abosi, to concede to a unified Nigeria. En route, she is brutally raped by Nigerian soldiers and witnesses the atrocities of torture and starvation that the Nigerian command is inflicting on the Igbo refugees fleeing their homes for Biafra. By the time she reaches Biafra to make her request, the Ibos have almost lost the war and the Nigerians have withdrawn the offer. Having learned class oppression by sharing the experiences of her people at war, Debbie decides to collect her notes from the journey into a memoir called *Destination Biafra.* "Oh, white man," she asks, "don't you understand your own language now?" (230). Learning, like Nnu Ego, that the privatization of public interests is leading to mass starvation and death, Debbie's turn toward identity in literature is defined as her new awareness of the Nigerian public, an awareness that opens the possibility of acting in defiance against foreign control, systematic starvation, militarism, new forms of imperialism, market exploitation, and damaging representations. As Debbie forsakes her marriage agreement with a British military advisor along with her attachments and contractual working arrangements with both the British and Nigerian governing classes, she concludes: "No, I am not ready yet to become the wife of an exploiter of my nation" (245).

Today, the same now well-supplied, technologized, and modernized military that stamped out Biafra, now under the front of a "freely elected" civilian government, is still mobilized against democratic organizing and political movements for self-determination, particularly in the case of environmentalist opposition. For example, on 4 January 1999, a helicopter known to be used by Chevron Corporation[19] swept over two Nigerian villages—Opia and Ikenyan—spraying bullets.[20] Four people were killed. The attack was in response to a massive demonstration in May of Chevron's presence in the Nigerian Delta where the unarmed Oguni villagers were protesting against the environmental damage Chevron was causing (nine people were killed then), followed by Chevron's allegations that some youths from the village had threatened to occupy one of their rigs (Goodman and Scahill). As Emecheta concluded in the final paragraphs of *Destination Biafra*, "Nigeria badly needed that stability [provided by an ample supply of guns and bombs imported for the purpose of ending the resistance in Biafra] to allow foreign investors to come in and suck out the oil" (245). The continued defense of the public through its institutions is necessary to stave off chronic war for the purpose of resource and labor control. There is a growing need to look at the ways cultural production has been appropriated into the service of corporate expropriation, imperialist military conquest, and market hegemony, and how culture has envisioned the social production of power as well as the public's options.

CHAPTER 5

Homework
School in Serowe

At the year 2000 Republican convention in Philadelphia, Laura Bush called
for mothers to read to their children at an early age. This reduction of a
public function to the private sphere was certainly not absent on the Democratic platform that year. The Gore campaign and the Democratic Party
similarly evoked family tenderness and love to sell their political agenda.
Two of the Gore children spoke about how much they loved their parents,
one even telling of how her father taught her to build an igloo without ex-
plaining how they got enough snow to build one in Tennessee. Tipper Gore
showed a heart-warming video about her life and love with Al, boasting of
how they have been in love with each other for thirty years, ever since they
first set eyes on each other. Clearly, this was an attempt to offset the Clinton legacy of dubious morality and infidelity. However, it also serves the
same purpose as Laura Bush's speech in selling hard politics in the name of
love. Not subject to partisan differences, the sanctimonious and caring
family is supposed to replace the need for a welfare state or a social net, and
serves to justify, in political rhetoric, structural adjustment programs both
in the United States and abroad. What makes Laura Bush's speech alarm-
ing (though not unique and certainly not party-exclusive) is how she uses a
story about education as central to "compassionate conservativism," or
rather, her "politics of care," through which she constructs a neoliberal
philosophy. Likening teaching to mothering, Laura Bush explicitly linked
family values, increased attention to early childhood (but not to welfare),
to the curtailment of the federalist state, the growth of the military, and the
need to remove federal regulations on capital flows, in other words, to the

need to defend aggressively the expansion of markets for U.S. goods in the interests of providing and protecting an ideal, blissful and untouchable privacy.[1] The Republican innovation was to privatize the public sphere by privatizing the classroom, as the soon-to-be first lady spoke in front of a Dubya joining her through video teleconferencing from a midwestern elementary school. By transforming the role of the teacher into a mothering relation, by reducing the public role of socializing citizens to sentimental or familial pictures of private love, this moral, even emotional vision of teaching as nurturing serves to show education as a private rather than a public responsibility.

Alongside sweatshops, service provision, child care, nursing, care for the elderly, and the like, the feminization of teaching is part of a broader public discourse creating unequal distributions of wealth, power, and value in the workforce. Subjected to ideologies of the private sphere, the feminization of certain sectors of labor subjects these labor markets to wage depression. Teaching, like other types of feminized caretaking and nurturance jobs, seems to be a labor of love and devotion rather than a difficult job deserving adequate compensation, the right to organize, benefits, safety regulations, labor provisions, governance, and contracts. Furthermore, as Nelly Stromquist and Karen Monkman have pointed out,

> Part-time jobs represent about one-fifth of jobs in the OECD [Organization for Economic Cooperation and Development] economies; under globalization, these jobs also have a tendency to increase. Flexible time and part-time work favor women because they accommodate women's needs[...] [T]he neoliberal project that accompanies current globalization processes depends on women retaining their "traditional" family-oriented identities without undermining their availability for the labor market to provide low-wage competition. (9–10)

Representations of feminized labor benefit labor flexibility which, in turn, increases corporate profitability.

The image of privatized teaching serves two simultaneous and interacting functions: 1) to demonize or diminish a public or political culture; and 2) to create a sentimentalized sphere of labor separate from political concerns or public controls and solely responsive to private interests. As Henry Giroux points out, in the U.S. case, "[T]he continued devaluation of education as a public good points to the need for educators to work together to reclaim schools as democratic public spheres" (2000: 26).[2] Defining teaching through an ideology of mothering—redefining public interests as private problems and private responsibilities—feeds a common knowledge that favors the privatization or corporatization of a wide range of social functions and democratic institutions, from corporate-sponsored curricula, charter schools, and vouchers to welfare-to-work programs, the development of private investor accounts to replace Social Security, faith-based or volunteerist initiatives, police outsourcing, and military subcontracting, for example.

Ideas about how education might have other functions besides preparing students for a global, technologized labor market in the service of corporate power are becoming, in this critical political juncture, unspeakable.[3] In part, the ideological mechanisms through which corporate values reign unquestionably assume a gendered division of labor. Through bolstering a wide-ranging separation between public and private laboral spheres, gender rhetorically creates wage and value differentials that lower the costs of production or that maintain a reserve labor market.[4] Contends Saskia Sassen,

> The expansion of downgraded manufacturing sector, be it the garment sweatshops in New York city of the high-tech production plants in the Los Angeles region, can be seen to generate a demand for low-wage women workers . . . Similarly, the expansion of low-wage service jobs, particularly pronounced in major cities . . . generates a demand for low-wage workers . . . [M]any of these jobs have been historically and/or culturally typed as women's jobs . . . There is, then, a correspondence between the kinds of jobs that are growing in the economy generally, and in major cities particularly, and the composition of immigration—largely from low-wage countries and with a majority of women. (128–129)

Feminizing the kinds of employment that can be labeled as traditionally and historically domestic weakens their competitive status, cheapening such currently mainstay jobs as teaching and caring for children as well as clothing manufacturing, precision assembly, and clerical support service. Additionally, popular understandings of femininity that associate women with the traits of domesticity are often currently upheld as the limits to the public authority of the nation-state, setting the nation-state as the enemy of people's private interests and freedoms when it is still the dominant guarantor of citizens' rights against private corporate interests.

This chapter shows how some feminist psychological educational theory has neglected a serious consideration of how feminism can build a vision of a non-gender-exploitative alternative to the present. I criticize some psychology-based educational theory which, under the name of feminism, upholds a "politics of caring" as a methodological imperative while neglecting how this same "politics of caring" sets in place political ideas about labor that are detrimental to women. In contrast, I offer a reading of a feminist text that considers education's central task as constructing a politics of the public. South African novelist and educator Bessie Head's ethnographic study *Serowe: Village of the Rain Wind* (1981)[5] presents the history of a community in Botswana as it builds a school to train workers for a postcolonial economy. Head documents the construction of a school as a public alternative to privatization, profit motivation, exploitation, or the earning of surplus to benefit people not involved directly in production.

There is another body of feminist scholarship on education which is more sociologically based. Most of these studies tend to be empirical and/or ethnographic, often participant-observer and written as "qualitative" rather than "quantitative" analysis in that they tend to collect self-descriptions of their subjects rather than quantifiable categories. Such studies for the most part seem to me to be flawed in the narrowness of their focus, as they tend to shy away from the broader political context in which the categories of observation acquire meaning. For example, one such study, Holland and Eisenhart's "Women's Ways of Going to School: Reproduction of Women's Identities as Workers," questions why girls in elementary school want to engage in boy-takes-girl extracurricular activities even when their teachers were "promoting asexual 'good student' roles" and so not reproducing gender-coded behavior: "We interpreted the gender emphasis of the students to be a reaction, in part, to the school-promoted age hierarchy that defined them as children. When they found opportunities to engage in more "adult" activities, such as cross-gender relationships, they did so" (268). Though seemingly divergent from the more psychology-based studies of feminist research on education in its focus on the social, this conclusion likewise centers the domestic by isolating the classroom as a miniature of the entire social field and gender as an individual choice. In other words, gender is something kids can choose to be or not to be in defiance of the authority of teachers but without regards to the even greater authority of, for example, the mass media. The idea would mean that if teachers taught traditional gendered-behavior, the students in defiance would all choose to be gender-benders or gender outlaws, as if the relationship between the teachers' lessons about gender and the students' adoptions of gender codes were confined inside a social test tube with controlled parameters. The question of why kids choose heterosexualized and gendered codes of behavior replaces the more important question about who makes these codes, who genders them, whose interests do they serve, and in what way do they serve particular interests. Seemingly clueless about certain poststructuralist contributions to the study of identity such as Judith Butler's, such a perspective presumes the truth of gender as prior to the identification with it. In defining a field, empiricism tends to create categories of objects—quantifiable as well as qualifiable—that can be observed through a set of regularizable parameters, so that the ultimate complexity of forces in the contemporary social world get reduced to a few variables with a few measurable pathways of interaction at the expense of the political and economic structures that ultimately produce these variables only as part of a broader set of meanings and power.

Another example of the more sociologically based empiricist educational studies is Lois Weis and Doris Caronell-Medina's "Learning to Speak Out." Again, this analysis claims its feminist clout by observing how identities are formed in relation to broken homes and private lives, and how they can be healed through peer-group discussions that substitute for public institutional supports. The article looks at an abstinence-only urban public education program to show that, contrary to what some scholarship says, "such curricula can potentially be used in[…] progressive ways" (27) because they can "encourage young women across race and ethnicity to explore their own gendered subjectivities and, most of all, to resist the violence and control they feel lies ahead of them" (27). Such an accomodationist approach—we hate what we've got but we got it and there is nothing we can do about it so we might as well make the best of it, or rather, redefining a patriarchal practice as "feminist"—reinforces the gender oppressions it identifies by only suggesting therapeutic, private solutions to public problems. For example, in a gossipy section similar to other sections where "data" is presented, one of their informants, a white girl Connie, talks about the poverty that has stricken her family—"We live in a really small house" (36)—to the point where her mother and all of her sisters are on welfare, and then about how she does not want to follow such a course. The researchers conclude by comfortably asserting that Connie has found a safe and protective space for sharing her experience in her abstinence-only group. However, they never consider that Connie is not likely to find herself on the welfare roles, not because her friends give her solace but because the welfare roles are likely no longer to exist as welfare timetables shrink, programs cut, and welfare turns into workfare. The turn toward the personal and the emotional, the focus on the private home as the source of identity, the eclipsing of the political with the therapeutic—all these theoretical tendencies in this ethnographic encounter mean that the real-world reasons for the conditions of alienation described by Connie and her peers fall outside of the study's parameters: housing shortages, school poverty, urban poverty, unemployment and under-employment, welfare cuts, and, indeed, abstinence-only programs.

The consequences of the shift toward neoliberalism and privatization are clearly harsh on women, from single mothers who have been cut from the welfare roles in rich countries to, for example, the rural Mexican women whose local economies have been wiped out by multinationals and who are subsequently forced to seek employment in border zones of industrial production where they work for low wages without contracts, security, benefits, safety protections, or the rights to organize. As Saskia Sassen points out, "[W]hile forty-two percent of all women as compared to 34.4 percent of all men held jobs in the two lowest earnings classes in 1970, this share had increased to fifty-two percent for women and only to 35.7 percent for the men by 1980 . . . And all the gains in the two highest income strata were obtained by men, while women actually lost some representation" (122). The economic system currently expands itself by restructuring labor markets in conformity with what in the industrial age defined women's domestic values and modes of working: private domestic production, outsourcing, temporary work, piece work, and the like. "[I]n 1995, the United Nations maintained that . . . [a]s a result of globalization and world market integration, 'women were able to gain more jobs than men while losing in terms of equal pay and quality of employment. Women's economic position did not improve relative to men and probably deteriorated'" (Wichterich, 28). Women are even sought after, by corporate headhunters, because they promise lower production costs, sometimes even providing and paying for their own work spaces and equipment by producing at home, ensuring, as then–UN Secretary Boutros Boutros-Ghali announced at the 1995 Beijing Conference on Women, that 70 percent of the world's poor are women.[6] Contends Saskia Sassen, talking about the corporate recruitment of women in industrial zones for export manufacturing:

> The most obvious reason for the intensive recruitment of women is firms' desire to reduce costs, but there are other considerations as well: young women in patriarchal societies are seen by foreign employers as obedient and disciplined workers, willing to do tedious, high-precision work and to submit themselves to work conditions that would not be tolerated in the highly developed countries. (41–42)

Women are caught at these low ends of the economic ladder partly through a symbolic production of gendered attributes linked to the domestic sphere, attributes such as subservience, attention to detail, obedience, and affective allegiance, which benefit the expansion of corporatism. These same attributes are turned into virtues in stories of the good mother, encouraging a morality of menial labor.

Since the 1960s critical and other types of education theory has been concerned with the role of schools in reproducing the economic power structure and, particularly, its class relations. Following on Althusser's theories of State Apparatuses and interpellation and Bourdieu's analysis of state legitimation and the reproduction of "cultural capital" in schools, much has been written in pedagogical theory about how schools reproduce class domination and yet are also sites of struggle over meaning.[7] Feminists have contributed to this critique by showing the ways that schools reproduce sexual difference, from the structure and content of the curriculum to the propagation of student career expectations to the widespread allegation that teachers perform intellectual work inadequately. Such research presents empirical data that show that teachers pay less attention to girls and call on them less, or that curricular materials are less likely to provide them with role models, or that they are less likely to be encouraged in high-level math and science courses. Besides their valuable insistence on sex/gender equity law compliance, these feminists have suggested solving these problems by making teachers more aware of sex/gender issues through teacher testing, training, and the promotion of multicultural education.[8]

What such studies neglect, however, is how this valuing of economic and corporate assimilation as a way out of sex/gender oppression is the means by which sex/gender oppression becomes more socially entrenched, how education reproduces not only class position but also the entire economic structure through which class oppression is set in place. As feminist critic Kathlene Weiler puts it, "[T]here has been an implicit assumption that changes of texts and practices will lead to changes in social relationships and that girls and boys will then be equal within capitalist society. Implicit in this view is the concept that sexism exists within the realm of ideas, and that if those ideas are changed, then social relationships will also change. Such a view ignores the constraints of the material world" (1988: 29). In other words, there is no sense that if women succeed in their math and science courses, they could go on, as the next generation of engineers, to build the military equipment that enforces the ruinous rules of the IMF, or to patent, under corporate trademarks, pharmaceutical products which will, therefore, become more inaccessible to the world's poor, and particularly to poor women. As Elaine Unterhalter has pointed out, "Over the past two decades, in some of the poorest countries of the world there have been enormous increases in the proportion of girls at school. However these increases have not been accompanied by any concomitant change in the sexual division of labour or women's position in the employment structure" (71). Katha Pollitt confirms this observation on a global level: "In numerous countries—Jamaica, the Philippines, some Latin American nations—women are better educated than men. But nowhere does that fact result in on-the-job equality." Insisting that girls should excel within the current educational agenda does not subvert or even question how this educational agenda is furthering the class warfare that is ensuring the impoverishment of women worldwide, increasing the number of women working because their labor costs less to those profiting from it.

Teaching girls calculus or physics or providing them with computers will not in itself end sex/gender oppression but might, without further critical or feminist engagement, reinforce it, assimilating girls into an economic system that exploits sex/gender difference for a profit. As Michael Apple pointed out as early as the 1970s, the "high-status" position of math and science was not only a result of the increasing technologization of high-status careers, but, as well, a product of the economic structure of society and the distribution of poverty. Now, as technical knowledge is more pervasive at all levels of economic production, such knowledge is often valued more than the arts and humanities because of economic utility—the way, for example, it can turn students into entrepreneurs, but also because it makes the very idea of knowledge instrumental in preparing students for a twenty-first-century service-oriented workforce. Additionally, math and science appear as discrete units of knowledge that can then be accumulated and tested (42). Assessment testing has been increasingly dominating the public school curriculum, even more emphatically after George W. Bush implemented his "No Child Left Behind" educational reforms, and has been the rationale for multiple school closings, especially in poor areas, for taking curricular control away from teachers and scripting lessons. In other words, teaching math and science to girls does not necessarily lead to the liberation of women but rather reproduces sex/gender attributes in the workforce, undervaluing "women's work" through its further feminization, its loss of control, its de-intellectualization, and its service orientation. Additionally, even with noted successes in girls' math and science achievement in recent years, women have still only attained 14 percent of management and administrative jobs and 6 percent of upper management jobs worldwide, as women still mostly find themselves in agriculture or service-level jobs (71 percent), now, of course, with higher productivity because of their technical knowledge (Lim). Reaffirming the class system on which corporate exploitation works, the ideology bolstered in science and math teaching does not, then, guarantee the end of sex/gender oppression.

Serowe

The southern cape regions of Africa where Botswana lies tell of histories stricken with intertribal warfare and colonial incursions from British, German, and Boer interests. In 1896, Botswana was made into a British protectorate in order to head off the invasions of John Rhodes, who wanted to annex it to Rhodesia. South Africa wanted to annex Botswana as a "native homeland" after 1909, resenting British influence on their borders. As a result, South Africa encouraged black immigration to settle in Botswana, not requiring passports, and many, like Bessie Head, went there, living in exile until they could figure out ways to move to other places in Africa or Europe. The British, increasingly apprehensive about South Africa's racial policies after the official enactment of apartheid in 1948, started to put in place the institutions for independence, including the Bechuanaland Democratic Party in 1960, which awakened political consciousness by extending voting rights to everyone, including women and blacks, and finally granted independence in 1966. The hands-off policies of the London-headed governance meant that the tribal peoples interviewed by Head often confessed to liking the colonial administration, where power was left in the hands of local chiefs, better than the government after the 1966 independence, when political affairs were directed from the faraway capital.

Serowe: Village of the Rain-Wind chronicles how the processes of decolonization are instituted within the formation of a school, from when teachers met students to share ancestral lore under a tree to a more systematized curriculum tied to nationalistic, locally based productivity. The descriptions given by Head's informants focus on how schooling contributes to forging indigenous identities in defiance of capitalist encroachments. Maintains Head in *A Woman Alone:*

> Botswana had experienced a history without parallel in southern Africa. If the indigenous people had lost their lands, they would have lost everything and become slaves and a source of cheap labour to any white exploiter at hand. Of a country totalling 220,000 square miles, 112,503 square miles remained under the ancient traditional African land tenure system. The 104,069 square miles ceded to the British Crown still remained effectively under the traditional land tenure system. (198)[9]

Within this impetus to reproduce tradition as an antidote to capital, women's work was essential because it used tradition—even changing tradition—as the basis for constructing public works. Rob Nixon observes, "[Head] was neither a cultural preservationist nor an advocate of modern nationalism as a progressive force. Increasingly, she saw the issues of precolonial, colonial, and postcolonial experience through the optic of women's relation to male authority structures, property, and the land" (160). Male authority lay in household economies, family production, tribal justice, and the conjugal control of the bride price abolished in the late nineteenth century. Women's opposition to male authority appears as forming a broader connection to developing a public sphere: "I have always done housework," tells Sekgabe Ntshwarisang, a traditional housebuilder. "The skill of homebuilding was taught to every young girl from about the age of eighteen. [. . . I]f [a woman] liked help and wanted the house quickly, she would say to the other women: 'Come and join me in the work. I'll give you half a bag of corn or one pot of our milk.' [. . . T]his is what my mother taught me" (50). Rob Nixon has pointed out that the building of this public is identified with redistributive land policies: "[Head's] writings suggest . . . that the core colonial issue of land is ineradicably gendered. While passionately supporting the idea of independence, she came to feel firsthand women's and men's unequal access to the fruits of nationhood" (160).

As Head explains the principle concern with thinking about education in Serowe, "The . . . painful question . . . is whether it is wise to create a skilled labour force that will eventually be exploited by the rich manufacturers, starting the cycle of poverty all over again at another level" (146). The answer is to create a school which becomes an operating cooperative for craft and agricultural production, a means of financial backing for local development projects, an active catalyst for job opportunities, which allow for participant control over the means of symbolic and material production, a democratic forum to critique the mechanisms of oppression and then to discuss political options, and a community occupied in understanding its future production as connected to a rich cultural heritage of opposition.

When Head arrived from South Africa in 1964, schools restricted to the education of white traders' children had just been opened up to the black population. This contrasted to the segregated schools in neighboring South Africa where, after 1948, the racial division of labor was in strict concordance with the racial division of educational agendas.[10] Botswana is the only country in southern Africa where girls' access to primary and secondary education is not shamefully comparable to the poorest countries in the world, as it was in South Africa under apartheid (Unterhalter, 71). For the people of Serowe, the education of women is necessary for conceiving an economy resistant to exploitation by "rich manufacturers," white supremacy, and economic dependence. "Many women," explains the elementary school teacher Keitese Lethoko, "make a lot of money brewing and selling traditional beer and since they can purchase all their own needs, they feel no need for a husband" (62). Head explores how women use tradition in order to maintain control over their productivity and transform the broader economic situation, which leaves women's labor in less productive, less skilled, and more low-paying niches.

Bessie Head's first novel, *When Rain Clouds Gather* (1969), explored the possibilities of a radical economic change through educating women toward collective involvement and public responsibility. In this novel, the British agriculturalist Gilbert Balfour came to Botswana to begin organizing cooperative farming. He discovered, however, that such a project would be impeded with the current division of labor where the men left the village for most of the year in order to tend the far-grazing of cattle while the women stayed home but lacked scientific knowledge for profitable agricultural production. "He felt that he had stumbled," Gilbert ruminates, "on to one of the major blockages to agricultural progress in the country. The women were the traditional tillers of the earth, not the men . . . But when it came to programmes for improved techniques in agriculture, soil conservation, the use of pesticides and fertilizers, and the production of cash crops, the lecture rooms were open to men only" (29). Closer to tradition, the women were also closer to developing a viable public sphere of production. Gilbert arranged for the women together to learn the construction of mud huts to dry tobacco leaves as cash crops for export. Such a revaluing of women's housework as substantial and even central for the community's well-being produced a political culture where the community, led by the women, joined together to overturn the power of an unjust chief. "Perhaps all change in the long run," Gilbert concludes, "would depend on the women of the country and perhaps they too could provide a number of solutions to the problems he had not yet thought of" (38).

Homework

Much Western feminist writing on education, particularly that based in psychology, has, unfortunately, been less sensitive to how ideological understandings of gender are used to implement and maintain the way productive forces operate and their power enforced to keep the public sector in check by keeping women's labor marginalized, excluded, subordinated, and undercompensated. Instead, feminist contributions to pscyhological theories of education tend to affirm an oppressive order of labor by insisting that the present order of gender needs validation to give women a better "recognition," "self-concept," or more "self-esteem." What is needed, such writers claim, is more attention to traditionally female roles, particularly in terms of elevating private, domestic, loving life as a model for liberatory knowledge. "The project of this text," begins, for example, Madeleine Grumet, "is to draw that knowledge of women's experience of reproduction and nurturance into the epistemological systems and curricular forms that constitute the discourse and practice of public education . . . I am suggesting that there is a dialectical relation between our domestic experience of nurturing children and our public project to educate the next generation" (149–50). Following on nineteenth-century conceptions of an organic feminine morality,[11] such theories say that female nurturance, a politics of caring, or women's relational ethics[12] undermines the domination put in place by objective, rational knowledge.

Such writing, however, does not acknowledge the vast amount of academic and feminist analysis on how such traditional values were fashioned as behavior codes for the dominant elite, nor how they have been shifted to control and punish poorer and nonwhite women. As bell hooks has pointed out, such premises that women's identities are defined through domestic roles assumed a privilege that most women were denied, as "only women with leisure time and money could actually shape their identities on the model of the feminine mystique" (1984: 2). Such metaphors of femininity, Anne McClintock among others has shown, turned up in narratives of progress and practices of hygiene instruction, spiritual guidance, and socialization where "imperialism [came] into being through *domesticity*" (32).[13] Kristin Ross has shown, as well, how domesticity worked to make colonial power and colonial torture of Algerians comfortable and familiar to French citizens: "Algeria, like France, will be the scene of some violent housecleaning[. . . E]veryday words and everyday places—kitchens and bathrooms—were beginning to take on new and horrific dimensions. The dark underside of French comfort emerges most clearly in the settings described in[. . .] the personal accounts of torture at the hands of the French military[. . .] The new techniques that were revolutionizing the countryside in France—the arrival, that is, of bathtubs (running water) and electricity—were putting a modern, more hygienic touch on torture as well" (108–113).

Still clinging to an ideal of domestic femininity as signifying the absence of power, many contemporary writers on feminist education have neglected to consider how, as McClintock emphasizes, "the colonies [. . .] became a theater for exhibiting the Victorian cult of domesticity" (34), nor how such mobilizations of femininity champion a decentering of authority that has recently become the ideological platform supporting privatization and voiding the power of democratic institutions through which the public has traditionally asserted its political decisions. Implicated in devaluing public involvement both at home and abroad as well as devaluing the thinking of education as a public good, such a celebration of femininity as the limit of governance has contributed to formulating Third World corporate work regimes of cheap labor as well as public disinvestments and limits to the Keynsian economic remedies of government stimulation and job creation.

Among the most influential of such writers, Elizabeth Ellsworth and Deborah Britzman advocate a feminist politics of the irrational based in the Oedipal domestic rather than a rationality conceived, in the democratic tradition, as public deliberation. For these writers, the irrational, the emotional, or the Unconscious—in other words, the pre-Symbolic mother-child dyad in Lacanian psychoanalysis—constitutes a "great refusal" to the bourgeois authority of the teacher's rational voice and renders communication impossible, a community of shared meanings and goals unrealizable, as the irrational constantly intervenes: "The hatred and fear of one's own implication in what's being taught," claims, for example, Ellsworth, "about the histories and operations of racism or sexism, for example, or about the Holocaust . . . can make forgetting or ignoring or not hearing an active, yet unconscious, refusal" (1997: 57). Suggesting that *not* learning about racism would be an act of radical opposition to authority, deliberately not differentiating between the exercise of authority and authoritarianism, Ellsworth alleges that by dismantling sense and logic in the name of recognizing feelings, rather than by developing analytical and critical practices of dissent, women would be freer. As Wendy Brown puts it,

> [C]ontemporary discourses of empowerment too often signal an oddly adaptive and harmonious relationship with domination insofar as they locate an individual's sense of worth and capacity in the register of individual feelings, a register implicitly located on something of an otherworldly plane vis-à-vis

> social and political power. In this regard, despite its apparent locution of resis-
> tance to subjection, contemporary discourses of empowerment partake
> strongly of liberal solipsism—the radical decontextualization of the subject
> characteristic of liberal discourse that is key to the fictional sovereign individu-
> alism of liberalism. Moreover, in its almost exclusive focus on subjects' emo-
> tional bearing and self-regard, empowerment is a formulation that converges
> with a regime's own legitimacy needs in masking the power of the regime.
> (22–23)

Furthermore, an analytic that situates power in self-esteem reproduces a commercial order that banks on the promotion of anxieties, lack, and inadequacy in order to sell consumer goods as satisfaction while masking that it is doing so.

The "feminist" argument that wants to valorize the home as a womanly space of love and caring has not stuck to investigating pedagogical meth-ods, but has also advocated curricular adjustments. Patricia J. Thompson writes of the virtues of keeping domesticity separated from notions of po-litical authority as a path toward feminist liberation: "in a society defined by men, women have been both invisible and voiceless. To the home eco-nomics professional . . . such ideas have special poignancy" (184). Thomp-son makes her argument in favor of home economics by separating the public sphere of suffrage politics (as represented by figures such as Susan B. Anthony) from the private sphere of what she calls a Hestian politics based on women's experience, focused on the domestic. In public school home economics classes today, students learn to sew on buttons, or com-bine into mostly heterosexualized pairs in order to care for an egg as practice for later caring for a child. As Henry Giroux states in an interview with Lilia Bartolome, "[W]e have to be vigilant about pedagogical ap-proaches that endorse notions of caring that either prevent the engage-ment of pertinent political issues at work in multicultural education or serve to produce other forms of 'benevolent' oppression' " (102). Talking about teaching as a practice of caring often means thinking about teaching as a set of methods, as when organizing classroom desks in the form of a circle is deemed the vehicle for democratic participation in politics. Such formalistic methods are evaluated as "working" or "not working" rather than in terms of what they work for, in whose interests they work, and what kinds of knowledge or learning are fostered. Home economics is a skill-based practice of self-care maintaining the female sphere as a haven from the political, the economic, and the rational, and thus fueling corpo-rate ideologies where freedom resides in the expansion of private power rather than in public alliances and supports. It also promotes ideas about tasking, piecework, and the like, ideas that make seem apolitical the pre-dominantly female forms of labor under newly dispersed manufacturing strategies. The current defensiveness of the stable, sanctified family unit—

spanning from the Christian Right to the mass media and Hollywood to feminist equal-pay-for-housework awareness campaigns, from antiabortion/antiwelfare politics to gay and lesbian marriage/gay and lesbian adoption advocacy—demonstrates that the idea of the home itself is struggled over as a projection of broader mechanisms of power and structures of domination in the social field.

Current home economics teaching does not talk about how the construction of domesticity fueled the unequal wage system of industrialization. As Nancy Fraser argues: "The construction of breadwinning and caregiving as separate roles, coded masculine and feminine respectively, is a principal undergirding of the current gender order" (61). Nor does home economics address how the field was conceived as a resistance to the subordination of women, calling for them to be assimilated into the hierarchies of rational knowledge and factorylike functionalism, instead of as a validation of domesticity's moral superiority because of its happy evasion of an oppressive rationality, as Barbara Ehrenreich and Deirdre English have shown. Nor does it talk about how learning about home management has been a vehicle of structural adjustment programs and sweatshop arrangements through which new forms of corporate imperialism are currently reorganizing Third World economies: "All over the world, home-based work (carried out by women) is an important source of employment. In seven African countries, 55 to 77 percent of enterprises are home-based" (Stromquist and Monkman). Rather, home economics today is designed to include women's naturalized experience of domesticity, nurturance, and relationships as the eternal and loving entrenchment of the current organization of labor, continuing in the legacy of industrialization where, as Jane Bernard Powers has pointed out, the central question in girls' education was whether to prepare girls for short-term industrial labor or to focus solely on home economics and domestic care, so that "the work skills they were trained in [would] be applicable to homemaking" (33). As Grace Chang indicates, "[T]he[. . .] state mediates the conflicting demands of capitalism for women to provide two functions: to remain in the home to reproduce and to maintain the labor force, and to undertake traditionally 'female' low wage work in the paid labor force" (70).

As globalization demonstrates, and as the history of home economics indicates, capitalist oppressions of women thrive on the expansion and affirmation of a naturalized, domestic sphere. Chandra Mohanty offers two examples of situations where women's labor is more easily exploitable because it is defined as the work of housewives in the private sphere. The first tells of lacemakers in Narsapur, India, where women work in "leisure time" out of their homes for the profit of the men who export and sell the finished items. The second describes the system of electronics assembly in California's Silicon Valley, where mostly immigrant women work in tedious, temporary jobs defined as supplementary to men's work even when they earn more. "Both kinds of work are done in the home, in isolation, with the worker paying her own overhead costs (like electricity and cleaning) with no legally mandated protections (such as minimum wage, paid leave, health benefits, etc.)" (1997: 17). *Clearly, women's experience is not invisible; it has been recognized. The problem then is not simply the marginalization of women's voices and experiences, but rather the way the current organization of capital transforms these voices and experiences into the central rationality of the new economy.*

By situating the private sphere as the locus of production, companies are able to bypass labor laws as well as to avoid labor organizing and other types of protections, stoppages, or auxiliary expenditures like providing child care, protecting the environment, and ensuring safety. Moreover, often without contracts or the heavy machinery of industrial factory space, systems of domestic labor ensure the possibilities of quick hirings and firings so they can respond quickly to the ever quickening changes of mass consumerism. Christa Wichterich paints homeworking as central to the expansion of the global economy, to the detriment and increased exploitation of women:

> Homeworking—for example, as ancillary work for the clothing sector or for electronics or precision engineering—is a kind of black hole in the industrialized economies, with piece-rates equivalent to much less than the legal minimum wage. Women are often offered loans on favourable terms to purchase a sewing machine of their own; they then have to cover all the electricity and repair costs. "Homeworking" . . . is women's work almost by definition . . . Sometimes homeworkers slave away more than twelve hours a day and seven days a week, for an hourly rate of around US$1.75. (23)

There is clearly a connection between corporate demands for labor flexibility and the paranoic demands for stable family life and home by politicians and religious leaders alike, even at a time when housing itself is becoming less affordable or available to many, especially in cities like New York, while in cities like Chicago, poor immigrants and people of color are being removed from their homes to make room for gut-rehab condos and gentrification.

Furthermore, immigrant women are recruited in the United States and elsewhere as home care helpers because, as Grace Chang observes, "Dominant US ideology identifies women as caretakers and women of color/Third World women especially as servants to nurture and clean up after First World elites" (113). Chang argues that a strategy of labor control is implemented in order to attract workers in certain low-wage positions without providing benefits, income supports, living wages, social services, or enforcing rights. Clearly, educating girls (and/or boys) in an ethics based on private caring human relationships and nurturance rather than principles of abstract justice and rational critique is not giving them the tools that they need to combat women's subordination and economic dependency.

Furthermore, the recourse to women's experience in such feminist views uses a conservative view of gender to bolster liberalization and public sector cutbacks. Even as Laura Bush was lauding the pedagogical virtues of the mother-child dyad, protestors demanding more fair and equitable housing and health care policies were denied marching permits from the City of Philadelphia, labeled "radicals" and arrested, the civil rights of some violated and many held for several days without access to telephones, on trumped-up charges, and at exorbitant bail-out rates.[14] Surely, the Republicans and the Philadelphia administration make it clear that elevating domesticity, nurturance, and home-sweet-home to a sacred position within politics does not guarantee that women's needs will be met.

The symbolics of feminine domesticity and nurturance insist that private power should expand without regard for public controls, community interests, social demands, or the basic necessities of the disadvantaged. However, privatization is beneficial to neither women nor children. Current education initiatives are failing not principally because of the breaking apart of traditional families, but rather because of the inavailability of textbooks, overcrowded classrooms, deteriorating buildings, cuts in the provision of breakfasts and lunches to poor children, the insufficiency of standardized tests as an objective guiding content choices, making public schools compete for funds with other better-off public and private schools, corporate interventions in lesson design, or the system's inability to make the curriculum relevant to many students' experiences, in other words, in the complete disregard for the nurturance and care of children.

Serowe

I only took Brecht's dictum: We must help.

—Bessie Head

In *Serowe: Village of the Rain-Wind*, students are not simply trained in skills for integration in a global corporatist, privatized economy. The education they received in primary and secondary was also meant to instill in students the idea of reciprocal service and cooperative responsibility. The age regiments used for tribal initiation (*bogwera*) were turned into work regiments that could be called upon to do collective labor, such as building schools, in the service of self-help and community development. The work Brigades were each dedicated both to teaching and to practicing a certain field or skill like building, gardening, weaving, basket making, and tanning, and each part of a "broadly based creative, educational programme" (145).

The program was supposed to be self-sufficient, with the gardening Brigade growing enough food for the entire school, the building Brigade erecting all the buildings. "The wonder of it is how eager and prepared very poor people are to share everything with each other—some work groups like the pottery house and the stone masons have higher earnings than the others and often tend to carry everyone else on their backs" (171–172). Learning to perform household chores did not isolate women or subject them to a specific type of domestically oriented exploitation. As one schoolteacher explains, "[T]he children were taught not to despise the traditional tasks of their parents—they stamped corn, worked in the gardens, baked their own bread, milked their own cows—all the food they ate. And all the students, boys and girls, had to take a compulsory course in agriculture and domestic science" (85). The purpose of such an education was to make students "feel under some compulsion to fight hunger, poverty and ignorance in their country . . . [W]e will certainly discourage any notion that education is just a ladder which ambition climbs to privilege" (136). This agenda was implemented by leading students to be "agents of progress" (137), showing how their position within a working society was part of a global support of public culture.

Alongside their involvement in the Brigades, students were required to take a course of Developmental Studies:

> We study local production and economic institutions like banks, how advertising manipulates us all, how our local Consumers' Co-operative Society Stores work, how prices in the local supermarket vary with supply and demand, and so on . . . [W]e try to create a greater awareness of their own privileged position in society and to instil sympathy for the less privileged. Always we try to use active, question-centred teaching methods; the aim is to avoid getting the students simply to repeat what the teacher or some book has told them, and instead to think for themselves. This is helped by the fact that much of the course material is controversial—we cover topics as planned or market economies, the workings of a one-party state, and so on . . . [Development Studies] is linked to a programme of manual work . . . whereby the students make some contribution to the upkeep and development of their school and the local community. (141)[15]

As described here, the course makes it clear that the school opens up a public forum for both understanding world capitalism and thinking outside of it, creating, as Zymunt Bauman has articulated the politics of public life in a democracy, a "space where private problems meet in a meaningful way—that is, not just to draw narcissistic pleasures or in search of some therapy through public display, but to seek collectively managed levers powerful enough to lift individuals from their privately suffered misery; the space where such ideas may be born and take shape as the 'public good,' the 'just society' or 'shared values' " (1999: 3–4).

The politics of the public sphere in Botswana seem to offer it certain amounts of leverage vis-à-vis the global politics of imperialism. Diamonds were discovered in the Botswana territory after Independence, allowing a greater prosperity in Botswana than in many other African nations, including a greater per-capita income in real terms, because Botswana has been able to maintain national ownership of the mines. Currently, however, it is estimated that one-third of Botswana's population is dying or has died of AIDS, and this situation is confounded, the PBS *NewsHour* has reported, by the breakdown in the institution of marriage and by a traditional conservatism when it comes to talking about matters of sex. In face of this crisis, the national government in Botswana has been able to do more for its suffering population than other African governments because its national income is higher. The government has treated AIDS and AIDS education as a public concern and has invested in innovative outreach programs, including utilizing the existing structures of labor in the national mines to spread preventative information and treatment medication, often coming up against the interests of multinational pharmaceutical companies and global intellectual property rights laws.

Clearly, to use *Serowe* as a model for radical educational reform in the United States has its problems.[16] Bessie Head's work has been criticized as utopian for "attempts to construct models of idealized societies" and for providing "avenues for escape into the timeless-fantasies of the imagination as a means of resolving or escaping actual harrowing life experiences" (Ogwude). However, as Henry Giroux has argued, utopianism has often "been a driving force of dominant powers, extending from the Christian church, which proclaims it as one of the three cardinal virtues, to corporate management teams that use posters, financial incentives, and other rewards to manipulate workers by fostering a hope that cancels out forms of despair and resentment" (2001: 110). Certainly, as discussed in chapter 4, the idea of a utopian future has been mobilized on the part of right-wing neoliberals to talk about the market and privatization as the harbinger of equality, freedom, and the disappearance of social problems, illness, and economic hardship, when in actuality, the so-called free market simply sweeps the problems of its own making—e.g., pollution, poverty, and war—under the rug, uncountable in standard double-entry accounting, often disassociated from its causes and from those responsible. Acccording to Giroux, the left needs to claim back utopias "as a crucial component for those who want to reclaim a notion of ethical advocacy and radically charged politics that provides the basis for reimagining and struggling for a substantive and vital democratic social order 'grounded in broad-based civic participation and popular decision making'" (2001: 119). Head's construction of a public sphere is saturated in just this sort of utopian thinking.

The utopian drift of Bessie Head's writing, however, limits its potential application to an actual educational future in three ways. The first is that Bessie Head refused the label of feminist on a number of occasions, because, she said, "The world of the intellect is impersonal, sexless" (Eilersen, 238). This position is, historically and culturally, simply untenable. The gendering of intellectual work needs to be looked at as part of a general gendering of labor, and as a mechanism for solidifying such epistemological commonplaces as the relegation of women's work and thought to the bodily labor of reproducing the species while attributing to masculinity the directive powers for thinking through the world's future.[17]

Additionally, Bessie Head's attitude toward race is sometimes escapist, seeming to want to outdo racism and apartheid by imagining it away. "If I had to write one day," she explains, "I would just like to say people is people and not damn white, damn black. Perhaps if I was a good enough writer I could still write damn White, damn Black and still make people live. Make them real, Make you love them, not because of the colour of their skin but because they are important as human beings" (Eilersen, 55). Bessie Head's novel about teaching, *Maru* (1971), talks about a Masarwa woman teacher who overcomes racial discrimination in the village by proving herself noble, appealing, and marriageable, thereby offsetting any discussion about how racism furthers the interests of certain classes and certain codes of class, nor about how overcoming racial discrimination, as shown in *Serowe*, would take more than an assertion of individual will. This idea that racism can be combated and overturned through an appeal to the human bypasses a history of racial oppression and colonialism where racialism and racism were enforced in the name of the human. This is not to say that a humanist politics is historically made unlikely, but rather that humanism needs to allow for recognizing racial differences in order to become political. As Bessie Head herself points out, "It's not so much a question of being black as of having control of life's learning" (as cited in Driver, 176). In the United States and around the world, having "control of one's learning" is very much a question of race.

Furthermore, though Bessie Head had a short-lived involvement with the PAC (a more militant, pan-Africanist, and nationalist wing of the African National Congress), she also repudiated Marxism, even while professedly dedicating herself to combating poverty and hunger.[18] Not instead espousing any other type of broad-based economic reform or political theory or theories of social change, she thereby limited the types of historical perspectives and theoretical programs for change she could use to supplement, contextualize, and globalize her visions for development. Untutored in the possibilities of dialectical or revolutionary transformation, Bessie Head's politics were sometimes disappointingly, often cynically, and quite mistakenly tied into her studies of Eastern religions and, specifically, reincarnation: "The only thing that will break South Africa," she wrote, "is the supernatural and unknown . . . the unexpected sort of judgement day . . . No one can fight evil in the ordinary way with ordinary weapons. So I hold out for the miracle" (Eilersen, 197). White domination stood for an evil that would be eradicated in cosmic combat with good spirits, but would always return in another form.

However, Head's vision of the construction of a public sphere can become a call for federal responsibility toward the public and specifically toward empowering its institutions rather than marginalizing them. I am not suggesting here a "human capital" model of education, where investments in students are made for the future job market, but rather a model where students learn how they can have a relative say in their own conditions of life and what can be the democratic and public institutions that support them. Unlike in Botswana, many of the problems hitting public schools in the United States today have to do with unfair public funding distributions leading to overextended teaching loads, inadequate facilities, standardized curricula, reassigning teachers, large classrooms, closing schools, the contracting of public schools to private companies, and the like. The defunding of, say, schooling in the inner cities needs to be looked at in relation to a broader defunding of the public sphere in general, from the closing of public parks to the dismantling of public supports in the welfare system. As Henry Giroux points out, in the U.S. case,

> The increasing influence of corporate power in commercializing youth and eliminating the noncommercial spheres where youth meet and develop a sense of agency and autonomy is certainly related to corporate culture's attempts to turn institutions of public and higher education over to the imperatives of the market. Moreover, the continued devaluation of education as a public good points to the need for educators to work together to reclaim schools as democratic public spheres. (2000: 26)[19]

Schooling in Serowe is not about turning kids into corporate drudges in an economy that disenfranchises them, nor is it about isolating the limits to government in order to define freedom of expression alone as contrary to power. Rather, schools are about reimagining public power on a global scale.

Head looks at the school itself as at the center of global politics, as it helps to establish a democratic public sphere, exposing the political conservatism of the current system, which focuses on isolated information and personal skills, denying the possibilities of collective association, political awareness, public association, public works, global critique, and resistance. As well, Bessie Head is able to offer an idea of education spearheading economic transformations, new ways of economic organization and distribution, and equity linked to the development of a public sphere. Bessie Head's educational vision provides a way of thinking about work that is not all about personal ambition, advancement, and autonomy, nor is it about creating comfort zones of love or raising self-esteem. Rather, schooling here should forward a public agenda, providing an education geared toward establishing a knowledgeable, democratic, civic, global vision rather than a privatized, depoliticized, consumerist bliss where private power is deified to produce consent for privatization, deregulation, and exploitation. Feminism must overcome the instrumentalization of gender, which justifies unequal economic and political distributions, work agendas, and private accumulation and continues to make women's domestic labor exploitable for cheap at exponentially increasing rates.

CHAPTER **6**

Conclusion

World, Class, Women has criticized some ways that feminist agendas are being constructed, particularly as expressed within the field of feminist pedagogy and the theoretical perspectives that support it. It challenges the ways that the feminist subject, as the bulwark of feminist empowerment, is fashioned around the idea of privacy separated from political power. It indicates that such an idea of privacy—focused as it is on workplace, professionalism, family, and home—precludes a necessary thinking of the direction of the public to set future agendas, supporting instead a set of meanings that undergird private power in the form of corporate accumulation, commercialism, and global management. Some of the terms that *World, Class, Women* identifies in this way are: identity, independence, emotions, caring, domesticity, irrationality, the personal, the Imaginary, desire, consumption, the Unconscious, marginality.

World, Class, Women shows how these terms are wielded in order to support such practices as privatization, deregulation, outsourcing, contracting, the cheapening of labor, the move toward service labor, and the infiltration of global corporations into local economies. It then talks about how all these neoliberal systems of labor management are contributing to the impoverishment of women. It uses education to discuss the vital demand to counter neoliberal governance through constructing a public, democratic sphere. It uses gender to indicate how the building of a public sphere requires the breaking apart of the coded schemes of privacy and private ownership that women and women's labor often have been corralled to represent. It suggests the dangers to sovereignty, the environment, feminism, racial justice, and peace if the corporate order would continue to diminish public institutions and their power in order to build its own empire and indiscriminately pursue its own interests. It leads us to think about how in the current moment, our very ideas of political agency are powerfully inflected by the interests of oil, media, manufacturing, and other large industries as seen in many popular beliefs about labor, citizenship, diversity, family, ethnicity, schools, and childhood.

The unimaginability of the public within much of contemporary politics is leading to crisis. For example, the unilateralism of the Bush administration is reducing politics to images of personal vendetta or human interest, even as it is undermining the multilateralism necessary for world health, debt relief, aid, development, and schemes to end poverty and hunger that have fallen from the public agenda. President Bush's $10 billion pledge in his 2003 State of the Union address to fight AIDS in Africa was followed in February with the administration trying to block a congressional decision to provide an additional $150 million to a Global Fund to fight AIDS (essentially freezing the level of contribution to that of previous years) as well as a $500 million cut in international child health programs, at the same time building a lobby against an agreement that would loosen patent controls on pharmaceuticals in order to facilitate generic imports or domestic manufacturing capability (Booker).

I conclude by again emphasizing the limitations of grounding theory in a politics of the private and the importance of thinking globally about the role of the public. In the face of corporate pressures and the corporate-controlled structural adjustment programs of the IMF, which are strangling public health and child protections among other public functions, the demise of the welfare state—the traditional compromise between labor and capital—has led to an insufficiency of institutions to defend human, environmental, health, and labor rights. These institutions have not been replaced by global structures of governance or democracies but only with management agreements, loan administration, and militarization. Free trade is being institutionalized in treaties which form into governing bodies, and these agreements have been able to override, in many occasions, national governance in issues of taxation, tariffs, policing, social service expenditures, environment, labor, military functions, and the like.

As the state has often historically functioned as an arm of capital and as one of the main locations of domination in both socialist and capitalist camps, it is right to be suspicious of it. As Samir Amin has observed, "Our real world is and will for a long time remain founded on a grand contradiction between the globalization of the economy, based on a truncated market system which included trading in commodities and capital but excludes migration of labor power, and the persistence of the national state as the structure for the regulation of politics and social life" (1997: 49–50). The current model of the nation-state certainly does back the initiatives of accumulation and consolidation which are fueling the technology sector and defense companies, among others. As well, the nation-state is instrumental in the enormous growth of global militarism, the arms trade, weapons subcontracting, and the like, reaching beyond national borders as it expands hegemonically and territorially to an unprecedented degree even as it encourages militaristic cultures in foreign countries where its interests are at stake.

Though it is uncontestable, as Neil Lazarus notes, following Immanuel Wallerstein, that capitalism created itself as "a *world system* from the outset" (24) with a tendency to "create a world market" (25), it is equally clear that the rise and consolidation of corporate power in the last decades has seriously and fundamentally changed the nature of governance, the institution of the nation-state, and the relationship between public law and private interest. For example, even before September 11, under new trade agreements like NAFTA and the proposed FTAA, private companies were allowed to sue state and national governments if they wrote laws inflicting damage to future profits. In the 1999 case *Methanex v. United States*, a Canadian methanol plant filed suit against California for phasing out the production of a gas cleaner that contaminated drinking water in Santa Monica.[1] Such actions will set precedents for future suits, meaning not only that local public governments will not be able to pass legislation that protects the public from corporate pollutants, but also that, for example, educational companies could take legal action against public schools, even in other countries, for "unfair competition" because they receive "government subsidies." Severely restricting the nation-state's abilities to build its public institutions, encourage domestic production, and to invest long-term in future prosperity (as did the welfare state), "free-trade" arrangements, more often than not, let corporate activity transcend the laws and responsibilities of a nation-state.

Control of public institutions, spaces, and meanings are struggled over in a democratic society. Though capital growth has always relied on the state, the current phase of capital has witnessed, as Zygmunt Bauman has observed, a shrinking of representative government institutions that might check some of the expansionary power of capital:

> We may say that, with extant political institutions no longer able to slow down the speed of capital movements, power is increasingly removed from politics— a circumstance which accounts simultaneously for growing political apathy, the progressive disinterestedness of the electorate in everything "political"

> except the juicy scandals perpetrated by top people in the limelight, and the waning of expectations that salvation may come from government buildings, whoever their current or future occupants may be. (1999: 19)

It is necessary to think the public as both autonomous from the state and as connected to it. It is also necessary to think of other ways of fashioning other subjects and other languages to describe this process through terms like democracy and public education that still carry the force of politics and participation. Ideas about identity and resistance must take into account the global nature of contemporary capitalism, the rise of private over public power, the dispersed sites of identification in global consumer culture where needs for labor are in constant flux, and the insufficient scope of the model of a territorially defined nation-state as the future keeper of essential democratic values. It is necessary to start thinking about what such institutions of democratic governance—elections, courts, schools, etc.—would look like if instituted on a global plain. Public institutions presently provide a context for viable political participation and opposition as well as (up until now) the most powerful policy-tool for redistributing income, rights, and social promise in more equitable ways. Because of its historical analysis of the shaping of private and public spheres through the Enlightenment and industrialization, feminism can and must contribute to challenging the private appropriation of imagining public power and, also, to shaping the democratic hopes of the public's global future.

Notes

Introduction

1. I am sympathetic to Ella Shohat's use of the term "Third World": "The term *postcolonial* carries with it the implication that colonialism is now a matter of the past, undermining colonialism's economic, political, and cultural deformative traces in the present. The postcolonial inadvertently glosses over the fact that, even in the post–cold war era, global hegemony persists in forms other than overt colonial rule. As a signifier of a new historical epoch, when compared with *neocolonialism,* the term *postcolonial* comes equipped with little evocation of contemporary power relations; it lacks a political content that can account for the 1980s- and 1990s- style U.S. militaristic involvements in Granada, Panama, and Kuwait-Iraq and for the symbiotic links between U.S. political and economic interests and those of local elites" (132). Meanwhile, "[d]espite differences and contradictions among and within Third World countries, the term *Third World* contains a common project of (linked) resistances to neocolonialisms[. . .] Perhaps, it is this sense of a common project around which to mobilize that is missing from the post(anti)colonial discussions. If the terms *postcolonial* and *postindependence* stress, in different ways, a rupture in relation to colonialism and *neocolonial* emphasizes continuities, *Third World* usually evokes structural commonalities of struggles. The invocation of the Third World implies a belief that the shared history of neocolonialism and internal racism forms sufficient common ground for alliances among such diverse peoples" (138).

Chapter 1

1. Giroux' thinking here is in line with a tradition of U.S. democratic thinking. Thomas Jefferson: "I hope we shall crush in its birth the aristocracy of our moneyed corporations, which dare already to challenge our government to a trial of strength and bid defiance to the laws of our country." Abraham Lincoln (1864): "I see in the near future a crisis approaching that unnerves me and causes me to tremble for the safety of my country. As a result of the war, corporations have been enthroned and an era of corruption in high places will follow, and the money power of the country will endeavor to prolong its reign until all wealth is aggregated in a few hands, and the Republic is destroyed. I feel at this moment more anxiety for the safety of my country than ever before, even in the midst of the war" (as cited in Danaher, 42).
2. Most famous for the short story "The Yellow Wallpaper" (1892), about women's hysteria and postpartum depression, and the novella *Herland* (1915), a feminist utopia where women, isolated in a mountain range, have learned to produce and reproduce without men.

3. Walkerdine and Lucey, however, make the mistake of blaming the Frankfurt School for attributing the irrational to the working classes, and so helping to fashion the need for the regulation of working-class mothers. In particular, they fault Horkheimer and Adorno for talking about the masses as irrational: "The working-class family began to be blamed for the production of a regimented authoritarianism. Before and after the war, natural democracy was asserted with a new vigour. We argue that the Frankfurt School's position on fascism builds upon precisely what we are opposing: that the masses really are mad and irrational and that what has to be asserted is the rule of the rational. In particular, the guarantees of democracy were to be assured by a science of mothering which held women responsible for the future of the next generation" (1989: 42). The matter in Horkheimer and Adorno is of course more complicated: the irrational grants power to the rational, and capitalism itself works through irrationality, as the next chapter on Harry Potter indicates. Not only does Walkerdine and Lucey's interpretation misrepresent the history of critical theory, but it also presents reason as operating purely as repression, even in terms of the way it assigns meanings. This completely denies the Frankfurt School's insight that reason can be used against itself for the goals of emancipation.

4. According to Yannis Stavrakakis, this is not a fair or complete interpretation of Lacan. For Stavrakakis, the purpose of communicational gaps in Lacan is not to make communication impossible, but to invoke the possibility to create out of the wreckage a total utopian fantasy, "a dream, however, that was designed as a perfect solution to the inherent division of the social" (115), allowing the recuperation of complete communication. Additionally, the Lacanian concept of the Symbolic allows a place for the social, something which has been erased by Ellsworth's secluding of the teacher-student dyad within a force field of the psyche.

Chapter 2

1. Farah Mendlesohn: "[W]hen Harry's parents died, they left him substantial amounts of money. In normal circumstances, any court would release some portion of that money for his care. Instead, Harry's proper guardians, the wizards and their government, deliberately choose to leave him to unknown relatives who are expected to care for him without recompense or assistance[...] And while the Dursleys are vile, the wizardly decision not to provide financial support for their care of Harry is not based upon this judgement, for the wizards provide no evidence that they have taken this into account" (172).

2. Rowlings gives generously to the National Council for One Parent Families, Maggie's Centres of Edinburgh, which gives counseling support to cancer victims and their families, and the MS Society of Scotland.

3. John Williams, "Look, Child Poverty in the Wealthy Countries Isn't Necessary," *The International Herald Tribune,* 24 July 2000. See also Chris Hartman, ed., "Facts and Figures": "nine states have reduced child poverty rates by more than 30% since 1993. These states include Tennessee, Michigan, Arkansas, South Carolina, Mississippi, Kentucky, Illinois and New Jersey. Michigan is a prime example of a national trend, in that even the recent dramatic improvement did not counter the losses of the previous 15 years, in which its poverty rate increased 121%. In California, the number of children living in poverty has grown from 900,000 in 1979, to 2.15 million in 1998. (Columbia University)."

4. Both Joan Acocella in *The New Yorker* and children's media critic Jann Lacoss have remarked on the correspondence between the Harry Potter series and the Russian formalist's work on the folktale.

5. See "Carpentier's Magical Conception" in *Infertilities: Exploring Fictions of Barren Bodies.*

6. See "Rivers of Fire: Amoco's Impact on Education" by Robin Truth Goodman and Kenneth J. Saltman in *Strange Love: Or How We Learn to Stop Worrying and Love the Market* (Lanham, MD, and Boulder, CO: Rowman & Littlefield, 2002).

7. See Schapiro, 18.

8. According to a follow-up study on the Fourth World Conference on Women and The World Summit for Social Development, the number of women in the workforce in OECD Countries grew by twice that of men in the 1980s. In Europe, women have made up seven million of the eight million newly employed. Women migrate more for work, and women in developing countries work longer hours, while they compose 80 percent of those working in export pro-

cessing zones. Women also work more in service jobs (71 percent in the Carribean; 60 percent in developing countries) and agricultural jobs (80 percent in sub-Saharan Africa; 50 percent in Asia). Meanwhile, women compose only 14 percent of administrative and management jobs and less than 6 % of senior management jobs worldwide (Lim).

9. Though Marcuse was talking about the cold war and the way ordinary people were lured into accepting its insane premises of détente and mutual destruction by investing in expensive, luxury fallout shelters replete with TVs, the theory can be applied similarly to today's insanity of war where there is a growing post–September 11 commercial market for high-tech "panic rooms," manifesting people's "inner life" identification with the advertising, public relations, opinion polls, media blitz, and political speech that introduces and reproduces afterimages of terror as the rationale behind expanded U.S. aggressions in places having no tie to the terrorist attack.

10. Marcuse's romanticization of the alienation of the working classes builds into a nostalgia for what he seems to see as the good ol' days of exploitation. Nevertheless, Marcuse's theory does, I believe, provide a way of thinking through why the powerless, the disenfranchised, the working classes, and the alienated often currently identify with the irrational workings of power.

Chapter 3

1. Keri Hulme has also acknowledged the support of other institutions such as the New Zealand Literary Fund, ICI, Otago University, the Maori Trust, Auckland University Press and the literary journal *Islands.*

2. "Mobil de Venezuela, an affiliate of Mobil Corporation, was established in 1994. It is involved in all aspects of the Venezuelan petroleum industry, from a joint venture with PDVSA and Veba Oel to produce 120,000 barrels a day of heavy oil from the Cerro Negro field in the Orinoco tar belt by 2001 to exploration on the La Ceiba block on the southeastern shore of Lake Maracaibo. The company has also begun Phase 1 engineering for a new olefins plant in Jose in a 50/50 joint venture with Pequiven. Mobil is also the leading brand among private lubes marketing companies and recently entered the Venezuelan fuels market with plans to brand over 200 service stations in the next three years" (*Business Wire*).

3. *The Bone People* is, to date, the only Pegasus novel originally written in English. Mobil's promotion explicitly states that part of its purpose is to counter "the one-way flow of translated fiction in the U.S."

4. On the global level, this tendency on the part of MobilExxon to destroy public forums, decision-making power, and institutions in order to privatize the economy in its own interest has further escalated currently into a war where MobilExxon and its compatriots like ChevronTexaco, ConocoPhillips, BPAmoco, and Kellogg Brown and Root, a subsidiary of Halliburton, have been bidding for contracts to clean up Iraq and secure the oil wells (Reuters).

5. "For the past thirty years, the world price of oil has been "managed" by governments, albeit with haphazard results. The price was maintained by the OPEC cartel of oil-producing nations, with discreet consultations from the United States and other industrial powers. Before OPEC, the world price of oil had been managed since the thirties by the fabled Seven Sisters, global oil corporations that still have an influential voice in the conversations. Oil-price diplomacy, for obvious reasons, is mostly done in deep privacy" (Greider).

6. This is most likely related to the oil industry's most pressing promotional and customer relations problem: how to dull public fears over oil spills.

7. As history creeps forward toward increasing technologization and increasing centralized control of capital, politics goes from Social Democracy to Labour to Socialism and the factory replaces the fields in a flash without distinction, as though it made no difference who the faces were as long as the historical currents of capitalist transformation eeked on in their mysterious way.

8. In fact, the voice of property is the promise of democracy, which, in turn, is the promise to do business: "What it's all about is the fact that the land has no rightful heirs. Who are the owners? The occupants are a few peasants who till their plots with no titles of ownership that give them anything; that's why I don't believe in democracy" (Ana Teresa Torres, 200).

9. Chavez had been democratically elected in 1998 with an 80 percent approval rating. His popularity had since fallen to around 30 percent. His drop in popularity has been variously attributed to the slowness of his regime's ability to deliver on promises of reform to the poor as much as by the media's onslaught of negative attention. Many have speculated that the high numbers of participants in the strike and in the protest resulted from the closing of businesses affiliated with the oil industry even while most of the people who could go to work (because their places of work remained open), did so. See Wilpert, Wilpert, and Lebowitz. Though it is yet unclear how the political turmoil in a country that ships almost as much oil to the United States as Saudi Arabia is related to the broader "war on terror," it is broadly accepted that the current rise in price of gas at the pump which encouraged prowar sentiment in the United States was fueled, so to speak, by Venezuela's crisis.

10. It is still unclear who shot first, though most of the dead were Chavez supporters (Wilpert, "Coup in Venezuela").

11. "If marriage still too often resembles a master/subject relation, this is due in large measure to its social embeddedness in relation to sex-segmented labor markets, gender-structured social-welfare policy regimes, and the gender division of unpaid labor" (Nancy Fraser, 228).

12. "In 1971, 90 percent of international financial transactions were related to the real economy—trade or long-term investment—and 10 percent were speculative. By 1990 the percentages were reversed, and by 1995 about 95 percent of the vastly greater sums were speculative, with daily flows regularly exceeding the combined foreign exchange reserves of the seven biggest industrial powers, over $1 trillion a day, and very short-term: about 80 percent with round trips of a week or less. Prominent economists warned over 20 years ago that the process would lead to a low-growth, low-wage economy, and suggested fairly simply measures that might prevent these consequences. But the principal architects of the Washington consensus preferred the predictable effects, including very high profits. These effects were augmented by the (short-term) sharp rise in oil prices and the telecommunications revolution" (Noam Chomsky, 24).

13. "[A]s a race, we *like* fighting" (original emphasis; Keri Hulme, 338).

14. "The White Nation has offered the concept of 'multiculturalism' to Pacific Island people," Donna Awatere adds. "The hidden agenda of this offer is to align Pacific Peoples to the White Nation[. . .]. However the "multiculturalism" offered to Pacific peoples is not decision-making power, it is another lizard's trick, a continuation of white power dressed up in tapa cloth. True multiculturalism would mean that Pacific Island people must be part of the economic, political and philosophical policy making systems. This will *never* occur under white sovereignty" (37–40).

15. "The state's upholding of these[. . .] narratives of identity has meant that small tribes . . . have been forced to bury their historical traditions and tribal identities and adopt those of larger, more powerful tribes if they are to compete for resources," concludes Maxwell (197).

16. The Chicago Cultural Studies Group has convincingly pointed out that "[i]t is far from clear whether a multicultural emphasis in education will result in a more democratically critical society or rather in one with more subtle international administrative abilities" (115).

17. Advocates for environmental reform have pointed out that the oil industry as a whole is in the business of expanding hegemonic, neo-colonial controls through expanding the areas of extraction. "According to the San Francisco–based Transnational Resource and Action Center (TRAC), 'Big Oil's long-term strategy is still dictated by the urge to explore.' New exploration as well as oil or gas pipelines threaten the survival of peoples in the Amazon basin, Southeast Asia, and North America. BP Amoco, the world's largest solar company, is committed to spending $5 billion in the next 5 years on oil exploration and production in the sensitive environment of Alaska alone. This dwarfs the trifling sum of $45 million recently spent on its solar business division[. . .]. Other companies such as the combined Exxon-Mobil, the world's largest oil corporation, are doing even less to develop renewables. In the global economy, the unsustainable expansion of corporate activities into ever-larger markets means that there is an almost irresistible force driving the formation of megacompanies of all types[. . .]. At Exxon and Mobil, job losses will exceed 9,000. As TRAC notes, Exxon had already been cutting jobs at the rate of 4 per cent every year for over a decade" (Cromwell).

18. In 1998, the richest 1 percent of the population owned 42.1 percent of stocks, mutual funds and retirement accounts. The bottom 90 percent owned 36.6 percent (Wolff).

19. "Thrown into this chiastic field a phenomenon I invoke often: the shift into transnationalism in the early seventies through the computerization of the big stock exchanges. Of course, changes in the mode of production of value do not bring about matching changes in the constitution of the subject. But one is often surprised to notice how neatly the ruses change in that arena that engages in coding subject-production: cultural politics. And the universities, the journals, the institutes, the exhibitions, the publishers' series are rather overly involved here. Keeping the banal predictability of the cultural apparatus in transnational society firmly in mind, it can be said that the shift into transnationalism brought a softer and more benevolent Third Worldism into the Euramerican academy[. . .]. It is in this newer context that the postcolonial diasporic can have the role of an ideologue. This 'person' [. . .] belonging to a basically collaborative elite, can be uneasy for different kinds of reasons with being made the object of unquestioning benevolence as an inhabitant of the new Third World[. . .]. This produces a comfortable 'other' for transnational postmodernity[. . .]. In fact, most postcolonial areas have a class-specific access to the society of information-command telematics inscribed by microelectronic transnationalism. And indeed, the discourse of cultural specificity and difference, packaged for transnational consumption along the lines sketched above, is often deployed by this specific class" (Spivak, "Who Claims Alterity?" 275–276). Spivak cites as evidence the National Governors' Report issued in Washington on February 24, 1989, which "calls for more language learning and culture learning, because otherwise the U.S. will be "outcompeted" (290).

20. "America is moving from a country in which companies guaranteed an employee's pension through a defined 'set of benefits' to a country in which many companies now just guarantee a defined 'contribution, and the individual manages his or her own money and shifts it around, according to where he or she can get the best return. And with people now living longer, and wondering whether Social Security will be there when they want to retire, they are not only turning to these mutual funds and pension funds in an aggressive manner but also managing them very aggressively for higher returns" (Thomas Friedman, 51).

21. "He could never imagine his great-grandfather, who had taken part in several feasts of people, as a cannibal. He remembered the old man only as a picture of a silver-haired fiercely dignified chief. He'd always imagined cannibals to be little wizened people, with pointy teeth. 'We're meat, same as anything else,' his grandmother had said" (Keri Hulme, 335).

22. Frequently, blockages to democracy are exhibited in the press, by the national or international spin-weavers, and/or through culture, as resulting from unbridgeable gulfs between ethnic groups, or, as post–cold war cultural logic suggests, from the resurgence of ancient ethnic rivalries or incompatible cultural practices. As Michel Feher has shown, throughout the 1990s, the masters of the international community continually claimed that all post–cold war world conflicts "were about "tribal" disputes—over land, resources, ethnic or religious supremacy, and so forth—rather than rival ideologies and adverse political projects" (Feher, 40). Yet, as E. Ike Udogu has argued "a focus on ethnicity obscures the fact that . . . , ethnic movements may be encouraged and incited to action by the political "princes" who accede to power and use it to further their individual and group interests. In a way, therefore, ethnicity becomes a mask for class privileges" (Udogu, 159–172).

Chapter 4

1. "[I]n most countries we have surveyed, the value of extralegal real estate alone is many times greater than total savings and time deposits in commercial banks, the value of companies registered in local stock exchanges, all foreign direct investment, and all public enterprises privatized and to be privatized together" (86).

2. "[T]hey hold these resources in defective forms: houses built on land whose ownership rights are not adequately recorded, unincorporated businesses with undefined liability, industries located where financiers and investors cannot see them. Because the rights to these possessions are not adequately documented, these assets cannot readily be turned into capital, cannot be traded outside of narrow local circles where people know and trust each other, cannot be used as collateral for a loan, and cannot be used as a share against an investment" (2000: 5–6).

3. Burbules and Torres: "The broader economic effects of globalization tend to force educational policies into a neoliberal framework that emphasizes lower taxes; shrinking the state

sector and 'doing more with less'; promoting market approaches to school choice (particularly vouchers); rational management of school organizations; performance assessment (testing); and deregulation in order to encourage new providers (including on-line providers) of educational services" (20). Also, "Corporations are becoming so powerful that many are creating their own postsecondary and vocational education programs. Burger King has opened 'academies' in fourteen U.S. cities, and IBM and Apple are contemplating the idea of opening schools for profit . . . [C]orporate influence over the nation-state is exercised indirectly, through intellectual leadership, instilling policymakers a new set of values and setting limits on the nation-state's range of options, which is a more effective strategy in changing policy priorities than the explicit threat of punitive sanctions. The new values . . . promote less intervention and greater reliance on the free market, and more appeal to individual self-interest than to collective rights" (8–9).

4. Saltman: "Urban and largely nonwhite schools are being targeted for military invasion in the form of retired soldiers being installed as teachers. Brainchild of the Clinton administration, the 'Troops to Teachers' program was designed to provide work for retired soldiers and at the same time to provide 'good role models' and disciplined instruction for children in understaffed urban public schools . . . The militaristic turn has a highly assimilationist economic efficiency justification for education. Within such a view, discipline and the emphasis on strong self-discipline translate into an undemocratic form of social decision making, as the social good becomes determined by the rule of private power not of the students' or most citizens' making" (2000: 91–92).

5. The Nigerian government has identified literary production as dangerous to its hold on power, as in 1995, before widespread international outcry, it executed nine poets who were Oguni environmental activists, and then exiled its most celebrated novelists. Writes Howard W. French for the *New York Times:* "Nigeria's military Government charged a Nobel laureate, Wole Soyinka, and 11 other dissidents with a series of bombings of army installations . . . The Government of Nigeria's military ruler, Gen. Sani Abacha, has already drawn strong international condemnation for the November 1995 execution of prominent author Ken Saro-Wiwa . . . Although he has never condemned the bombings, Mr. Soyinka has denied any connection with them."

6. Criticized for rampant corruption and for leading the country to 7,000% inflation during his 1985–1990 presidency, Garcia was still gaining momentum on an anti-IMF platform for presidency in 2001, an election which he lost by a slim margin to Alejandro Toledo.

7. For an analysis of de Soto's influence on Mario Vargas Llosa's 1990 bid for presidency, see the chapter "Mario Vargas Llosa and the Rape of Sebastiana" in my *Infertilities: Exploring Fictions of Barren Bodies*.

8. For an in-depth and insightful analysis of how the language of school choice feeds corporate interests, see Kenneth J. Saltman's *Collateral Damage: Corporatizing Public Schools— A Threat to Democracy:* "In the context of the current educational reform debates, placing radically different programs under the same rubric [of school choice] risks forwarding one particular version of school choice, namely market-based choice, at the expense of careful consideration of the competing versions and their underlying social visions. This is because the current educational reform debates have come to be monopolized by the language and logic of the market" (33).

9. Chomsky (1999): "Adam Smith's praise of the division of labor is well known, but not his denunciation of its inhuman effects, which will turn working people into objects 'as stupid and ignorant as it is possible for a human creature to be,' something that must be prevented 'in every improved and civilized society' by government action to overcome the destructive force of the 'invisible hand.' Also not well advertised is Smith's belief that government 'regulation in favour of the workmen is always just and equitable,' though not 'when in favour of the masters.' Or his call for equality of outcome, which was at the heart of his argument for free markets" (39).

10. "Since the mid-1970's, the most fortunate one percent of households have doubled their share of the national wealth. They now hold more wealth than the bottom 95 percent of the population." (Chris Hartman, ed., "Facts and Figures," (18 Sept. 2000)). In the United States alone, "by far the richest country in the world and the homeland of the world's wealthiest people, 16.5 per cent of the population live in poverty; one fifth of adult men and women can neither read nor write, while 13 per cent have a life expectancy shorter than sixty years" (Bauman, *The Individualized Society*, 115).

11. Valerie Walkerdine, too, talks about how children needed to be free from coercion and allowed to play like the animals in order to achieve adult normality: "The old ways had to be outlawed to make room for natural reason. Children, therefore, were taught facts, but were left alone to interact with their environment. The horror of child labor was to be no more. Classroom work was replaced by play—the *proper* medium of expression for children, the most basic and animal-like of unconscious fantasies and the recapitulated development of the species" (19). This advent of naturalism in educational theory and practice led, Walkerdine contends, to the gendering of teaching: "It is the female teacher who is to *contain* this irrationality and to transform it into reason" (21). Yet, Walkerdine never mentions the relation between these ideas and imperialist exploitation, racism, and the cheapening of the labor force.

12. This is a fictive name, combining the names of two authors – feminist geographers Julie Graham and Katherine Gibson – who, "[f]ollowing in the footsteps of many women writers who have played with authorship and naming, [...] became [...] a single writing persona" (xi).

13. For an explanation of Milken's Wall Street crimes and the rise of his corporate education empire "Knowledge Universe," see the first chapter of Goodman and Saltman's *Strange Love: Or, How We Learn to Stop Worrying and Love the Market*: "In the 1980s, Michael Milken was sent to prison for his illegal financial dealings—fraud and insider trading. However, his legal activities in the junk bond market were destructive to companies, to retirees, and to the general public. He was a major factor in the Savings and Loan collapse which cost the public billions. He invented the junk bond market, and after failing to reap sufficient rewards from personally investing in junk bonds, he profited enormously by selling risky junk investments to publicly backed savings and loans. He promoted and pioneered the use of junk in hostile corporate takeovers which destroyed businesses, labor unions, and job security while only enriching a tiny corporate elite, and prominently contributed to the rise of the corporate media monopoly. He promoted greed as a public virtue and still claims that his destructive profit-seeking behavior is the essence of democracy. Since his early release from prison, Milken has been building the first education conglomerate which is aimed at transforming public education into an investment opportunity for the wealthy by privatizing public schools, making kids into a captive audience for marketers, and redefining education as a corporate resource rather than a public good vital to the promotion of a democratic society" (39).

14. "Extralegal businesses are taxed by the lack of good property law and continually having to hide their operations from the authorities . . . Moreover, because extralegal entrepreneurs live in constant fear of government detection and extortion from corrupt officials, they are forced to split and compartmentalize their production facilities between many locations, thereby rarely achieving important economies of scale. In Peru, 15 percent of gross income from manufacturing in the extralegal sector is paid out in bribes, ranging from 'free samples' and special 'gifts' of merchandise to outright cash. With an eye always on the lookout for the police, underground entrepreneurs cannot openly advertise to build up their clientele or make less costly bulk deliveries to customers" (2000: 155). This contention removes responsibility for poverty and deprivation from producing nations, basically insisting that richer nations, or rather the nations De Soto himself identifies as within the Western bubble of successful capitalism, neither caused nor can alleviate the structural indigence defining the current historical juncture.

15. For in-depth analyses of Guatemala's postwar "socialist" experiment and of the subsequent U.S. reprisal, see Richard Immerman's *The CIA in Guatemala: The Foreign Policy of Intervention* and Stephen Schlesinger and Stephen Kinzer's *Bitter Fruit: The Untold Story of the American Coup in Guatemala*.

16. This was the same cutlass given to him for cutting grass on the Railway.

17. Blackmore: "Whereas modernization based on rapid expansion of mass education and women-friendly self-help programs during the 1980s rapidly improved girls' education participation rates in African, Asian, and Latin American states, structural adjustment policies in the 1990s advocating a weak state and strong market forces have reasserted male privilege in the market . . . The new international economic orthodoxy of structural adjustment, which focuses on balanced national budgets and 'export-oriented industrialization' based upon increasing female participation as semiskilled and unskilled labor, often means education is complicit in the production of the 'docile and unskilled worker in foreign-controlled enterprises.' Such policies continue to assume a gender-neutral postcolonial

state and a gender-neurtral education system, ignoring the historically constituted class/ gender/race inequalities of past regimes. Regardless of structural variations in education (centralization or decentralization), the gendered division of labor persists, and has perhaps been exacerbated in particular anglophone states, with educational restructuring. Regardless of their educational achievement, women are still disadvantaged in the education market" (136–137).

18.   In the words of *New York Times* foreign correspondent Thomas Friedman, "The hidden hand of the market will never work without the hidden fist—McDonald's cannot flourish without McDonnell Douglas, the designer of the F-15. And the hidden fist that keeps the world safe for Silicon Valley's technologies is called the United States Army, Air Force, Navy, and Marine Corps" (373).

19.   Clearly, Chevron is not the only culprit here. Soyinka has described secret profiteering agreements between the Nigerian political elite and Shell. Educational theorist Peter McLaren has indicated Shell's involvement: "[O]ne of the many glorious companies supported by investments from universities is Shell, which has confessed to paying the Nigerian government for military assaults against opponents of multinational oil companies resulting in the 1995 executions of nine Ogoni activists who opposed Shell, including Nobel Peace Prize nominee [poet and environmental activist] Ken Saro Wiwa" (2000: 26). Soyinka has also described secret, corrupt profiteering agreements between the Nigerian political elite and multinational transportation and shipping sectors, where they were able to manipulate both import licencing and currency rates (82).

20.   "Abroad, Chevron engages in destruction of indigenous cultures and ecosystems; murder of nonviolent activists in Nigeria; obstruction of any meaningful efforts to address global warming; and repeated labor violations. Closer to home, Chevron is one of the worst corporate polluters in California. Here in the Bay Area, its Richmond refinery earned top billing from a recent study by the Environmental Protection Agency, which designated the Richmond plant as the nation's biggest toxic waste producer, releasing about 1 million pounds of poison to the air and 500,000 pounds to the Bay. 'From the forests of Colombia to the platforms of Nigeria down to the waters and workers of our own Bay, large petrochemical corporations display callous disregard for human life and the future of this planet,' says [a member of a U.S.-based] Solidarity Committee. 'We have witnessed toxic spill after toxic spill. We have seen our fellow workers perish in refinery "mishaps," and we have watched oil companies take off their gloves and get directly involved in the murder of indigenous peoples the world over . . .'" (Dyer).

Chapter 5

1.   The scene of nurturing evoked by Laura Bush softens the severe violence of a militarized world under corporate management etched by then-vice-presidential candidate, Gulf War leader Dick Cheney, and others—on all sides of the political spectrum—talking about the need for military strengthening for the advantage of markets rather than working people. The idea of the government's role as a protector and provider of citizens' basic freedoms is dwarfed under a vision of an expansive capitalism defended by force.

2.   This corporatization of schooling affects not only the way schools are funded through voucher plans or direct corporate sponsorship of specific programs as well as whole schools, but also the content of curriculum. See, for example, Robin Truth Goodman and Kenneth J. Saltman, *Strange Love: Or How We Learn to Stop Worrying and Love the Market.* Boulder: Rowman & Littlefield (2002).

3.   See Manning: 17.

4.   "[T]he assumption that certain characteristics are natural to women—such as nurturance, caring, sensitivity, etc.—leads women into certain jobs and not others" (Weiler, 36).

5.   Bessie Head researched and wrote *Serowe: Village of the Rain Wind* in 1973. It was supposed to be published in Johannesburg and London as well as in the United States, but there was a controversy about an issue in taxation having to do with Head's being denied citizenship in Botswana. Though by law she should have been taxed only in Botswana, she felt that the

publishers were plotting against her to make her pay taxes in Britain as well. Angrily, she canceled the agreement, not to get the offer from Heinemann publishing until 1981. Eilersen, Head's biographer, attributes this decision to her mental illness and acute paranoia, but, at the same time, she cites letters from the intended London publishers that clearly indicate that an unjust double taxation would ensue: "As far as your earnings here are concerned, there would appear to be no way round the tax problem because of the lack of a double taxation agreement between Botswana and Britain" (178), even though there was a double taxation agreement. The other cause of the delay was that Head wanted to ensure that all of her informants received a published copy.

6. "Women face discrimination and marginalization in subtle as well as in flagrant ways. Women do not share equally in the fruits of production. Women constitute 70 per cent of the world's poor" (567). Katha Pollit has noted that in the five years plus since Beijing, women's overall situation has not improved: "[T]he overall picture . . . is not a happy one: staggering rates of poverty, domestic violence, suicide."

7. Bowles and Gintis's *Schooling in Capitalist America,* for example, argues, "The educational system helps integrate youth into the economic system, we believe, through a structural correspondence between its social relations and those of production. The structure of social relations in education not only inures the student to the discipline of the work place, but develops the types of personal demeanor, modes of self-presentation, self-image, and social class identification which are the crucial ingredients of job adequacy" (131). Reproductive theory has been criticized for its lack of attention to a theory of agency. Giroux and Aronowitz, for example, provide an in-depth, historical analysis of reproduction theory, showing its shortcomings in its failure to address hegemony, or the ways subjects negotiate meanings within institutional and social contexts. "Schools are not solely determined by the logic of the workplace or the dominant society," they assert, "they are not merely economic institutions but are also political, cultural, and ideological sites that exist somewhat independently of the capitalist market economy" (68). "[W]hat is needed here," attests Kathlene Weiler, "is an examination of the way in which these meanings and forms of power are negotiated and worked out in the actual lived reality of teachers and students in schools" (1988: 36). I am interested here in how the work relation underlies many other types of oppression within a global capitalist society, and I want to explore how other types of work relations offer other, perhaps more equitable or more just, possibilities to change a variety of oppressive relations.

8. See the AAUW report *How Schools Shortchange Girls: A Study of Major Findings on Girls and Education.* New York: Marlowe & Company, 1995.

9. *A Woman Alone* is a posthumous collection of autobiographical writings. Head was starting to compile research for an autobiography commissioned by Heinemann when she died unexpectedly of hepatitis in 1986.

10. In 1950, the Bantu Education Act centralized African education under government control. Different tribal regions were administered by different agencies, and everyone would be taught in his/her native tongue. In 1959, the apartheid government passed the Extension of the University Education Act, which established ethnic colleges for the various black groups. In 1963, the Coloured Persons' Education Act established an Educational Council to bring the education of Coloured children under government controls. Nevertheless, starting in the 1970s, global capital was putting pressure on the educational system because apartheid's segregation policies did not allow for the labor flexibility required by the new economy. Resumes Bill Nasson, "We can distinguish fundamental changes in the nature of industrial production and the labor process during the 1970s, with increasing concentration and centralization of capital, rapid technological innovation in the shape of expanded mechanization and automation, and the growing expulsion of unskilled and some semi-skilled labor from the workplace. . . . The process of deskilling and reskilling under the imperatives of monopoly capital has been intensifying pressure for an invigoration of black schooling, and for a general restructuring of education to meet more fully the changing needs of the occupational hierarchy. Anxiety over acute skill shortages in the labor market has crystalized around the argument that older apartheid education policies are responsible for structural instabilities in the market economy" (163–164). As a result, following the Soweto riots in the late 1970s, schools in South Africa became one of the primary places for "young people to contest the very legitimacy of the capitalist market order" (148). In other

words, education was not simply reproducing the values of an oppressive social system but was also providing spaces for contestation which succeeded finally in irreparably weakening the apartheid regime. At the same time, much black education fell under the control of foreign investors. It is unlikely that restructuring black education to conform to the needs of a global market for labor in the new technologies will actually lead to liberation. As Eric Molobi indicated at the time, "Big business began to promote investment in Black education, setting up private schools, tutorial schemes, and training programs for the black staff. Their aim is to depoliticize education and to get on with the job. Education, we are told, should be left up to the private sector and invisible hands of the free enterprise system. Yet who believes multinationals are democratic institutions or apolitical in their operations and intents?" (13). As Sibusiso Nkomo and Renosi Mokate warn, it is not likely that "racial discrimination will be competed out of the market place" (407) if those with backgrounds in political activity are turned down categorically from scholarship programs.

11. See my own discussion of how this conception of the feminine served as a justification for empire in "Conrad's Closet," *Infertilities: Exploring Fictions of Barren Bodies,* Minneapolis: University of Minnesota Press, 2001. For further historical perspectives on how practices of child caring, bearing, and rearing helped to support both ideologies and material power relations of eighteenth- and nineteenth-century colonial rule, see Anna Davin, "Imperialism and Motherhood," *History Workshop: A Journal of Socialist Historians* 5 (Spring 1978): 9–65 and Anne Laura Stoler, *Race and the Education of Desire: Foucault's* History of Sexuality *and the Colonial Order of Things,* Durham and London: Duke UP, 1995.

12. These attributions of the feminine are borrowed from feminist psychoanalytic object relations theory. See, for example, Nancy Chodorow, *The Reproduction of Mothering: Psychoanalysis and the Sociology of Gender,* Berkeley: University of California Press, 1978.

13. Anne Laura Stoler has, as well, raised the issue of how domesticity set in place some of the mechanisms of colonial control: "[T]he emergence in the nineteenth-century[. . .] of an intensified discourse on bourgeois respectability and sexual morality carried with it a new interest in the domestic milieu and scrutiny of the privatized habitus in which European bourgeois values could be cultivated[. . . T]he assertion of a bourgeois order[. . .] was never distinct from the changing definition of who was European. Cultural competencies and sexual practices signaled the lines of descent that secured racial identities and partitioned individuals among them" (45).

14. Schwartz: "More than 400 people were arrested, the vast majority of whom were held for several days without access to telephones, and some for as long as two weeks. Actions that are usually summary offenses were met with charges of multiple misdemeanors and felonies, and initial bail amounts for some protesters soared as high as $1 million. But nearly a year later, almost all the cases have been heard, and over 95 percent of them have resulted in not-guilty verdicts or dismissals or thrown out in pretrial hearings[. . .] Even in the cases of arrestees dubbed "ringleaders" by the police and saddled by the DA's office with the most serious charges and highest bails, the prosecution had little to back up its claims [. . .] During the criminal trials evidence surfaced that supported the protesters' belief that there was a coordinated law enforcement effort to cripple their protests and muzzle their messages during the convention. The *Philadelphia Inquirer* reported that the FBI helped local and state police coordinate plans for responding to the demonstrations, and this July the Philadelphia Police Department acknowledged infiltrating protest planning meetings, monitoring e-mail discussion lists and taking photographs of those they suspected would participate in demonstrations. Less widely reported was a municipal court judge's public announcement of a citywide plan for preventive detention[. . .] Philadelphia's handling of last summer's demonstrations illustrated the convergence of two disturbing trends: an increased crackdown on dissent and a strict redefinition of the rights of those who use what is popularly known as public property" (5–6).

15. Clearly, education is not isolated from the field, of politics in which the ways people labor, as well as laboring people themselves, are valued. Neither is it formulated as a way for certain students to acquire "cultural capital" to maintain and reproduce their class status, nor to encourage their integration within a managerial enclave, which will assure their abilities to acquire more and better goods for personal consumption.

16. It is glaringly evident that vocational and technical training would not be adequate to the very diverse and flexible economy in the United States today. Teaching kids to milk and

graze cattle or to assemble looms will not be a sufficient agenda for an educational system mired in a world of global technologies, for example. Such an agenda would further engrain a class system based in the division between a liberal-arts-educated ruling elite and a manual-labor-educated workforce locked out of power. Neither would an expansion of current service-learning programs—where students donate (for credit) a designated amount of time to "volunteer" work in the community—succeed in challenging hierarchies of power, but rather to inculcate, in the name of charity and patronage, social hierarchies and condescending distances between the helpless and the helping, the needy and those with excess time to give, while also putting responsibility for social problems onto the laps of individual citizens rather than public institutions, legal structures, and politics.

17. However, certainly, there have been some critics who have maintained that her works are, indeed, feminist. See, for example, Bazin, who attempts to show a feminist revolution in Bessie Head's work, particularly in *A Question of Power* (1974), by exploring how the novel portrays a woman's coming to awareness under patriarchy. I find talking about a feminist revolution in terms of the interior consciousness of a fictional character a rather weak type of hope. Driver argues that Bessie Head's work is feminist because it inserts a woman's voice into a patriarchal community in order to create a different kind of community. It is very clear, however, as Laura Bush's example warrants, that simply making women's voices heard is not enough to challenge gender oppression without simultaneously reforging power relations and relations of property.

18. In fact, when Patrick van Rensburg invited Head to return to Serowe in 1976 to reestablish the garden, "She felt," her biographer Eilersen explains, ". . . that it was wrong not to receive payment for work done, or to make the garden a paying affair by selling the produce and sharing the profits . . . , demonstrating that she actually had little sympathy for the cooperative ideas which she had praised in her writing" (184). Indeed, Head even wrote a paper asking why Van Rensburg had to "ask the poor, who have to meet school fees, and many household needs, to come to Boiteko [the name of the development project] and work for no salary? [. . .]If there is no money to help subsidise projects, Boiteko ought to close down. It is a cruel and evil farce. I have behind me four years of back-breaking labour for nothing for Boiteko and I know it leads to misery and starvation. I am sick of the farce and I will not delude 13 bright girls into believing that Boiteko offers them anything in its present form. It offers them nothing but poverty, hard work and starvation and I am not going to be a part of this evil game any more" (as cited in Eilersen, 185).

19. This corporatization of schooling affects not only the way schools are funded through voucher plans or direct corporate sponsorship of specific programs as well as whole schools, but also the content of curriculum. See, for example, Robin Truth Goodman and Kenneth J. Saltman, *Strange Love: Or How We Learn to Stop Worrying and Love the Market.* Boulder: Rowman & Littlefield, 2002.

Chapter 6

1. See Greider, 21.

Works Cited

ACIL Economics, Policy and Strategy Consultants. "Barriers to Entry to the New Zealand Downstream Oil Market: A Report to New Zealand Ministry of Commerce." Canberra, Sydney, Brisbane and Perth: Crown Copyright, 1997.

Acocella, Joan. "Under the Spell: Harry Potter Explained." *The New Yorker* (31 July 2000): 74–78.

Adler, William M. *Mollie's Job: A Story of Life and Work on the Global Assembly Line.* New York: Scribner, 2000.

Adorno, Theodor W. *Kant's Critique of Pure Reason.* Standford: Standford UP, 2001.

Ahmad, Aijaz. *In Theory: Classes, Nations, Literatures.* London and New York: Verso, 1992.

Alexander, M. Jacqui, and Chandra Talpade Mohanty. "Introduction: Genealogies, Legacies, Movements." In *Feminist Genealogies, Colonial Legacies, Democratic Futures.* Eds. M. Jacqui Alexander and Chandra Talpade Mohanty. New York and London: Routledge, 1997.

Althusser, Louis. "Ideology and Ideological State Apparatuses." *Lenin and Philosophy and Other Essays.* Trans. Ben Brewster. London: NLB, 1971.

American Association of University Women. *How Schools Shortchange Girls: A Study of Major Findings on Girls and Education.* New York: Marlowe & Company, 1995.

Amin, Samir. "Africa: Living on the Fringe." *Monthly Review* (March 2002): 41–55.

———. *Capitalism in the Age of Globalization: The Management of Contemporary Society.* London and New York: Zed Books, 1997.

Andrade, Susan Z. "Rewriting History, Motherhood, and Rebellion: Naming an African Women's Literary Tradition." *Research in African Literatures* 21, no. 1 (Spring 1990): 91–110.

Ansen, David. "The Trouble With Harry." *Newsweek* (19 November 2001): 70.

Apple, Michael W. *Ideology and Curriculum.* London: Routledge & Kegan Paul, 1979.

Arnot, Madeleine, Miriam David, and Gaby Weiner. *Closing the Gender Gap: Postwar Education and Social Change.* Cambridge, UK: Polity Press, 1999.

Aronowitz, Stanley, and Peter Bratsis. "State Power, Global Power." *Paradigm Lost: State Theory Reconsidered.* Eds. Stanley Aronowitz and Peter Bratsis. Minneapolis and London: University of Minnesota Press, 2002.

Awatere, Donna. *Maori Sovereignty.* Auckland: Broadsheet: 1984.

Barlow, Maude. *The Free Trade Area of the Americas: The Threat to Social Programs, Environmental Sustainability and Social Justice, A Special Report by The International Forum on Globalization (IFG).* Ed. Debi Barker. San Francisco: International Forum on Globalization (IFG), 2001.

Baudrillard, Jean. *The Consumer Society: Myths & Structures.* London: Sage, 1998.

Bauman, Zygmunt. *Globalization: The Human Consequences.* New York: Columbia UP, 1998.

———. *The Individualized Society.* Cambridge, England and Malden, MA: Polity Press, 2001.

185

———. *In Search of Politics.* Stanford, CA: Stanford UP, 1999.

Bazin, Nancy Topping. "Venturing into Feminist Consciousness." In *The Tragic Life: Bessie Head and Literature in South Africa.* Ed. Cecil Abrahams. Trenton, NJ: Africa World Press, 1990.

Bederman, Gail. *Manliness & Civilization: A Cultural History of Gender and Race in the United States, 1880—1917.* Chicago and London: Chicago UP, 1995.

Belenky, Mary Field, Blythe McVicker Clincy, Nancy Rule Goldberger, and Jill Mattuck Tarule. *Women's Ways of Knowing: The Development of Self, Voice, and Mind.* Boston: Basic Books, 1986.

Berlant, Lauren, and Michael Warner. "Sex in Public." *Critical Inquiry* 24, 2 (Winter 1998): 547–566.

Blackmore, Jill. "Globalization: A Useful Concept for Feminists Rethinking Theory and Strategies of Education." *Globalization and Education: Critical Perspectives.* Eds. Nicholas C. Burbules and Carlos Alberto Torres. New York and London: Routledge, 2000.

Booker, Salih, William Minter, and Ann-Louise Colgan. "Policy Report: Africa Policy Outlook 2003." *Foreign Policy In Focus* (March 2003). http://www.fpif.org.

Block, Jennifer. "Christian Soldiers on the March." *The Nation* (3 February 2003): 18–21.

Bourdieu, Pierre. *Masculine Domination.* Trans. Richard Nice. Stanford, CA: Stanford UP, 2001.

Bourdieu, Pierre, and Jean-Claude Passeron. *Reproduction in Education Society and Culture.* London and Beverly Hills: Routledge and Kegan Paul, 1983.

Bousquet, Marc. "The Informal and the Informational." *Workplace: A Journal for Academic Labor* 5, 1 (October 2002). http://www.louisville.edu/journal/workplace/issue5p1/bousquetinformal.html.

Boutros-Ghali, Boutros. "The Beijing Delcaration and the Platform of Action." *Issues in Feminism: An Introduction ot Women's Studies.* Ed. Sheila Ruth. London and Toronto: Mayfield Publishing, 1988.

Bowles, Samuel, and Herbert Gintis. *Schools in Capitalist America.* New York: Basic Books, 1976.

Briggs, Laura. *Reproducing Empire: Race, Sex, Science, and U.S. Imperialism in Puerto Rico.* Berkeley, Los Angeles, London: University of California Press, 2002.

Britzman, Deborah P. *Lost Subjects, Contested Objects: Toward a Psychoanalytic Inquiry of Learning.* Albany: State University of New York Press, 1998.

Brown, Wendy. *States of Injury: Power and Freedom in Late Modernity.* Princeton, NJ: Princeton UP, 1995.

Burbules, Nicholas C., and Carlos Alberto Torres. "Globalization and Education: An Introduction." *Globalization and Education: Critical Perspectives.* Eds. Nicholas C. Burbules and Carlos Alberto Torres. New York and London: Routledge, 2000.

Burgos, Elizabeth. *Me llamo Rigoberta Menchu y asi me nacio la consciencia.* Mexico City: Siglo Veintiuno Editories, 1985.

Business Wire. "Venezuelan Author Ana Teresa Tores Wins the 1998 Mobil Pegasus Prize for Literature." 15 October 1998. http://www.businesswire.com/webbox/bw.101598/839033.htm.

Butler, Judith. *Antigone's Claim: Kinship Between Life & Death.* New York: Columbia UP, 2000.

Campbell, Ian. "Global View: U.S. Consumer Debt-Burdened?" United Press International. 23 September 2002. http://www.upi.com.

Chang, Grace. *Disposable Domestics: Immigrant Women Workers in the Global Economy.* Cambridge, MA: South End Press, 2000.

Charterjee, Partha. *The Nation and Its Fragments.* Princeton: Princeton UP, 1993.

Chicago Cultural Studies Group. "Critical Multiculturalism." *Multiculturalism: A Critical Reader.* Ed. David Theo Goldberg. Oxford, UK, and Cambridge, MA: Blackwell, 1994.

Chodorow, Nancy J. *Feminism and Psychoanalytic Theory.* New Haven and London: Yale UP, 1989.

———. *The Reproduction of Mothering: Psychoanalysis and the Sociology of Gender.* Berkeley: University of California Press, 1978.

Chomsky, Noam. *Profit Over People: Neoliberalism and Global Order.* New York, Toronto, London: Seven Stories Press, 1999.

Cockburn, Alexander. "Concerning Pee-Wee, Townshend and Ritter." *The Nation* (17 February 2003): 9.

Cockrell, Amanda. "Harry Potter and the Secret Password: Finding Our Way in the Magical Genre." *The Ivory Tower and Harry Potter: Perspectives on a Literary Phenomenon.* Ed. Lana A. Whited. Columbia, MO, and London: University of Missouri Press, 2002.

Cole, David. *No Equal Justice: Race and Class in the American Criminal Justice System.* New York: The New Press, 1999.

Cromwell, David. "Local Energy, Local Democracy." 15 August 2000. http://www.zmag.org/ZSustainers/ZDaily/2000–08/15cromwell.htm.

Danaher, Kevin. *10 Reasons to Abolish the IMF & World Bank.* New York: Seven Stories Press, 2001.

Davin, Anna. "Imperialism and Motherhood." *History Workshop: A Journal of Socialist Historians* 5 (Spring, 1978): 9–65.

Davis, Angela. *Women, Race & Class.* New York: Vintage Books, 1981.

De Soto, Hernando. *The Mystery of Capital: Why Capitalism Triumphs in the West and Fails Everywhere Else.* New York: Basic Books, 2000.

———. *The Other Path: The Invisible Revolution in the Third World.* New York: Harper & Row, 1989.

Dillabough, Jo-Anne, and Madeleine Arnot. "Feminist Political Frameworks: New Approaches to the Study of Gender, Citizenship and Education." *Challenging Democracy: International Perspectives on Gender, Education and Citizenship.* London and New York: Routledge-Falmer, 2000.

Douglas, Lee. "Oregon Law Would Jail Protestors as Terrorists." Reuters (2 April 2003). http://reuters.com.

Dresang, Eliza. "Hermione Granger and the Heritage of Gender." *The Ivory Tower and Harry Potter: Perspectives on a Literary Phenomenon.* Ed. Lana A. Whited. Columbia, MO, and London: University of Missouri Press, 2002.

Driver, Dorothy. "Reconstructing the Past, Shaping the Future: Bessie Head and the Question of Feminism in a New South Africa." In *Black Women's Writing.* Ed. Gina Wisker. New York: St. Martin's Press, 1993.

During, Simon. *Modern Enchantments: The Cultural Power of Secular Magic.* Cambridge, MA, and London: Harvard UP, 2002.

Eagleton, Terry. *The Ideology of the Aesthetic.* Oxford, UK, and Malden, MA: Blackwell Publishers, 1990.

Ebert, Teresa L. *Ludic Feminism and After: Postmodernism, Desire, and Labor in Late Capitalism.* Ann Arbor, MI: University of Michigan Press, 1996.

Ehrenreich, Barbara, and Deirdre English. *For Her Own Good: 150 Years of the Experts' Advice to Women.* Garden City, NY: Anchor Press/Doubleday, 1978.

Eilersen, Gillian Stead. *Bessie Head: Thunder Behind Her Ears, Her Life and Writing.* Portsmouth, NH: Heinemann; London: James Currey; Cape Town & Johannesburg: David Philip, 1995.

Elliot, Anthony. *Concepts of the Self.* Cambridge, UK: Polity, 2001.

Ellis, Diane. "The Effect of Consumer Interest Rate Deregulation on Credit Card Volumes, Charge-Offs, and the Personal Bankruptcy Rate." *FDIC* 98-05. March 1998. http://www.fdic.gov.

Ellsworth, Elizabeth. *Teaching Positions: Difference, Pedagogy, and the Power of Address.* New York and London: Teachers College Press, 1997.

———. "Why Doesn't This Feel Empowering? Working Through the Repressive Myths of Critical Pedagogy." *The Education Feminism Reader.* Ed. Lynda Stone. New York and London: Routledge, 1994.

Emecheta, Buchi. *Destination Biafra.* Portsmouth, NH: Heinemann, 1982.

———. *The Joys of Motherhood.* Portsmouth, NH: Heinemann, 1979.

Enloe, Cynthia. "Masculinity as Foreign Policy Issue." *Foreign Policy in Focus* 5, 36 (October 2000). http://www.foreignpolicy-infocus.org.

Fanon, Frantz. "Algeria Unveiled." *A Dying Colonialism.* Trans. Haakon Chevalier. New York: Grove Press, 1965.

———. "Concerning Violence." *The Wretched of the Earth: The Handbook for the Black Revolution That Is Changing the Shape of the World.* Trans. Constance Farrington. New York: Grove Press, 1968.

Fasman, Jona. "Freedom Coke: The Arab World's Foolish Boycott of American Food." *Slate* (25 March 2003). http://www.msn.com.

Feher, Michel. *Powerless By Design: The Age of the International Community.* Durham and London: Duke UP, 2000.

Fisher, Berenice Malka. *No Angel in the Classroom: Teaching Through Feminist Discourse.* Lanham, MD, and Boulder, CO: Rowman & Littlefield, 2001.

Fløgstad, Kjartan. *Dollar Road.* Trans. Nadi Christensen. Baton Rouge and London: Louisiana State UP, 1989.

Florida Department of Education. "Just Read, Florida!" *Florida Department of Education* (7 February 2003). http://www.fldoe.org/specialfeatures/2003_02_07_read.asp.

Foucault, Michel. *The History of Sexuality: Volume I: An Introduction.* Trans. Robert Hurley. New York: Vintage Books, 1990.

Fraser, Lindsey. *Conversations with J. K. Rowling.* New York: Scholastic, 2000.

Fraser, Nancy. *Justice Interruptus: Critical Reflections on the "Postsocialist" Condition.* New York and London: Routledge, 1997.

———. *Unruly Practices: Power, Discourse and Gender in Contemporary Social Theory.* Minneapolis: University of Minnesota Press, 1989.

Freire, Paulo. *Pedagogy of the Oppressed.* Trans. Myra Bergman Ramos. New York: Continuum, 1970.

French, Howard W. "Nigerian Nobel Winner Faces Treason Charges." *New York Times* (13 March 1997): A6.

Friedman, Thomas L. *The Lexus and the Olive Tree.* New York: Farrar, Straus & Giroux, 1999.

Galeano, Eduardo. *Open Veins of Latin America: Five Centuries of the Pillage of a Continent.* Trans. Cedric Belfrage. New York: Monthly Review Press, 1973.

———. *Upside Down: A Primer for the Looking-Glass World.* Trans. Mark Fried. New York: Picador, 1998.

Gallop, Jane. *Anecdotal Theory.* Durham and London: Duke UP, 2002.

Gibson-Graham, J. K. *The End of Capitalism (As We Knew It): A Feminist Critique of Political Economy.* Malden, MA, and Oxford, UK: Blackwell, 1996.

Gilman, Charlotte Perkins. *Benigna Machiavelli.* Santa Barbara, CA: Bandanna Books, 1994.

———. *Women and Economics: A Study of the Economic Relation Between Men and Women as a Factor in Social Evolution.* Mineola, NY: Dover Publications, 1998.

Giroux, Henry A. *Border Crossings: Cultural Workers and the Politics of Education.* New York and London: Routledge, 1992.

———. *Public Spaces, Private Lives: Beyond the Culture of Cynicism.* Lanham, MD, and Boulder, CO: Rowman & Littlefield, 2001.

———. *Stealing Innocence: Youth, Corporate Power, and the Politics of Culture.* New York: St. Martin's Press, 2000.

———. *Teachers As Intellectuals: Toward a Critical Pedagogy of Learning.* Granby, MA: Bergin & Garvey, 1988.

Giroux, Henry, and Stanley Aronowitz. *Education Still Under Seige.* Granby, MA: Bergin & Garvey, 1993.

"Going on down: Nigeria." *The Economist* (8 June 1996): 46.

Goodman, Amy and Scahill, Jeremy. "Killing for Oil in Nigeria." *The Nation* (15 March 1999): 6–7.

Goodman, Robin Truth. *Infertilities: Exploring Fictions of Barren Bodies.* Minneapolis and London: University of Minnesota Press, 2001.

Goodman, Robin Truth, and Kenneth J Saltman. *Strange Love: Or, How We Learn to Stop Worrying and Love the Market.* Lanham, MD, and Boulder: Rowman & Littlefield, 2002.

Gray, John. *False Dawn: The Delusions of Global Capitalism.* New York: The New Press, 1998.

Greene, Maxine. "Lived Spaces, Shared Spaces, Public Spaces." *Construction Sites: Excavating Race, Class, and Gender Among Urban Youth.* Eds. Lois Weis and Michelle Fine. New York and London: Teachers College Press, 2000.

———. *Releasing the Imagination: Essays on Education, the Arts, and Social Change.* San Francisco: Jossey-Bass Publishers, 1995.

———. *Teacher as Stranger: Educational Philosophy for the Modern Age.* Belmont, CA: Wadsworth Publishing Company, 1973.

Greider, William. "Oil on Political Waters." 23 October 2000. http://www.thenation.com/greider.

———. "The Right and US Trade Law: Invalidating the 20th Century." *The Nation* 15 October 2001: 21–29.

Grumet, Madeleine. "Conception, Contradiction, and Curriculum." In *The Feminist Education Reader.* Ed. Lynda Stone. New York and London: Routledge, 1994.

Habermas, Jurgen. *The Structural Transformation of the Public Sphere: An Inquiry into a Category of Bourgeois Society.* Trans. Thomas Burger with Frederick Lawrence. Cambridge, MA: The MIT Press, 1989.

Hamelin, Christine. " 'Fitted to His Own Web of Music': Art as Renaming in *The Bone People.*" *Australian & New Zealand Studies in Canada* 10 (December 93): 106–20.

Haraway, Donna J. *Modest_Witness@Second_millennium.FemaleMan_Meets_ Oncomouse: Feminism and Technoscience.* New York and London: Routledge, 1997.

Hardt, Micheal, and Antonio Negri. *Empire.* Cambridge, MA, and London: Harvard UP, 2000.

Hartman, Chris, Ed. "Facts and Figures." (18 September 2000). http://www.inequality.org/factsfr. html.

Hayden, Tom. "Seeking a New Globalism in Chiapas." *The Nation* (7 April 2003): 18–23.

Head, Bessie. *Maru.* Oxford: Heinemann, 1971.

———. *A Question of Power.* Oxford: Heinemann, 1974.

———. *Serowe: Village of the Rain-Wind.* Oxford: Heinemann, 1981.

———. *A Woman Alone: Autobiographical Writings.* Oxford: Heinemann, 1990.

———. *When Rain Clouds Gather.* Oxford: Henemann, 1969.

Henke, Suzette. "Keri Hulme's *The Bone People* and *Te Kaihau:* Postmodern Heteroglossia and Pretextual Play." *New Zealand Literature Today.* Eds. R. K. Dhawan and William Tonetto. New Dehli: Indian Society for Commonwealth Studies, 1993.

Hennessy, Rosemary. *Materialist Feminism and the Politics of Discourse.* New York and London: Routledge, 1993.

Herman, Edward S., and Robert W. McChesney. *The Global Media: The New Missionaries of Corporate Capitalism.* London and Washington: Cassell, 1997.

Hogan, Patrick Colm. *Colonialism and Cultural Identity: Crises of Tradition in the Anglophone Literatures of India, Africa, and the Carribean.* Albany: SUNY Press, 2000.

Holland, Dorothy C., and Margaret A. Eisenhart. "Women's Ways of Going to School: Cultural Reproduction of Women's Identities as Workers." *Class, Race, & Gender in American Education.* Ed. Lois Weis. Albany, NY: SUNY Press, 1988.

hooks, bell. *Feminist Theory from Margin to Center.* Boston, MA: South End Press, 1984.

———. *Teaching to Transgress: Education as the Practice of Freedom.* New York and London: Routledge, 1994.

Horkheimer, Max, and Theodor W. Adorno. *Dialectic of Enlightenment.* Trans. John Cumming. New York: Continuum, 1991.

Houppert, Karen. "You're Not Entitled! Welfare 'Reform' Is Leading to Government Lawlessness." *The Nation* (25 October 1999): 11–31.

Huggan, Graham. "Opting out of the (Critical) Common Market: Creolization and the Post-Colonial Text." *Kunapipi* 11, 1 (1989): 27–39.

Hulme, Keri. *The Bone People.* New York: Penguin Books, 1983.

Immerman, Richard H. *The CIA in Guatemala: The Foreign Policy of Intervention.* Austin: University of Texas Press, 1982.

Irigaray, Luce. *Speculum of the Other Woman.* Trans. Gillian C. Gill. Ithaca, NY: Cornell UP, 1985.

Jaggar, Alison M. "Love and Knowledge: Emotion in Feminist Epistemology." In *Gender/Body/Knowledge: Feminist Reconstructions of Being and Knowing.* Eds. Alison M. Jaggar and Susan R. Bordo. New Brunswick and London: Rutgers UP, 1989.

James, Joni. "Educator Says Colleges Need to be Graded." *Wall Street Journal* (6 September 2000).

Jameson, Fredric. "Notes on Globalization as Philosophical Issue." *The Cultures of Globalization.* Eds. Fredric Jameson and Masao Miyoshi. Durham and London: Duke UP, 1998.

———. "Third-World Literature in the Era of Multinational Capitalism." *Social Text* 15 (1986): 65–88.

Jefferson, Stebbins. "Test College Kids? Don't Stop There." *Palm Beach Post* (3 May 2003).

Kalyvas, Andreas. "The Stateless Theory: Poulantzas's Challenge to Postmodernism." *Paradigm Lost: State Theory Reconsidered.* Eds. Stanley Aronowitz and Peter Bratsis. Minneapolis and London: University of Minnesota Press, 2002.

Kaplan, Cora. "Pandora's Box: Subjectivity, Class and Sexuality in Socialist Feminist Criticism." In *Feminisms: An Anthology of Literary Theory and Criticism.* Eds. Robyn R. Warhol and Diane Price Herndl. New Brunswick, NJ: Rutgers Univeristy Press, 1991.

Karp, Stan. "Let Them Eat Tests." *Rethinkingschools.Org* (Summer 2002). http://www.rethinking schools.org.

Kelley, Robin D. G. *Yo' Mama's Disfunktional!: Fighting the Culture Wars in Urban America.* Boston: Beacon Press, 1998.

Klees, Steven J., Irene Rizzini, and Anthony Dewees. "A New Paradigm for Social Change: Social Movements and the Transformation of Policy for Street and Working Children in Brazil." *Children on the Streets of the Americas.* Ed. Roslyn Arlin Mickelson. London and New York: Routledge, 2000.

Kristeva, Julia. *The Sense and the Non-Sense of Revolt: The Powers and Limits of Psychoanalysis.* Trans. Jeanine Herman. New York: Columbia UP, 2000.

Kumar, Anita. "College FCAT? Failure Could Hurt Alma Mater." *St. Petersburg Times* (1 May 2003). http://www.sptimes.com/2003/05/01/state/College_FCAT_Failure_shtml.

Lacan, Jacques. "The Mirror Stage as Formative of the Function of the I as Revealed in Psychoanalytic Experience." *Ecrits: A Selection.* Trans. Alan Sheridan. New York: W. W. Norton & Company, 1977.

Lacoss. Jann. "Of Magicals and Muggles: Reversals and Revulsions at Hogwarts." *The Ivory Tower and Harry Potter: Perspectives on a Literary Phenomenon.* Ed. Lana A. Whited. Columbia, MO, and London: University of Missouri Press, 2002.

Lather, Patti. *Getting Smart: Feminist Research and Pedagogy With/in the Postmodern.* New York and London: Routledge, 1991.

———. "Ten Years Later, Yet Again: Critical Pedagogy and Its Complicities." *Feminist Engagements: Reading, Resisting, and Revisioning Male Theorists in Education and Cultural Studies.* Ed. Kathleen Weiler. New York and London: Routledge, 2001.

Lazarus, Neil. *Nationalism and Cultural Practice in the Postcolonial World.* Cambridge, UK: Cambridge UP, 1999.

Le Cam, Georges-Goulven. "The Quest for Archetypal Self-Truth in Keri Hulme's *The Bone People:* Towards a Western Re-Definition of Maori Culture?" *Commonwealth* 15, 2 (Spring 1993): 66–79.

Lebowitz, Mike. "Venezuela's National Union of Workers." *Z-Net* (2 April 2003). http://www.zmag.org.

Leistyna, Pepi. *Defining and Designing Multiculturalism: One School System's Efforts.* Albany: SUNY Press, 2002

Lim, Lean Lim. *More and Better Jobs for Women—An Action Guide. An ILO Follow-up to the Fourth World Conference on Women and The World Summit for Social Development.* Geneva: ILO, 1996.

Locke, John. *Two Treatises of Government.* Ed. Peter Laslett. Cambridge, UK: Cambridge UP, 1960, 1967, 1988.

Lozada, Carlos. "Poverty Solved: No Muss, No Fuss. *The American Prospect* 12, 4 (26 February 2001). http://www.prospect.org.

Lyderson, Kari. "Payday Profiteers: Payday Lenders Target the Working Poor." *Multinational Monitor* 22, 10 (Oct. 2001). http://www.thecriticalvoice.com/payday.html.

Macedo, Donaldo and Barolome, Lilia I. *Dancing With Bigotry: Beyond the Politics of Tolerance.* New York: St. Martin's Press, 1999.

Maher, Frances A. and Tetreault, Mary Kay Thompson. *The Feminist Classroom: An Inside Look at How Professors and Students Are Transforming Higher Education for a Diverse Society.* New York: Basic Books, 1994.

Mann, Bill. "The Threat of Bad Consumer Debt." *Fool on the Hill* (19 January 2001). http://www.fool.com/news/foth/2001/foth010119.htm.

Manning, Steven. "The Corporate Curriculum." *The Nation* (27 September 1999).

Marcuse, Herbert. *One-Dimensional Man: Studies in the Ideology of Advanced Industrial Societies.* Boston: Beacon Press, 1964.

Maxwell, Anne. "Ethnicity and Education: Biculturalism in New Zealand." *Multicultural States: Rethinking Difference and Identity.* Ed. David Bennett. London and New York: Routledge, 1998.

McChesney, Robert W. "Introduction." In *Profits over People: Neoliberalism and Global Order.* By Noam Chomsky. New York: Seven Stories Press, 1999.

McLaren, Peter. *Che Guevara, Paulo Freire, and the Pedagogy of Revolution.* Lanham, MD, and Boulder, CO: Rowman & Littlefield, 2000.

McRobbie, Angela. "Good Girls, Bad Girls? Female Success and the New Meritocracy." *British Cultural Studies: Geography, Nationality, and Identity.* Ed. David Morley and Kevin Robins. Oxford: Oxford UP, 2001.

Mendlesohn, Farah. "Crowning the King: Harry Potter and the Construction of Authority." *The Ivory Tower and Harry Potter: Perspectives on a Literary Phenomenon.* Ed. Lana A. Whited. Columbia, MO, and London: University of Missouri Press, 2002.

Metcalf, Stephen. "Reading Between the Lines." *The Nation* (28 January 2002).

Mickelson, Roslyn Arlin. "Globalization, Childhood Poverty, and Education in the Americas." *Children on the Streets of the Americas.* Ed. Roslyn Arlin Mickelson. London and New York: Routledge, 2000.

Miller, Mark Crispin. *The Bush Dyslexicon: Observations on a National Disorder.* New York: W. W. Norton & Co., 2001.

———. "Free the Media." *We the Media: A Citizens' Guide to Fighting for Media Democracy.* Eds. Don Hazen and Julie Winokur. New York: The New Press, 1997.

Mobil. "Pegasus Prize: Background." n.d. http://www.magnolia.com/pegasus prize/background. html.

Mohanty, Chandra Talpade. "On Race and Voice: Challenges for Liberal Education in the 1990's." *Cultural Critique* 14 (Winter 1990): 179–206.

———. "Women Workers and Capitalist Scripts: Ideologies of Domination, Common Interests, and the Politics of Solidarity." In *Feminist Genealogies, Colonial Legacies, Democratic Futures.* Eds. M. Jacqui Alexander and Chandra T. Mohanty. New York and London: Routledge, 1997.

Molnar, Alex. *Giving Kids the Business: The Commercialization of America's Schools* Boulder: Westview, 1996.

Molobi, Eric. "South Africa: Education Under Apartheid." *Bulletin* 20 (Summer 1987).

Morris, Rosalind C. "Modernity's Media and the End of Mediumship? On the Aesthetic Economy of Transparency in Thailand." *Millennial Capitalism and the Culture of Neoliberalism.* Eds. Jean Comaroff and John L. Comaroff. Durham and London: Duke UP, 2001.

Mouffe, Chantal. *The Return of the Political.* London and New York: Verso, 1993.

Nasson, Bill. "Modernization As Legitimation: Education Reform and the State in the 1980s." In *Pedagogy of Domination: Toward a Democratic Education in South Africa.* Ed. Mokubung Nkomo. Trenton, NJ: Africa World Press, 1990.

Natov, Roni. "Harry Potter and the Extraordinariness of the Ordinary." *The Ivory Tower and Harry Potter: Perspectives on a Literary Phenomenon.* Ed. Lana A. Whited. Columbia, MO, and London: University of Missouri Press, 2002.

Ngugi Wa Thiong'o. *Decolonising the Mind: The Politics of Language in African Literature.* London: James Currey; Nairobi: EAEP; Portsmouth, NH: Heinemann, 1981.

Nixon, Rob. "Refugess and Homecomings: Bessie Head and the Politics of Exile." In *Late Imperial Culture.* Eds. Roman de la Campa, E. Ann Kaplan, Michael Sprinker. London and New York: Verso, 1995.

Nkomo, Sibusiso and Renosi Mokate. "Education, Labor Power, and Socio-Economic Development." In *Pedagogy of Domination: Toward a Democratic Education in South Africa.* Ed. Mokubung Nkomo. Trenton, NJ: Africa World Press, 1990.

Noddings, Nel. "An Ethic of Caring and Its Implications for Instructional Arrangements." In *The Feminist Education Reader.* Ed. Lynda Stone. New York and London: Routledge, 1994.

———. *Starting at Home: Caring and Social Policy.* Berkeley, Los Angeles, London: University of California Press, 2002.

Nooteboom, Cees. *Rituals.* Trans. Adrienne Dixon. San Diego, New York, London: Harcourt Brace, 1983.

Ogwude, Sophia Abiajulu. "Protest and Commitment in Bessie Head's Utopia." *Research in African Literatures* 29, 3 (Fall 1998): 70–82.

Pollitt, Katha. "Women: Two Steps Forward, One Step Back?" *The Nation* (26 June 2000): 10.

Prentice, Chris. "Re-writing Their Stories, Renaming Themselves: Post-colonialism and Feminism in the Fictions of Keri Hulme and Audrey Thomas." *Span* 23 (September 1986): 68–80.

Press, Eyal. "Texaco on Trial." *The Nation* (31 May 1999): 11–16.

Propp, Vladimir. "Fairy Tale Transformations." Trans. C. H. Severens. *Readings in Russian Poetics: Formalist and Structuralist Views.* Eds. Ladislav Matejka and Krystyna Pomorska. Ann Arbor: University of Michigan Press, 1978.

Reuters. "Iraqis agree on role for oil majors, OPEC." Reuters (5 April 2003). http://www.reuters.com.

Ronell, Avital. *Stupidity.* Urbana and Chicago: University of Illinois Press, 2002.

Rose, Jacqueline S. "The Case of Peter Pan: The Impossibility of Children's Fiction." *The Children's Culture Reader.* Ed. Henry Jenkins. New York and London: New York UP, 1998.

Ross, Kristin. *Fast Cars, Clean Bodies: Decolonization and the Reordering of French Culture.* Cambridge, MA, and London: The MIT Press, 1995.

Rowling, J. K. *Harry Potter and the Chamber of Secrets.* New York: Scholastic, 1999.

———. *Harry Potter and the Goblet of Fire.* New York: Scholastic, 2000.

———. *Harry Potter and the Order of the Phoenix.* New York: Scholastic, 2003.

———. *Harry Potter and the Prisoner of Azkaban.* New York: Scholastic, 1999.

———. *Harry Potter and the Sorcerer's Stone.* New York: Scholastic, 1997.

Saltman, Kenneth J. *Collateral Damage: Corporatizing Public Schools—A Threat to Democracy.* Lanham, MD, and Boulder, CO: Rowman & Littlefield, 2000.

———. "Why Doesn't This Feel Political: Elizabeth Ellsworth, *Teaching Positions.* Teachers College Press, New York, 1997." *Journal of Critical Pedagogy* II, 1 (15 November 1998). http://www.lib.wmc.edu/pub/jcp/issueII-1/saltman.html.

Sassen, Saskia. *Globalization and Its Discontents: Essays on the New Mobility of People and Money.* New York: New Press, 1998.

Schapiro, Mark. "Big Tobacco: Uncovering the Industry's Multibillion-Dollar Global Smuggling Network." *The Nation* (6 May 2002): 11–20.

Schiffrin, André. "The Corporatization of Publishing." *We the Media: a Citizens' Guide to Fighting for Media Democracy.* Eds. Don Hazen and Julie Winokur. New York: The New Press, 1997.

Schlesinger, Stephen and Kinzer, Stephen. *Bitter Fruit: The Untold Story of the American Coup in Guatemala.* New York: Doubleday, 1982.

Schwartz, Deb. "Philadelphia Law." *The Nation* (3/10 September 2001): 5–6.

Scott, Joan. " 'Experience.' " *Feminists Theorize the Political.* Eds. Judith Butler and Joan W. Scott. New York and London: Routledge, 1992.

Seller, Anne. "Whose Women's Studies? Whose Philosophy? Whose Borderland?" *Knowing Feminisms: On Academic Borders, Territories and Tribes.* Ed. Liz Stanley. London: Sage, 1997.

Shalom, Stephen R. "The U.S. Response to Humanitarian Crises." *Z-Net* (September 1991). http://www.lbbs.org.

Shohat, Ella. "Notes on the 'Post-Colonial.' " *The Pre-Occupation of Postcolonial Studies.* Eds. Fawzia Afzal-Khan and Kalpana Seshadri-Crooks. Durham and London: Duke UP, 2000.

Showalter, Elaine. "Presidential Address 1998: Regeneration." *PMLA* 114 (May 1999): 318–325.

Simecka, Martin M. *The Year of the Frog.* Trans. Peter Petro. Baton Rouge and London: Louisiana State UP, 1993.

Sleeter, Christine E. *Multicultural Education as Social Activism.* Albany: SUNY Press, 1996.

Smith, Sean. *J. K. Rowling: A Biography.* London: Michael O'Mara Books Limited, 2001.

Soyinka, Wole. *The Open Sore of a Continent: A Personal Narrative of the Nigerian Crisis.* New York and Oxford: Oxford UP, 1996.

Spivak, Gayatri. "Diasporas Old and New: Women in the Transnational World." *Revolutionary Pedagogies: Cultural Politics, Instituting Education, and the Discourse of Theory.* Ed. Peter Pericles Trifonas. New York and London: RoutledgeFalmer, 2000.

———. "Who Claims Alterity?" *Remaking History.* Eds. Barbara Kruger and Phil Mariani. Seattle: Bay Press, 1989.

Stavrakakis, Yannis. *Lacan & the Political.* London and New York: Routledge, 1999.

Stead, C. K. "Keri Hulme's *The Bone People,* and the Pegasus Award for Maori Literature." *Ariel: A Review of International English Literature* 16, 4 (October 1985): 101–108.

Stoler, Anne Laura. *Race and the Education of Desire: Foucault's 'History of Sexuality' and the Colonial Order of Things.* Durham and London: Duke UP, 1995.

Stratton, Florence. "The Shallow Grave: Archetypes of Female Experience in African Fiction." *Research in African Literatures* 19, no. 2 (Summer 1988): 143–169.

Stromquist, Nelly P. and Monkman, Karen. "Defining Globalization and Assessing Its Implications on Knowledge and Education." *Globalization and Education: Integration and Contestation across Cultures.* Eds. Nelly P. Stromquist and Karen Monkman. Lanham, MD, and Boulder, CO: Rowman & Littlefield, 2000.

Taft Group. "Top Givers in the Top 9 Categories—1999." http://www.taftgroup.com/taft/.

Taylor, Charles. "The Politics of Recognition." *Multiculturalism: A Critical Reader.* Ed. David Theo Goldberg. Oxford, UK, and Cambridge, MA: Blackwell, 1994.

Teare, Elizabeth. "Harry Potter and the Technology of Magic." *The Ivory Tower and Harry Potter: Perspectives on a Literary Phenomenon.* Ed. Lana A. Whited. Columbia, MO, and London: University of Missouri Press, 2002.

Thompson, Patricia. "Beyond Gender: Equity Issues for Home Economics Education." In *The Feminist Education Reader.* Ed. Lynda Stone. New York and London: Routledge, 1994.

Tompkins, Jane. "Pedagogy of the Distressed." *College English* 52, 6 (October 1990): 653–660.

Torres, Ana Teresa. *Doña Inés Vs. Oblivion.* Trans. Gregory Rabassa. New York: Grove Press, 1999.

Udogu, E. Ike. "The Allurement of Ethnonationalism in Nigerian Politics: The Contemporary Debate." *Journal of Asian and African Studies* 29, 3–4 (July–October 1994): 159–172.

Uhlfelder, Steve. "It's Time to Hold Universities Accountable for Quality." *Tallahassee Democrat* (24 January 2003).

Umeh, Marie. "Introduction: (En)Gendering African Womanhood: Locating Sexual Politics in Igbo Society and Across Boundaries." *Emerging Perspectives on Buchi Emecheta.* Ed. Marie Umeh. Trenton, NJ: African World Press, 1996.

Unterhalter, Elaine. "Can Education Overcome Women's Subordinate Position in the Occupation Structure?" *Education in a Future South Africa: Policy Issues for Transformation.* Eds. Elaine Unterhalter, Harold Wolpe, and Thozamile Botha. Trenton, NJ: Africa World Press, 1992.

Viswanathan, Gauri. *Masks of Conquest: Literary Study and British Rule in India.* Delhi: Oxford UP, 1998.

Walkerdine, Valerie. "Progressive Pedagogy and Political Struggle." *Feminisms and Critical Pedagogy.* Eds. Carmen Luke and Jennifer Gore. New York and London: Routledge, 1992.

Walkerdine, Valerie, and Helen Lucey. *Democracy in the Kitchen: Regulating Mothers and Socializing Daughters.* London: Virago, 1989.

Wallerstein, Immanuel. *The Essential Wallerstein.* New York: The New Press, 2000.

Webby, Elizabeth. "Keri Hulme: Spiralling to Success." *Meanjin* 44, 1 (March 1985): 14–23.

Weiler, Kathleen. "Rereading Paulo Freire." *Feminist Engagements: Reading, Resisting, and Revisioning Male Theorists in Education and Cultural Studies.* Ed. Kathleen Weiler. New York and London: Routledge, 2001.

———. *Women Teaching for Change: Gender, Class & Power.* New York: Bergin & Garvey, 1988.

Weis, Lois, with Doris Carbonell-Medina. "Learning to Speak Out in an Abstinence-Based Sex Education Group: Gender and Race Work in an Urban Magnet School." *Constructing Sites: Excavating Race, Class, and Gender Among Urban Youth.* Eds. Lois Weis and Michelle Fine. New York and London: Teachers College Press, 2000.

Welch, Mark. "Get Ready for Patriot Act II." *Alternet* (2 April 2003). http://www.alternet.org.

Westman, Karin E. "Specters of Thatcherism: Contemporary British Culture in J. K. Rowling's Harry Potter Series." *The Ivory Tower and Harry Potter: Perspectives on a Literary Phenomenon.* Ed. Lana A. Whited. Columbia, MO, and London: University of Missouri Press, 2002.

Wichterich, Christa. *The Globalized Woman: Reports From a Future of Inequality.* Trans. Patrick Camiller. New Melbourne: Spinifex Press; London and New York: Zed Books, 2000.

Williams, John. "Look, Child Poverty in the Wealthy Countries Isn't Necessary." *International Herald Tribune* (24 July 2000).

Wilpert, Gregory. "Coup in Venezuela: An Eyewitness Account." *Z-Net* (12 April 2002). http://www.zmag.org.

———. "An Imminent Coup in Venezuela?" *Z-Net* (10 April 2002). http://www.zmag.org.

Wokusch, Heather. "Leaving Our Children Behind." *CommonDreams.org* (8 July 2002). http://www.commondreams.org/views02/0708–08.htm.

Wolfensohn, James D. "The Other Crisis." 6 October 1998. http://www.worldbank.org/html/extdr/am98/jdw-sp/am98-en.htm.

Wolff, Edward N. "Recent Trends in Wealth Ownership, 1983–1998." April 2000. Table 6. <http://www.levy.org/docs/wrkpap/papers/300.html>.

Wollstonecraft, Mary. *A Vindication of the Rights of Woman.* Ed. Carol H. Poston. 2nd Edition. New York and London: W. W. Norton & Company, 1988/1975.

Woolf, Virginia. *Three Guineas.* San Diego, New York, London: Harcourt Brace & Company, 1938, 1966.

Wright, Melissa W. "The Dialectics of Still Life: Murder, Women, and Maquiladoras." *Millennial Capitalism and the Culture of Neoliberalism.* Eds. Jean Comaroff and John L. Comaroff. Durham and London: Duke UP, 2001.

Zembylas, Michalinos and Boler, Megan. "On the Spirit of Patriotism: Challenges of a 'Pedagogy of Discomfort.' " *Teachers College Record* (12 August 2002).

About the Author

Robin Truth Goodman is an assistant professor of English at Florida State University and a Global Fellow at the International Institute of the University of California at Los Angeles. Her previous publications include *Strange Love: Or How We Learn to Stop Worrying and Love the Market*, cowritten with Kenneth J. Saltman (Rowman & Littlefield, 2002) and *Infertilities: Exploring Fictions of Barren Bodies* (University of Minnesota Press, 2001).

Index